Praise for *Samurai William*
by Giles Milton

"A vivid, scrupulously researched biography . . . Milton offers a wonderful glimpse of Japan through foreign eyes."
—*The New York Times Book Review*

"An excellent history . . . *Samurai William* does not entirely revolve around Adams. It is at least as much a compact general history of sixteenth- and seventeenth-century Europe's contacts with Japan, and with the East in general, replete with weird sexual customs, threats of cannibalism, and sightings of strange creatures, not a few of them human. . . . Milton is an expert at seeking the detail that will shock as well as illustrate."
—*Minneapolis Star-Tribune*

"An impressive, intriguing history . . . Milton presents an enchanting account of the life and leisure, the violence and perfidies, the elegance and ambition of both the Japanese and the Europeans."
—*The Baltimore Sun*

"Adams's story is a grand one, fit to take its place beside any of the engrossing tales of travel, displacement, and personal discovery that pepper the years of Europe's apparently unending search for trade, religious converts, and empire. . . . Milton presents it with undisguised gusto . . . throughout the book readers will find a rich and delightfully varied roster of oddities about British character and behavior . . . there are countless striking vignettes of the hazards of travel at the time, and Milton has fun exploring the often disastrous sexual adventures of the British when they were ashore."
—*The New York Review of Books*

"Milton has a keen eye for the telling anecdote . . . best of all he brings personalities to life in a multidimensional way . . . Milton makes this armchair voyage to the Japan of four hundred years ago both stimulating and comfortable."
—*The Seattle Times*

"Giles Milton, again expertly navigating the eastern seas from which he brought us *Nathaniel's Nutmeg*, frames the tale of this first meeting between Japan and the West around Adams's remarkable career there."
—*The Economist*

"Milton couches considerable scholarship in a vivacious and colorful narrative that will appeal to lovers of historical adventure."
—*Publishers Weekly*

PENGUIN BOOKS

SAMURAI WILLIAM

Giles Milton is the author of *Big Chief Elizabeth*, *Nathaniel's Nutmeg*, and *The Riddle and the Knight*. He lives in London.

SAMURAI WILLIAM

·

The Englishman Who
Opened Japan

GILES MILTON

Penguin Books

PENGUIN BOOKS

Published by the Penguin Group

Penguin Group (USA) Inc., 375 Hudson Street, New York, New York 10014, U.S.A.

Penguin Books Ltd, 80 Strand, London WC2R 0RL, England

Penguin Books Australia Ltd, 250 Camberwell Road, Camberwell, Victoria 3124, Australia

Penguin Books Canada Ltd, 10 Alcorn Avenue, Toronto, Ontario, Canada M4V 3B2

Penguin Books India (P) Ltd, 11 Community Centre,
Panchsheel Park, New Delhi – 110 017, India

Penguin Books (N.Z.) Ltd, Cnr Rosedale and Airborne Roads,
Albany, Auckland, New Zealand

Penguin Books (South Africa) (Pty) Ltd, 24 Sturdee Avenue,
Rosebank, Johannesburg 2196, South Africa

Penguin Books Ltd, Registered Offices: 80 Strand, London WC2R 0RL, England

First published in Great Britain by Hodder & Stoughton,
a division of Hodder Headline, 2002
First published in the United States of America by Farrar, Straus and Giroux 2003
Published in Penguin Books 2004

1 3 5 7 9 10 8 6 4 2

THE LIBRARY OF CONGRESS HAS CATALOGED THE
AMERICAN HARDCOVER EDITION AS FOLLOWS:
Milton, Giles.
Samurai William : the Englishman who opened Japan / Giles Milton.—1st American ed.
p. cm.
Originally published: Hodder & Stoughton, 2002.
Includes index.
ISBN 0-374-25385-4 (hc.)
ISBN 0 14 20.0378 6 (pbk.)
1. Adams, William, 1564–1620. 2. Japan—Officials and employees, Alien—Biography.
3. Great Britain—Officials and employees—Japan—Biography. 4. British—Japan—
Biography. 5. Pilots and pilotage—Great Britain—Biography. 6. Japan—
Relations—Great Britain. 7. Great Britain—Relations—Japan. I. Title.
DS869.A3 M54 2003
952'.024'092—dc21
[B]   2002072362

Printed in the United States of America
Designed by Abby Kagan

FOR AURELIA

Contents

THE VOYAGE TO

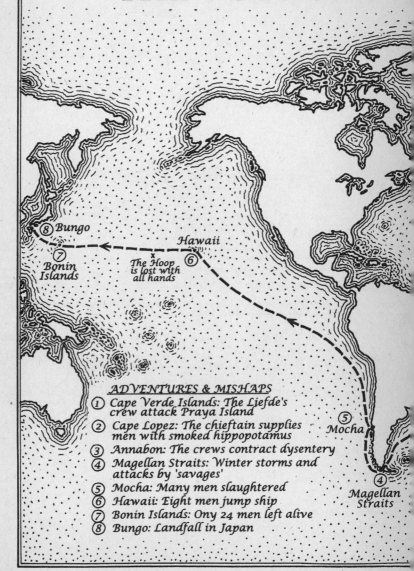

⑧ Bungo

Hawaii

⑦
Bonin
Islands

x
The Hoop
is lost with
all hands

⑥

⑤
Mocha

④
Magellan
Straits

ADVENTURES & MISHAPS

① Cape Verde Islands: The Liefde's
   crew attack Praya Island
② Cape Lopez: The chieftain supplies
   men with smoked hippopotamus
③ Annabon: The crews contract dysentery
④ Magellan Straits: Winter storms and
   attacks by 'savages'
⑤ Mocha: Many men slaughtered
⑥ Hawaii: Eight men jump ship
⑦ Bonin Islands: Ony 24 men left alive
⑧ Bungo: Landfall in Japan

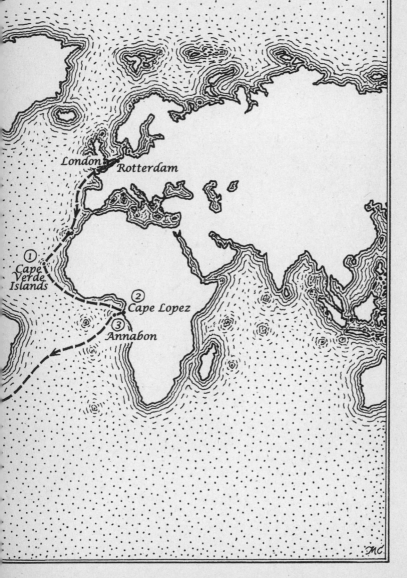

JAPAN: 1598–1600

London • Rotterdam

① Cape Verde Islands

② Cape Lopez

③ Annabon

A Note on Spelling

The language used by William Adams, Richard Cocks, and the other men is quirky and rich. But their eccentric spelling often makes their diaries and letters hard to read. I have modified and standardized some archaic spellings, while trying not to tamper too much with the piquancy of the original.

"Theyre" and "there" have been changed to "their" where appropriate; "ye" becomes "the." All names of people and places have been standardized, and some superscript letters have been lowered. The old-fashioned *v* has been replaced by *u*; and *i* has been changed to *j* where appropriate (so "iudge" becomes "judge"). William Adams frequently uses contractions; these have been spelled out in full.

I have also modernized some words whose original forms are so bizarre that they are almost unreadable. Those wishing to consult the diaries and letters in their original forms will find the relevant sources listed in the Notes and Sources.

SAMURAI WILLIAM

PROLOGUE

**T**HEY HAD REACHED the end of the world. A tremendous storm had pushed them deep into the unknown, where the maps and globes showed only monsters of the deep. The night sky sparkled, but the unfamiliar stars had proved a mischievous guide to these lost and lonely adventurers.

For almost two years, William Adams and his crew had braved wild and tempestuous oceans. They had clashed with spear-toting island chieftains, and suffered from sickness and empty bellies. Now, on April 12, 1600, these few survivors had once again sighted land, where they expected death at the hands of barbarous savages.

The bell of the great Manju-ji monastery clanged at dawn. As the weak spring sunlight spilled over the southern mountains, a dozen temples seemed to echo in reply. It was already light on the watery delta of the Oita River, but night still lingered in the palaces and pagodas of Funai. Their cuneiform roofs trapped the shadows. It would be several hours before daylight pierced the gridlike maze of walkways.

The strange vessel that was drifting helplessly into the harbor was in a terrible state of repair. Her sails were in shreds and her timbers had been bleached by the sun. With her stately poop and mullioned prow, she was quite unlike the junks that occasionally dropped anchor on the southern shores of Japan. No sooner had she been sighted than the alarm was raised and a small party of townsmen rowed out to view the vessel. Those who clambered aboard were greeted by a pitiful sight. A dozen adventurers lay helpless and groaning in their own filth. Many were covered in blotches—a sign of advanced scurvy—while others had been stricken with terrible tropical diseases. Their victuals had run out long ago and they had subsisted on the rats and other vermin that scavenged for scraps in the filthy swill in the hold of the vessel. Only William Adams was sufficiently coherent to greet the boarding party. He blinked in astonishment as he caught his first glimpse of a civilization that was older—and perhaps more sophisticated—than his own.

Adams immediately realized that these men had come not to their rescue, but to pillage the ship. He could only hope that he and his men would receive a welcome on shore. They had achieved the remarkable feat of crossing both the Atlantic and Pacific Oceans, negotiating the treacherous Magellan Straits en route. They had survived Antarctic blizzards and tropical storms, and had watched in horror as their friends and fellow crewmates had weakened and expired. Of a fleet of five ships, only one had made it to Japan. Of an estimated one hundred crew members, just twenty-four men were still alive. Of these, six were on the verge of death.

After more than nineteen months at sea, Adams had reached the fabled island of Japan, where no Englishman had ever before set foot. As he stepped ashore, he prayed that his voyage of discovery had at long last come to an end. In fact, it was just about to begin.

The adventurers of Elizabethan London knew almost nothing about Japan. When they unrolled their maps and gazed at the remote East, they saw only squiggles, dots, and grotesque sea monsters. Gerardus Mercator's 1569 map of the world depicted this kingdom as a lozenge-shaped blob with two tentacles of islands. Edward Wright's projection was little better. When he came to draw Japan, he delved deep into his imagination and came up with an island that looked like a misshapen prawn with a long fluffy beard. Although he took great pride in labeling his map "a true hydrographical description," he admitted that he had only accurately drawn "so much of the world as hath been hitherto discovered." That—alas—did not include Japan.

The bookish gentlemen elsewhere in northern Europe were equally ignorant as to the whereabouts, and people, of Japan. In the Low Countries, France, and the Holy Roman Empire the only information about this mysterious "kingdom" was to be found in the account of the great Venetian traveler Marco Polo. That was already three centuries old and was based on nothing more than hearsay. Polo himself had never been to Japan—a land he called Chipangu—but he had learned from the Chinese that the "people are white, civilised and well-favoured" and he noted that they were ferociously proud and "dependent on nobody." He added that no one—not even their neighbors the Chinese—dared to sail to Japan, for the distances were enormous and the dangers were great.

Forbidden kingdoms made for rich kingdoms in the minds of gentlemen adventurers, and distant Japan—the Land of the Rising Sun—was believed to glisten with gilded splendor. "The quantity of gold they have here is endless," wrote an excited Polo, "for they find it in their own islands." The emperor's palace was "entirely roofed with fine gold," while the windows glittered and twinkled, "so that altogether the richness of the palace is past all bounds and all belief."

Dozens of English adventurers were lured into uncharted seas by such tantalizing riches, placing their trust in the good Lord and a fair breeze. They studied their maps, consulted their charts, and

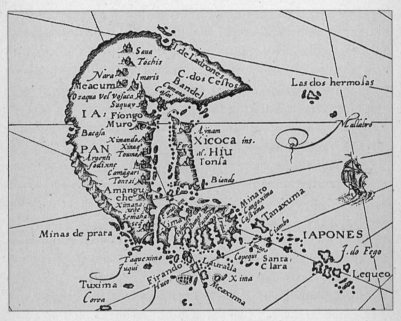

Inaccurate maps were the cause of many shipwrecks. This circa 1596 Dutch engraving, described by one captain as "very true," reproduces the prawn-shaped coastline of earlier charts.

concluded—quite logically—that the frosty Arctic Ocean offered the shortest route to the East. They little imagined that their fragile galleons would be battered by monstrous icebergs and translucent cliffs of ice. Sir Hugh Willoughby's 1553 expedition to the East had been the most spectacular failure. His vessel had been trapped in the icy jaws of the White Sea, to the north of Muscovy, and his men had frozen to death in an Arctic blizzard.

The Northwest Passage across the top of North America was believed to offer an even shorter route to Japan and China. But it, too, had displayed a voracious appetite for Elizabethan sea dogs. The route, wrote the Arctic adventurer George Beste, was so "freezing cold [that] not only men's bodies, but also the very lines and tackling are frozen." The seas were choked with ice even in midsummer, for tremendous storms would crack the polar ice cap and fling mountainous cliffs into the paths of their wooden vessels. "The ice enclosed us," wrote the mariner on one expedition, "that we could see neither land nor sea."

George Beste urged his countrymen on in their endeavors to reach the East, encouraging them with the lure of unimaginable wealth: "Whole worldes offer and reach out themselves to them that will first vouchsafe to possess, inhabit and till them." The riches of the world were there for the taking in the sixteenth century, and there were vast tracts of ocean that had never been crossed. "Yea, there are countreys yet remaining without masters and possessors, which are fertile to bring forth all manner of corne and grayne." Beste might have displayed slightly less enthusiasm had he known the perils of tropical seas. Elizabethan galleons were frail and entirely dependent on the whim of the winds and the swirl of the currents. There were no charts of the shoals and sandbanks of the East China Sea, and the mysterious island of Japan was said to be surrounded by unpredictable storms that swallowed ships with one watery gulp.

Portugal's plucky adventurers had proved rather more adept than their English counterparts at sailing to the farthest East. They had first rounded Africa's Cape of Good Hope in 1488, nudging their carracks into the uncharted waters of the Indian Ocean. They reached India just ten years later and, by 1511, had captured the Malay port of Malacca. Pushing farther and farther east, they conducted a covert trade in the coastal waters of China, trading silks and porcelains with Ming dynasty merchants. But as they rounded the plump underbelly of this great empire, they faltered and lost heart. Their resources were limited and their manpower was stretched. They were already operating in frontier territories, at the very limits of their capabilities, and they chose to go no farther.

More than thirty years would pass before the fearsome tropical winds carried the first foreigners to Japan. They would find themselves in a land that was unlike any other. There were ascetic monks and perfumed courtiers, exquisite palaces and lacquered temples. These newly arrived adventurers were stunned to discover that the Japanese indulged in leisure pursuits of the utmost refinement and had a system of ceremonial etiquette that was as complex as it was baffling.

Yet there was a dark side to this ancient civilization. Feudal lords and their armies fought battles on a scale unknown in Europe. The theater of war involved hundreds of thousands of warriors, and vanquished armies would commit ritual suicide rather than face the ignominy of surrender. Here, at the farthest end of the world, lay an enchanted but deeply melancholic land.

The story of Samurai William is one of the most remarkable of the Jacobean age. It tells of a civilization more sophisticated than anyone had previously dreamed of discovering, yet one that was to be rent asunder by conflicts manipulated by Europeans. It begins in 1544—almost sixty years before William Adams arrived in the Land of the Rising Sun—when the blustery monsoon caught the sails of a junk that carried a little band of Portuguese merchants. Their vessel had been blown far across the East China Sea until at last they caught sight of the forested island of Kyushu in southwestern Japan. So it was that, in 1544, three Portuguese adventurers stepped ashore in the ancient fiefdom of Bungo.

Chapter 1

AT THE COURT OF BUNGO

 NO ONE HAD EVER seen such strange-looking men. They had big noses, giant mustaches, and wore puffed and padded pantaloons. They also seemed to have little understanding of Japanese etiquette and manners. To the little crowd of onlookers gathered on Funai's quayside, these three seafarers appeared to have come from another world.

Their ship had been blown to Japan by the "great and impetuous tempest" that was playing out its last dance on the waters offshore. It was rare for junks to cross the East China Sea, and the arrival of this sea-battered vessel quickly attracted the attention of Funai's governor. He made his way to the port where the strangers—speaking through Chinese interpreters—explained that they "came from another land, named Portugal, which was at the further end of the world."

The governor was unsure how to react, and sent a message to the local ruler, the lord of Bungo, with news of their arrival. His lordship ordered that the men should be summarily executed, and he sent instructions for their possessions to be stolen and their vessel confiscated, fearing that they would cause no end of trouble if he kept them alive. This news caused something of a stir in the palace chambers, especially when it reached the ears of the lord's eldest son. He told his father that such an action would blacken the name of Bungo throughout Japan and added that he refused to tolerate such a murder.

The lord of Bungo reluctantly changed his mind, but congratulated himself later when he learned more about these men from "another land." He was told that they were well dressed and that they spoke with considerable delicacy. In the ordered and strictly hierarchical society of Japan, this was of the greatest importance, and his lordship was particularly pleased to learn that they were "clothed in silk, and usually wear swords by their sides, not like merchants." He composed a missive to the governor of the port, ordering that one or all of the men be brought to him immediately. "I have heard for a truth," he wrote, "that these same men have entertained you at large with all matters of the whole universe, and have assured unto you, on their faith, that there is another world greater than ours."

The lord of Bungo's sudden interest in the men was, it transpired, little more than idle curiosity. He was a lethargic individual who suffered from a variety of real and imagined illnesses and had long been taxed by ennui. "You know my long indisposition," he wrote in his letter, "accompanied with so much pain and grief, hath great need of some diversion." He promised that whoever visited his little court would be treated with the greatest honor and respect.

There was never any doubt as to which of the three Portuguese men would go to meet the lord of Bungo. Fernão Mendes Pinto, a garrulous adventurer, was immediately selected by the port's governor, who chose him because Pinto was "of a more lively humour, wherewith those of Japan are infinitely

The Japanese were fascinated but repulsed by Portuguese sea captains. These swaggering adventurers wore fabulous costumes, yet they rarely washed and showed scant regard for Japanese etiquette and manners.

delighted, and may thereby cheer up the sick man." His lively humor would, he explained, "entertain his melancholy, instead of diverting it."

Indeed it would. Pinto was an adventurer extraordinaire—an outlandish *fidalgo*, or nobleman—whose flamboyant costume hinted at the colorful persona beneath. He was a perennial romantic, a collector of yarns, who had left Portugal more than six years earlier in search of the bizarre and the absurd. When, many years later, he came to write up his travels, he gave his book an irresistible puff on the title page: "[I] five times suffered shipwrack, was sixteen times sold, and thirteen times made a slave."

His book, *Peregrinaçam*, or *Peregrination*, is packed with incident and high adventure, mostly involving the intrepid author. He wrote it for his family and friends, but it was soon printed and became a best-seller. It should have come with a cautionary note: Pinto was a plagiarist who thought nothing of passing off other men's exploits as his own. He claimed to have been the first European to reach Japan, yet it is now known—as he himself knew—that a few shipwrecked mariners had been washed up there in the previous year. Pinto altered dates, borrowed stories, and exaggerated his own bravado in order to make his tales more entertaining. Yet there is much that is true in his account of Japan. He certainly did sail to Bungo with his countryman Jorge de Faria, and his information on the Japanese coastline is largely correct. So, too, are the incidents that occurred during his time in the fiefdom, for they can be verified from other sources. The feudal lord's son, Otomo Yoshishige, later recounted a strikingly similar tale to a Japanese chronicler, who recorded it. The English translator of Pinto's book was not altogether wrong when he wrote that "no man before him . . . hath spoken so much and so truly of those oriental parts of the world."

Pinto was escorted to meet the lord of Bungo by a stately retinue of courtly retainers and ushers, who wore rich gowns and carried maces, their insignia of office. He was immediately struck by their sumptuous costumes, which were decorated with delicately embroidered petals and chased with golden filigree. Later visitors were rather more taken by the peculiar faces of the Japanese. They had "tiny eyes and noses," wrote the Jesuit padre Luis Frois, and they eschewed the fabulous mustaches so favored by the

Portuguese. Instead, they "plucked out [their] facial hair" with tweezers, leaving their skin smooth and shiny. Their hairstyles, too, were a cause of mirth. They shaved most of their heads, but left a ponytail "on the back part . . . long and bound together." Even the way in which the Japanese picked their noses was a cause for comment. "We pick our noses with our thumb or index fingers," wrote one, ". . . [while] the Japanese use their little finger because their nostrils are small."

Pinto was whisked into the great palace of Funai and taken straight to the private chambers where his lordship was languishing in bed. But as soon as the lord of Bungo set eyes on Pinto, he pulled himself up and gave a rare smile. "Thy arrival in this my country," he said, "is no less pleasing to me than the rain which falls from heaven is profitable to our fields that are sowed with rice." Pinto was quite taken aback by such an extraordinary greeting and recorded in his book that he was "somewhat perplexed with the novelty of these terms and this manner of salutation." But he soon recovered his composure and apologized for his momentary silence, explaining that it "proceeded from the consideration that I was now before the feet of so great a king, which was sufficient to make me mute an hundred thousand years." He added that he was "but a silly ant in comparison of his greatness."

Pinto may well have believed that the lord of Bungo was indeed the king of Japan, for it was some years before the Portuguese learned that Otomo Yoshiaki—for that was his name—was actually a feudal lord, one of sixty-six. His little fiefdom covered a small area of land on Kyushu, one of the four principal islands that made up the Japanese realm.

His lordship did nothing to correct Pinto's mistaken impression, nor did he show any interest in learning about the land from which Pinto had come. Instead, he spoke about his favorite subject—himself—using Pinto's Chinese intermediaries to inform his Portuguese guest of his illness. "Thou shalt oblige me to let me know whether in thy country, which is at the further end of the world, thou hast not learn'd any remedy for this disease where-with I am tormented." Gout was not his lordship's only problem. His stomach went into revolt every time he was presented with seafood and shellfish, and he told Pinto that his "lack of appetite . . . hath continued with me now almost these two moneths."

Pinto was alarmed to find himself being asked to administer medicine and he stalled for time, informing Yoshiaki that he "made no profession of physick." But, fearing that he would dis-appoint his lordship, he suddenly changed his tune and said that he had on board "a certain wood" that, when infused in water, "healed far greater sickness than that whereof he complained." This wood was brought to the palace, Pinto made a brew, and Yoshiaki, "having used of it thirty days together . . . perfectly re-covered of his disease."

Although the lord of Bungo quickly struck up a friendship with Pinto and seemed genuinely grateful for his medicinal po-tion, his fellow countrymen found little to praise in the early Eu-ropeans in Japan. "These men are traders of south-west Barbary," sniffed the author of the Japanese chronicle *Yaita-hi*. "They under-stand to a certain degree the distinction between Superior and In-ferior, but I do not know whether they have a proper system of ceremonial etiquette." Others were horrified to discover that these foreigners thought nothing of shouting at and cursing each other. "[They] show their feelings without any self-control," wrote one contemptuous scribe, "[and] cannot understand the meaning of written characters." Worse still, their clothing was filthy and stank of stale sweat, while their unshaven appearance was a cause for concern.

The Japanese probably would have dismissed the Portuguese without further ado, were it not for one important item that was stowed in the holds of their ships. This was a supply of weapons—muskets and arquebuses—and the destruction that they wrought was a cause of wonder to the Japanese. "They had never seen any gun in that country," wrote Pinto, "[and] they could not compre-

hend what it might be, so that for want of understanding the secret of the powder, they concluded that of necessity it must be
some sorcery."

The lord of Bungo quizzed Pinto about the number of gun-
men serving under the king of Portugal, thereby inviting his guest
to tell his tallest story so far. Pinto claimed that the Portuguese
king had approximately two million gunners at his disposal. "The
king was much abashed," wrote Pinto, adding with considerable
self-satisfaction that it was "a marvelous answer."

The lord of Bungo's son, Yoshishige, was quick to grasp the
value of such a powerful weapon in a land where wars were still
fought with swords and crossbows. Wishing to test the arquebus
for himself and fearful that Pinto would refuse his request, he
crept into his guest's chamber at night and stole it. It was a foolish
act. Young Yoshishige had little idea of how to load the gun, nor
was he sure how to fire it. He packed the barrel with a huge
quantity of powder, rammed in the shot, and applied the match.
There was a blinding flash and a huge explosion. "It was his ill-
hap that the arquebus broke in three pieces and gave two hurts, by
one of the which his right-hand thumb was, in a manner, lost."
The young prince looked at his shattered thumb, fainted, and "fell
down as one dead."

This was the worst possible news for Pinto. The prince's accident instantly caused turmoil and fury in the palace, and the object of this wrath was their uninvited guest. "They all concluded
that I had killed him," wrote Pinto, "so that two of the company,
drawing out their scimitars, would have slain me." But the lord of
Bungo stopped them, for first he wished to question Pinto more
closely. He ordered his guest to squat on his knees and his arms
were bound. Pinto was then quizzed by an interpreter while a
judge stood over him, clutching a dagger "dipped in the bloud of
the young prince." He was also given a swift lesson in the manner
of Japanese justice. In normal circumstances, convicted criminals
were mutilated in public, then flogged to death or beheaded. The

SEA OF
JAPAN

KOREA

HONSHU

Kamakuro
Sekigahara

Edo
(Tokyo)

Tokaido

TSUSHIMA

Yamaguchi

Kyoto

Osaka

Shizuoka

Hemi
(William
Adams's
country
estate)

Hirado

SHIKOKU

Bungo

Nagasaki

INLAND SEA

Kagoshima

KYUSHU

EAST
CHINA
SEA

RYUKYU
ISLANDS

Great Ryukyu
(Okinawa)

PACIFIC

OCEAN

0 ——— 150
miles

—▪—▪—Imperial Road

JAPAN

N
W   E
S

corpses were then left to rot as a grim warning to others. Pinto's punishment was to be no less gruesome. "If thou doest not answer to the questions I ask thee," said his inquisitor, ". . . thou shalt be dismembred into air, like the feathers of dead fowl, which the wind carries from one place to another, separated from the body with which they were joined whilst they lived."

The justices were itching to start chopping him to pieces, but the lord of Bungo had an altogether more sensible proposal. He suggested that since his guest had been the cause of young Otomo's accident, he should now be charged with bringing him back to life. He had provided a cure for the gout; it was possible, perhaps, that he could administer a different potion that would resurrect his son. For the second time since his arrival, Pinto found himself playing doctor—only this time his very own life was at stake.

Yoshishige looked as if he was beyond repair. He had collapsed on the floor, "weltering in his own blood, without stirring either hand or foot." But a cursory examination convinced Pinto that the wounds were not as serious as the assembled courtiers believed. The gash on his forehead looked terrible, but was actually "of no great matter," while the thumb, which was hanging from its tendons, could probably be saved. "Now, because the hurt of the right hand thumb was most dangerous," wrote Pinto, "I began with that, and gave it seven stitches." His handiwork was clumsy and the wound continued to ooze blood, so he applied a more traditional salve—"the whites of eggs . . . as I had seen others done in the Indies." The cure worked. The blood clotted, and the prince regained consciousness and began to recover. Within twenty days, he was completely better, "without any other inconvenience remaining in him than a little weakness in his thumb." The new technology—Pinto's muskets and arquebuses—had proved their deadly effect, and their future in Japanese warfare was guaranteed. Within a few months of the accident, local armorers were busy making copies of the weapons.

Present-giving was a way of life in Japan and involved much ceremony. The shogun and his courtiers expected costly and exotic gifts from European merchants.

Pinto was astonished by the refined manners of the Japanese, while Yoshiaki's retinue were appalled by the rough and uncouth table manners of the Portuguese. On Pinto's second visit to Japan, in 1556, he was invited to a stately banquet at which he quickly found himself the object of derision. "We fell to eating after our own manner," wrote Pinto, "of all that was set before us." He said that watching him eat "gave more delight to the king and queen

[than] all the comedies that could have been presented before them." The Japanese, it transpired, were "accustomed to feed with two little sticks . . . [and] hold it for a great incivilitie to touch the meat with one's hands." By the end of the meal, the good humor of the Japanese had turned to disdain, and the assembled courtiers "drove away the time at our cost, by jeering and gibing at us." The banquet ended abruptly when a Japanese merchant entered the room carrying a small stash of fake wooden arms. To the up-roarious mirth of the courtiers, he explained to Pinto and his men that since their hands "must of necessity smell always of flesh or fish . . . this merchandise would greatly accommodate us."

Pinto's first visit to Japan came to an end after a couple of months at Otomo's court. He had been fascinated by the richness and splendor of Japan and, although his account often reads like a medieval fable, it gave the world its first eyewitness description of the country. It also provided a graphic illustration of the amaze-ment that would soon be shared by those who followed in Pinto's footsteps. One newcomer would write home with the shocking news that the Japanese were a superior race in almost every re-spect: "You should not think that they are barbarians," he said, "for apart from our religion, we are greatly inferior to them."

Pinto survived his time in Japan by a mixture of bluff, bravado, and cheery good humor. Confined to the fiefdom of Bungo and never straying far from the coastline, he seemed unaware that sixteenth-century Japan was one of the most dangerous countries in the world. The Land of the Rising Sun was in the grip of the terrible *sengoku jidai*—the era of civil wars—in which power was determined by military prowess. "Men chastised and killed each other," wrote one early European visitor, "banished people and confiscated their property as they saw fit, in such a fashion that treachery was rampant and nobody trusted his neighbour." The land was nominally ruled by an emperor, the self-styled

Lord of Heaven, who lived in splendid isolation in the city of Kyoto. In the golden age of medieval Japan, he had presided over a vast hierarchy of courtly ladies and chamberlains who spent their waking hours indulging in aesthetic pursuits. Now, with the imperial coffers empty, many nobles had abandoned such ceremonial amusements and had withdrawn to the provinces, leaving the emperor to fend for himself. His palace was described by one Japanese chronicler as being indistinguishable from a peasant hovel; his remaining courtiers scratched a living by selling autographed verses and peddling antiques in Kyoto's back streets. Abdication was impossible, for the court could not afford the expense of the necessary rites and rituals. When the emperor Go-Tsuchimikado died in 1500, his rotting corpse remained unburied for six weeks due to the parlous state of the royal finances. The emperor currently on the throne, Go-Nara-tenno, fared only slightly better. His coronation had to be delayed for nine years because of insufficient funds. Even when he was enthroned, he was a puppet without any power. "The true king," wrote one, "but obeyed by no one."

The emperor's protector was the shogun, or "barbarian-quelling generalissimo," who was also the strongman of the feudal lords. But by the 1540s he, too, lacked any real authority, for the country had imploded into anarchy and was fought over by the hundreds of rival warlords, brigands, and mercenaries. The great *daimyo*, or feudal lords, like Otomo Yoshiaki, lord of Bungo, were engaged in constant internecine warfare, usurping each other's domains and slaughtering their families and kinsmen.

Effective power belonged to the most ruthless robber barons, banditti, and armed monks, who regularly laid waste the countryside. The success of these warlords depended to a great extent upon the strength of the *samurai*, or two-sworded warrior class, on their land. These warriors had, in the misty past, been utterly loyal to their overlord. "We will not die peacefully," was their mantra, "but we will die by the side of our king." But many could no longer be trusted, and those living in borderland regions were only too ready to switch allegiance to a more prosperous, or more successful, feudal potentate.

Armed monks presented another threat to the feudal lords and the shogun. Japanese chronicles recount numerous instances of monks laughing in scorn at threats to reduce their hilltop fortress-monasteries. Safely behind stout walls, these monks were in an impregnable position, and many had abandoned prayer in favor of a more raucous cycle of carousing, sodomy, and adultery. Yet not all was gloom in these turbulent times. A few of the greatest Zen Buddhist monasteries produced exquisite calligraphic scrolls. So, too, did the more educated feudal lords. Poetry, the Noh lyric dramas, and the courtly rituals of the tea ceremony also flourished in this troublesome period.

Despite the unrest and the power-jostling, the impoverished court continued to function with aloof grandeur and was held in enormous respect. "Though he [the emperor] lost his position and his services and his incomes four hundred years ago," wrote the Jesuit Luis Frois, "and is nothing more than an idol, he is still held in great respect." His shaven-headed *kuge*, or courtly nobles, were destitute of power, yet were accorded every possible dignity. In this strictly hierarchical society, their honorific titles were more than empty symbols; the most impoverished retainer, once ennobled by the imperial patent, would look down upon the mightiest robber baron with the utmost contempt. It was a peculiarly Japanese phenomenon; foreign arrivals could never quite understand how a powerful feudal lord, controlling two or three provinces, could be accorded so little respect simply because the emperor had not honored him with a position at court.

Pinto was soon followed by several other Portuguese adventurers. In the winter of 1547, Captain Jorge Alvarez visited the land and declared it to be far more impressive than coastal China or the islands of the East Indies. He wrote at length of the mountains and orchards, and concluded his report with a brief analysis of the

Japanese people. There was much to be celebrated. Captain Alvarez was pleased to note that "they are a white race" and "of good appearance," and he expressed his admiration for their diet, which consisted largely of boiled, glutinous wheat. "They eat it cooked as a gruel," he wrote, "and each time they eat very little."

They were pious, too, and would spend the greater part of each morning "with their rosary in their hand to pray." In old age, many retired to Buddhist monasteries to live the rest of their days in prayer and contemplation. It was a tantalizing vision to the churchmen of Portugal, and the only blemish came at the end of their prayer sessions when the monks would hitch up their kimonos "[and] engage in sodomy with boys whom they instruct."

Alvarez's report fascinated his countryman Francis Xavier, a young Jesuit who had spent more than eight years in India and the Malay archipelago. He saw a whole new world of missionary activity opening up and was even more excited when Captain Alvarez introduced him to an open-minded Japanese refugee called Anjiro. After converting to Christianity in 1548, Anjiro—along with his servant and a friend—accompanied Xavier to Japan.

The voyage was not without its difficulties. The junk carrying Xavier and his companions suffered a treacherous passage, dodging hurricanes and hidden reefs, pirates and shallows. When the captain's daughter fell overboard and drowned, the "pagan" Chinese crew engaged in diabolical rituals, sacrificing seabirds and smearing blood over the images of their goddesses. Finally, after three wearisome weeks at sea, Xavier and his companions sighted the forested coast of Kagoshima in southern Japan. It was August 15, 1549: the twenty-second day of the seventh month of the eighteenth year of the period known as Tembun.

Kagoshima lay some 130 miles to the southwest of Funai and was much more impressive. It was the capital of the Satsuma fiefdom, and its wooded hills were bedecked with many-storied pagodas with their distinctive concave roofs. Xavier arrived when it was looking its most picturesque. Just a week earlier, the inhabitants had celebrated the great Bon festival—the Buddhist All Souls' Day—and the city's graveyards had been sprinkled with fresh blossoms.

Xavier was delighted to discover that this island nation more than lived up to expectations. The Japanese, he wrote, were "of astonishing great sense of honour, who prize honour more than any other." He was disappointed, however, to discover that the Buddhist monks were "inclined to sins abhorrent to nature," but he felt convinced that Japan would prove fertile territory. "If we knew how to speak the language," he wrote, "I have no doubt that many would become Christians."

Kagoshima was situated in one of the most conservative provinces of Japan—a bastion of the ancient Shinto cult—and the city's alleys were decked with ancient wooden shrines with their characteristic double-beamed gateways. There were Buddhist temples as well: dimly lit altars whose gilded statues glittered in the candlelight. The city was home to all the principal sects, including the exotically dressed followers of the fanatical Hokke and the gray-robed monks of the Ji-shu. These lived together with female nuns and were rumored to spend their nocturnal hours in a frenzy of copulation.

Xavier headed for the great Fukosho-ji monastery, which lay just a short walk from the harbor. It was an exquisite spot, shaded with camphor trees and scented with plum blossom. The place was adorned with stone lanterns and a lotus pool, a dragon-gate bridge, and giant stone figures with hideous grimaces. Xavier made contact with the venerable superior, an eighty-year-old Zen Buddhist abbot called Ninshitsu, and found him to be an amiable man. Ninshitsu had long been troubled by the issue of the immortality of the soul and was fascinated by Xavier's preaching and simple piety. After a lengthy conversation, with Anjiro acting as interpreter, he led his guest into the meditation hall to watch the monks at prayer. When Xavier asked what they were doing, Ninshitsu gave a despondent shrug. "Some are counting up how

*The natives of Kyushu wore elaborate costumes, spoke courteously, and had
extremely refined manners. "[They] prize honour more than any other,"
wrote Francis Xavier.*

much they received during the past months from their faithful,"
he said, "others are thinking about where they can obtain better
clothes . . . In short, none of them is thinking about anything that
has any meaning at all."

The weather began to turn soon after Xavier's arrival in
Kagoshima. The autumnal breezes brought squally showers and
the days grew cooler. The chrysanthemums bloomed and died;
the harvested rice fields turned into mud-gray swamps; and the
oaks shed their leaves after a brief but spectacular burst of color.
Only the camphor trees in the grounds of the Fukosho-ji
monastery held their foliage in the chill north wind.

Xavier and his companions shivered in their cotton tunics.
Their lodgings were freezing, for the paper window panels did little to cut the icy blast that whipped off the sea. Winter brought

the first snows, which Xavier had not seen since leaving Portugal. He stayed indoors and spent his time doggedly studying Japanese, with which he was having great difficulties. His attempt to produce a phonetic Japanese catechism, written in Latin characters, was a disaster. Twice a day, he would clamber up the steep stone steps of the Fukosho-ji monastery and, seated at the far side of the dragon-gate bridge, overlooking the tranquil lotus pool, he would try to read aloud from his book. But the translation was poor and the Christian doctrine was unintelligible to the monks. Worse still, its clumsy style offended the ears of these highly educated men, and they laughed and said he was crazy.

His more private preaching—done with the help of his interpreter—had reaped a handful of converts. An impoverished samurai had been the first to be baptized; he took the name of Bernardo and devoted himself to studying the Bible. Anjiro's mother, wife, and daughter had also converted—along with the owner of Xavier's lodgings. But these were rare successes, and Xavier found that even sympathetic audiences were generally skeptical. He had tried to adopt and adapt Japanese words when he came to teach the local people about Christianity, but quickly mired himself in confusion. Japanese religious words were too laden with symbolism to convey the theology of the gospel.

So far, Xavier had not penetrated into inland Japan and his knowledge of the country was limited—like Pinto's—to the coastline. From the moment he had first set foot in Japan, he had intended to travel to the fabled imperial city of Kyoto—then known as Miyako—to seek permission to preach from the emperor himself. He also hoped to be granted an entrance into the famous university of Heizan in order to debate with, and convert, the erudite monks.

Toward the end of August 1550, he and his companions finally set off on a journey of great hardship. The first leg involved a dangerous sea voyage, braving storms and pirates, while the second stage entailed a treacherous trek over snow-capped mountains.

The mortification of the voyage left Xavier unfazed; indeed, he made it even more arduous by shunning the offer of a pack animal and subsisting on tiny quantities of roasted rice. "He was so absorbed in God," wrote one of his fellow travelers, "that he wandered off the way without noticing it, and tore his trousers and injured his feet without observing it." He made few converts en route, for he struck most observers as an eccentric figure whose impoverished demeanor won little respect in Japan. By the time he approached Kyoto, his sleeveless black surplice was torn to shreds, while his tiny Siamese cap—tied to his head with string— gave him the appearance of a jester.

Xavier had high expectations of the fabled imperial city. "We are told great things," he wrote, ". . . [and] are assured that it has more than ninety thousand homes, and that it has a great university." He had been told of monumental temples and monasteries, of golden shrines and pleasure houses where the emperor and his court engaged in intellectual tussles. The truth was very different. Kyoto lay in ruins—an expanse of crumbling dwellings and temples—for warfare, pestilence, and floods had left the city in a parlous state. The once-magnificent Sunflower and Moonflower Gates had been wrecked by a typhoon, and the clipped fringe of bamboo that surrounded the palace apartments had been swept away by floodwater. Princesses and courtly mistresses no longer spent their waking hours composing poetry. Now, they lurked by the perimeter fence in order to beg food from passing merchants. The emperor himself had withdrawn into the sanctum of his palace.

Had Xavier been allowed a peek inside those forbidden corridors, he would have seen an extraordinary sight. The puppet emperor actually looked and behaved like a puppet. He wore an extraordinary cap with giant earflaps, tassels dangled from each hand, and his straw sandals had nine-inch heels. "This gentleman never toucheth the ground with his foote," wrote one later visitor, "[and] his forehead is painted white and red."

Xavier was dispirited by his stay in Kyoto and realized that he would have to seek permission to preach from the great feudal lords if he was to have any success in Japan. It also dawned on him that his tattered gown and unkempt hair—the visible signs of his poverty—did not impress the Japanese. When he reached the city of Yamaguchi and requested an audience with the lord, Ouchi

Few Buddhist monks were impressed with Xavier's preaching. His clumsy attempts at speaking Japanese offended the ears of these highly educated, if impoverished, men.

Yoshitaka, he dressed in newly purchased silks and presented himself as ambassador of the governor of India. He also offered Ouchi the presents that had been intended for the emperor—a clock, some Portuguese wine, and two telescopes—and proceeded to dazzle the feudal court with his learning, giving lectures on astronomy and the geography of the world. Here, at last, was something that left an impression. "They do not know that the earth is round," he wrote, "nor do they know the course of the sun, and they ask about these things and others, such as comets, lightening, rain and snow." Xavier could see that Ouchi and his men delighted in his lesson "and regarded us as learned men, which was no little help in their giving credence to our words." By the time he left the city—on hearing that a ship was awaiting him at the port of Funai—he had converted some 500 souls. Ironically, many had been won over by his knowledge of astronomy, not of Christianity.

Xavier set sail from Japan in November 1551 after more than two years in the country. In that time, he had aged visibly and his hair had turned white. He put a brave face on the troubles he had experienced and wrote an upbeat letter to his fellow missionaries about his stay in the country. The Japanese, he said, "are the best who have as yet been discovered, and it seems to me that we shall never find among heathens another race to equal the Japanese." Although his contact with them had been limited, he had seen enough to conclude that "they are a people of very good manners, good in general, and not malicious."

While Xavier had been busy preaching, Portugal's merchants had been reaping their own, more profitable, harvest. They had discovered that the Japanese had a voracious appetite for Chinese silks and were prepared to pay enormous sums of money to acquire them. They could not buy silk themselves, for the Ming emperors in China, tired of piratical raids on their coastline, had forbidden any Japanese from landing on their shores on pain of death. An imperial decree described them as "thieves, birds of prey and rebels against the sovereign emperor of China." Such sentiments were music to the ears of the Portuguese. "The discord between China and Japan is a great help to the Portuguese," wrote one Jesuit monk, "[for] the Portuguese have a great means of negotiating their worldly business."

In or around 1555, the Portuguese secured a toehold on the tiny island of Macao, on the south coast of China, which gave them access to the great silk markets of Canton. With characteristic energy, they began buying vast quantities of silks in preparation for their first great trading mission to Japan, along with other "Chinish wares"—porcelain, musk, rouge, and rhubarb.

In 1555, a huge carrack laden with silks sailed to Japan under the command of Captain Duarte da Gama. She did brisk business on arrival and returned to Macao with such a vast quantity of silver that even the monks were left wide-eyed. "Ten or twelve days ago, a great ship from Japan arrived here," wrote the Jesuit padre Belchior. "She came so richly laden that now all other Portuguese and ships which are in China intend to go to Japan." The success of the voyage sparked a frenetic trade as Portugal's merchants entered this lucrative business. The profits were indeed staggering and commentators wrote excitedly about the enormous quantities of silver being exported from Japan. One quoted twenty million grams a year; another—Diogo de Couto—bragged that "the cargo . . . is all exchanged for silver bullion, which is worth more than a million of gold [cruzados]." A third said that the Portuguese were managing to cart off almost half of Japan's annual production of silver bullion.

The merchants in Macao built huge vessels to bring back their silver—unwieldy monsters of almost 2,000 tons. These *nao do trato*, or "great ships," were broad in the beam and had as many as four flush decks, with space for a staggering 120,000 cubic feet of silver bullion. They were veritable leviathans by the standards of the day, and they towered over the native junks. The way in which the trade was regulated was decidedly eccentric: the exclusive rights to the annual voyage to Japan were—quite literally—sold to the highest bidder in Macao. For the successful captains, the wealth and authority this brought them often went to their heads and they would swagger around the Japanese ports accompanied by armed retinues, fife bands, and Negro slaves. The Japanese had never seen anything like it.

Although they continued to label the Portuguese barbarians, the Japanese had the foresight to realize that these merchants had the wherewithal to bring them the silks they so fiercely craved. They also discovered that their best hope of attracting merchants to their fiefdoms was by currying favor with the Jesuit priests who arrived along with the bales of silk. The astute Otomo Yoshishige of Bungo was one of the first to grasp that trade and religion went hand in hand. He wrote to the Jesuit authorities in the most ingratiating terms, begging them to persuade merchants to harbor in his port. He assured them: "One of the reasons is that I will be able to install the fathers again . . . with greater favour than they obtained at first." But it was not the only reason. The lord of Bungo was desperate to lay his hands on Portuguese weaponry and requested "espera" guns, which fired twelve-pound shot. He argued that "if I have my kingdom prosperous and defended, [then] the church of god will likewise be so." In a decidedly saccharine afternote, he said that he had always enjoyed the company of the Portuguese and that his most treasured possession was a letter written by the queen of Portugal, "which I esteem so highly that I carry it in my breast as a relic."

Poor Yoshishige's request fell on deaf ears. Portugal's merchants and priests had discovered a far more suitable harbor on the northwestern shores of Kyushu: Nagasaki. From 1571, they began to direct their great ships into its deep, safe waters. "This place is a natural stronghold," wrote one, "and one which no Japanese lord could take by force." It was soon to prove as beneficial to the merchants as it was providential to the priests. The feudal lord of Nagasaki, Omura Sumitada, had converted to Christianity in 1562 and had taken the name Dom Bartolemeu. When he saw the quantities of silks, damasks, and porcelains arriving at his shores, he went one step further and declared his intention of making his fiefdom a purely Christian one, expelling all who would not conform to the new religion. This was swiftly achieved and a band of Jesuit monks, "accompanied by a strong guard . . . went around causing the churches of the gentiles"—the Buddhist and Shinto temples—". . . to be thrown to the ground." Within seven months, 20,000 people had been baptized, along with the monks of some sixty monasteries. The Jesuits were overjoyed and rejoiced at seeing these monks, "the very men who formerly regarded us as viler than slaves, . . . now [come to us] with hands and forehead on the ground in token of submission."

The Jesuits were aware that Dom Bartolemeu's actions were less inspired by Christian charity than business acumen. He did it, they recorded, "because he would thus ensure always having the Great Ship in that port, which would bring him great renown and make him a great lord through the duties and profits he would derive therefrom." He soon offered them an even more important concession. On June 9, 1580, he ceded them the port of Nagasaki, ostensibly so that they would have the necessary money to finance their mission. But Dom Bartolemeu himself was also a beneficiary. He would continue to receive all taxes and dues, and would be allowed to use Nagasaki as a place of refuge in time of danger.

So long as the Portuguese could keep their monopoly over Japan, they would reap rich rewards. What they did not know was that in the docks of Limehouse in London, preparations were under way for a voyage to the Land of the Rising Sun.

Chapter 2

ICEBERGS IN THE ORIENT

 THE WHARVES of Limehouse presented a forlorn sight at low tide. Their blackened timbers dripped and creaked and, in the half-light of dawn, the dockside looked like the skeletal frame of a wrecked galleon.

The church of St. Dunstan could be seen from the piers, while the Tower of London was visible to those on the river. Just a stone's throw upstream was Execution Dock, where crowds gathered to gawk at corpses hanging stiffly from the riverside gallows, whose water-blown bodies had been left as a grim warning. These were the remains of corsairs and filibusters who had been caught ransacking galleons and cargo vessels. If they were condemned and convicted, their punishment was terrible: they would be strung up and left "at the low water marke, there to remaine till three tides had overflowed them."

On normal days, the wharves did not come to life until first light, but on the morning of May 20, 1580, there was an unusual amount of activity in the hours before dawn. Limehouse was already busy as watermen and stevedores occupied themselves in preparation for the imminent departure of two tiny vessels. Their destination was unknown, but the cargo for these craft was so extraordinary that it was already drawing comment from the workers. In their holds were fine crystal goblets and pewter flagons, Venetian looking glasses and ivory combs. This was not the usual cargo of ships heading for strange and barbarous lands.

The vessels were owned by two of Elizabethan England's more extraordinary entrepreneurs. Sir George Barne was a serial adventurer who had been involved in "the discovery of new trades" for almost thirty years. His earliest venture—back in the 1550s—had been to Africa. He had subsequently dispatched several expeditions to Guinea, and on one occasion his men had returned with the head of an elephant and five black slaves. These slaves proved decidedly ungrateful at being separated from their families and complained, not without justification, that England was a land of perpetual drizzle. "The colde and moiste aire doth somewhat offend them," wrote the expedition chronicler. Now, after years spent expanding his trade network, Sir George had set his sights on the distant continent of Asia.

His partner, Sir Rowland Heyward, was also experienced in mounting expeditions to unknown lands. One of the founders of the Muscovy Company, which had opened trade with the vast realm of Ivan the Terrible, Sir Rowland had been granted extensive trading rights—not just to Moscow, but to such far-flung places as Astrakhan, Novgorod, and Kazan, the great Tartar city on the Volga. Sir Rowland had further petitioned the tsar, asking him for a building concession throughout his empire. A bemused Ivan duly obliged: "We have granted leave to the English merchant . . . to builde houses at Vologda, Colmogro [Kholmohovy] and the seaside; at Ivangorod, at Chcrell [Karelia], and in all other places in our dominions." Even this did not satisfy the insatiable Sir Rowland. Within a few years, he was touting for trade with

Persia, persuading Queen Elizabeth to introduce herself to the "emperor" and ask for trading rights to his empire.

Now, these two merchants had turned their attentions to the farthest East, to China and Japan, which were rumored to be lands of astonishing wealth. Sir Rowland knew that if he could be the first to stake his claim to these kingdoms, then fortune and fame would follow. He was undeterred by the logistical difficulties of such a voyage and undaunted by the distances involved. Together with Sir George, he began gathering all the available information, planning his project with his customary enthusiasm and gusto.

The two men soon found that much of the hard work had been done for them. Less than three years earlier, in 1577, an English enthusiast called Richard Willes had stumbled across two hitherto unknown documents that contained descriptions of both China and Japan. Aware that almost nothing was known about either nation and that he had laid his hands on gold dust, Willes decided to publish the information in a book entitled *A Historye of Travaile.*

The report on China had come into his hands by way of a Portuguese merchant who had been captured and imprisoned by mandarins of the Ming imperial court. It revealed that China was ruled by a powerful sovereign who meted out cruel and terrible punishments and that the population of this vast nation was expanding at an unsustainable rate. "The countrey is so well inhabited," recorded Willes, "that no one foote of grounde is left untilled." A large population meant a large potential market, and that was the best possible news for the London merchants. The eating habits of the Chinese were rather less appealing. They were reputed to munch their way through anything that moved, and Willes was astonished to learn that "frogs are solde at the same price that is made of hennes . . . as also dogs, cats, rats, snakes and all other uncleane meates."

The report on Japan was a great deal more optimistic. Willes had acquired a handful of private letters about "the Japonish nation," written by the Jesuit padre Luis Frois. These letters had been written to fellow Jesuits and were not intended to be studied—still less published—by "hereticke" Protestants. But Willes quickly realized their value and proceeded to translate them "word for word, in such wise as followeth."

The resulting publication caused considerable excitement among London's adventurers, for it revealed that Marco Polo had been right all along. Japan was a "glorious island among so many barbarous nations and rude regions" and was so fabulously wealthy that it had the means with which to pay—rather than barter—for trade goods. Although there was little gold—as Polo had promised—there was a "great store of silver mines," which produced thousands of tons annually. Even better news was the fact that the Japanese were quite unlike the savages and cannibals said to inhabit most of the islands of the East. The population was "tractable, civill, wittie, courteous [and] without deceit," and Willes could assure his readers that English merchants would be welcomed by a civilized nation who, "in virtue and honest conversation," outclassed any other people in the eastern hemisphere.

There were, of course, pitfalls to this enchanted kingdom. The coastline was extremely treacherous and there were rumors of "great piracie" in the waters around Japan. The weather, too, was said to be unendurably harsh. Willes recorded that "there falleth so much snow that the houses being buried in it, the inhabitants keep within doores." He informed his readers that the snow was often so deep and compacted that when the Japanese wished to venture outside, they had to "breake up the tiles" on the roofs of their houses. But even the bad news was tempered by good: a chill climate meant a huge potential market for English woollens.

Although the Japanese were said to be courteous and without deceit, they showed an alarming propensity for violence and brutality. They frequently strangled their own children—so as to avoid wasting precious food supplies—and had a strangely melancholic disposition. Ritual suicide—*seppuku*—was commonplace and often extremely bloody. Any man intent on taking his own life would dress in his finest silken costume, unsheathe an enormous curved sword, and, "lancing his body acrosse, from the breast downe all the belly, murthereth himselfe."

Although the inhabitants of the principal island of Japan were held to be extremely cultivated, the population of the wild northerly provinces—where Barne and Heyward's expedition was likely to make its first landfall—came from altogether more barbarous stock. The island of Hokkaido was said to be inhabited by "savage men, clothed in beasts skinnes, rough-bodied, with huge beards and monstrous muchaches." These mustaches were so big that they were said to be propped up with special forks during their customary drinking bouts.

When the two entrepreneurs learned of the potential riches of these Eastern realms, they decided to press ahead with their voyage without further ado, petitioning investors and gathering information. The most obvious route was to sail down the African coastline, round the Cape of Good Hope, and across the Indian Ocean. But this was fraught with danger. Portugal's merchant adventurers had been sailing this course for almost a century, controlling many of the best harbors and watering holes en route. They were not likely to welcome England's heretic mariners into harbors that they considered to be their own. The second option—sailing around the southern tip of South America and across the empty expanse of the Pacific—was scarcely more appealing. The rocky Straits of Magellan presented a formidable challenge to even the most talented of pilots, while the Pacific was as unpredictable as it was unknown. Worse still, the first landfall was likely to be the Philippines, which were firmly in the grasp of King Philip II of Spain.

Sir Rowland and Sir George decided that both these routes presented too great a risk. They were more familiar with the frosty North than the tropical South and argued that a voyage across the top of Russia, although undeniably dangerous, had the

Richard Willes's readers were astonished to learn about seppuku—*Japanese ritual suicide. The perpetrator would slice open his stomach with a curved sword, "from the breast downe all the belly."*

advantage of being relatively short. After consulting with the great expert on Elizabethan exploration, Richard Hakluyt, they came up with a plan that was as bold as it was simple. They would build a base on one of the Arctic's many islands—perhaps Vaygach Island, at the entrance to the Kara Sea—which could be used as a depot. Such a base could prove a lifesaver in the long winter months and could, in time, become a great trading entrepôt between England and the farthest East. It was an uncomplicated, straightforward idea that had the advantage of avoiding any clash with the Portuguese or Spanish. It would also help to avoid a disaster on the scale of Sir Hugh Willoughby's expedition of 1553.

Sir Rowland and Sir George knew that previous undertakings had failed because of "want of skill in the cosmographie and the arte of navigation." They decided, right from the outset, to hire the very best captains they could find. After a lengthy search, they settled on two hardy and dependable mariners, Arthur Pet and Charles Jackman, both of whom had already made lengthy voyages into Arctic climes. Jackman had taken part in two of Sir Martin Frobisher's voyages in search of a Northwest Passage, while Pet had considerable experience of the extreme north of Russia. Both men jumped at the opportunity to take part in yet another dangerous but exhilarating venture, and were joined by the London merchant Nicholas Chancellor, who hoped to be the first Englishman to make his fortune in the Far East.

Finding a crew proved rather more difficult. When Sir Rowland and Sir George mooted their project around the Thameside dockyards, they were met with a distinctly lukewarm response. Just thirteen men and two boys signed up. Although they had little prospect of enticing any more would-be adventurers onto their rolls, the two merchants decided to push on regardless. The exploration expert Richard Hakluyt was alarmed at the lack of men and warned that a few deaths could scupper the entire enterprise. "You must have great care to preserve your people," he advised, "since your numbers is so small and not to venture any one man in any wise."

Sir Rowland and Sir George hired two diminutive vessels, the *George* and the *William*, which were anchored "in the river of Thames against Limehouse." Next, they set to work on the detailed planning, beginning with a formal commission of employment for their two captains. The principal aim of the voyage was the "search and discoveries of a passage by sea . . . to the countries or dominions of the mightie prince, the emperour of Cathay, and in the same unto the Cities of Cambalu [Peking] and Quinsay [Hangchow]." Aware that the journey would push the crew to the extremes of endurance, they were instructed "to joine in friendship together, as most deere friends and brothers . . . to the furtherance and orderly performing of the same voyage." They were to love each other, pray for each other, and "bend yourselves to the uttermost of your powers to performe the thing that you are both employed for."

Richard Hakluyt was asked to prepare a detailed list of the supplies and cargo that the men would need, while Dr. John Dee, the acknowledged expert on mathematics and astrology, proffered advice on navigation and topography. He urged the men not to drop anchor when they reached Hangchow in China, but to "saile over to Japon Island, where you shall finde Christian men, Jesuits of many countreys . . . at whose handes you may have great instruction and advise." The maritime expert William Borough was also consulted. He had mapped at least part of the shoreline of the White Sea and begged Pet and Jackman to continue his work, telling them to make charts of "where the high cliffs are, and where lowe land is, whether sande, hils or woods." In return for their labors, they were allowed to give names to every bay and headland "at your pleasure."

Sir Richard and Sir George had put much thought into the sort of cargo that the vessels should carry to the Far East and agreed with Hakluyt's view that this expedition was much more than a mere trading mission. It was a floating exhibition of wares and products that would reveal the advanced and civilized state of Elizabethan England.

Hakluyt's notes reveal his sense of disquiet at the prospect of making contact with a heathen land that was also believed to be as civilized and sophisticated as Europe. Previous voyages had been to "rude" and "barbarous" lands, where adventurers found themselves confronting primitive "savages" dressed in stinking skins and carrying spears. William Hawkins's voyages to South America had brought Englishmen face to face with Indians whose pierced cheeks were studded with bone. William Towerson's expeditions to Guinea had discovered "wilde negroes" who chomped on raw flesh and lived in shacks made of mud. The more Englishmen saw of the world, the more they convinced themselves that faraway re-

Richard Hakluyt had heard rumors of the sophistication of the Japanese, especially noblemen (above). When Captains Pet and Jackman set sail, they took only the finest-quality goods.

gions were inhabited by primitive tribes who pranced around stark naked and showed off their "privy partes." Much of this was wishful thinking or blind prejudice. The inhabitants of the extreme north of America had shown themselves to be effective hunter-gatherers who most certainly did not eat one another, yet the accounts describe them as "ravenous, bloudye and man-eating" and mock them for showing an appreciation for simple objects like "belles, looking glasses and other toys." Even those living on the fringes of the British Isles were deemed primitive by the sophisticates of Elizabethan London. One group was held to be particularly backward—idolatrous, superstitious, and living in "barbarous ignorance." They were the Welsh.

Hakluyt knew that Pet and Jackman's voyage to the Far East would bring Englishmen into contact with altogether more cultured people, and he urged that only the finest-quality goods be taken on board. He insisted that the two captains take accurate scales and weights, which, he said, were used only by societies with "a certaine shew of wisdom." He suggested that they take a little collection of silver coins bearing the noble head of Queen Elizabeth I, "to be showed to the governours . . . which is a thing that shall in silence speake to wise men more than you imagine." He instructed them to take a map of England, but warned that it should not be *any* map. It must be one that was "set out in faire colours . . . [and] of the biggest sort." The men were also to take the finest examples of the work of England's blacksmiths: "locks and keyes, hinges, bolts, haspes &c., great and small, of excellent workmanship." They were to take spectacles (or "glazen eyes") and fine glassware; hourglasses and "combes of ivorie"; looking glasses from Venice; knitted gloves, pewter bottles, and leather buttons. Wool, England's chief export, was well represented: there were hand-knitted socks and gloves, as well as nightcaps and blankets. Other items stowed in the holds included seeds of sweet-smelling flowers, tinderboxes, bellows, and printed books. Every item was carefully selected to show that England was a rich, sophisticated, and highly cultured realm.

The *George* and the *William* slipped away from Limehouse in the spring of 1580. After a brief pause at Harwich to take on extra food supplies, the ships pushed on into the North Sea. Shortly after their departure, Richard Hakluyt received a reply to a letter that he had written to the esteemed Flemish cartographer Gerardus Mercator. It offered important advice to Pet and Jackman, and it was most unfortunate that it arrived several weeks too late. Mercator warned that one of the chief hazards of sailing to the north was the wild inaccuracy of the compass in such regions. "The neerer you come unto it [the North Pole]," he wrote, "the more the needle of the compasse does vary from the north, sometimes to the west and sometimes to the east." He said that compass variation was a cause of frequent disaster for Arctic explorers and informed Hakluyt that "if Master Arthur [Pet] be not well provided . . . or of such dexteritie that, perceiving the errour, he be not able to correct the same, I feare [that] he be overtaken with the ice."

Compass variation was not the only peril faced by Pet and Jackman. There was also the danger of icebergs whose underwater buttresses could easily puncture a hole in the fragile oak timbers of Elizabethan vessels. When Martin Frobisher had gone in search of the Northwest Passage just a few years earlier, his men had been forced to keep a sharp eye on the icebergs and "were brought many times to the extreamest pointe of perill." They had watched in horror as "planckes of timber, more than three inches thicke . . . were severed and cutte in sunder." Even in midsummer, when the Arctic was at its most clement, a strong northerly wind could send a flurry of icebergs into previously open waters.

The lack of clear skies was an additional hindrance to pilots whose equipment was dependent upon being able to take an accurate reading of the sun. "The sunne draweth near to the horizon in the north parts," explained one, "[and] it is there commonly shadowed with vapours and thicke fogges." In winter, the situation would become critical, for the land would be "deformed with horrible darkenesse and continuall nighte."

Despite the doom and gloom in London, Captains Pet and Jackman made rapid progress to the bustling port of Wardhouse, on today's border between Russia and Finland, where they picked up fresh supplies. The *William* also underwent urgent repairs, for her rudder was damaged and she was found to be "somewhat leake." It took a whole day to repair her hull.

Shortly after leaving Wardhouse, Captains Pet and Jackman had their first disagreement. For reasons that remain obscure, Jackman wished to put into the next port. Pet taunted him for cowardice and sneeringly informed his erstwhile friend "that if he thought himselfe not able to keepe the sea, he should doe as he thought best." He added that the crew of the *George* intended to press on alone. It was a remarkably foolish decision and one that explicitly broke the terms of their commission, which said, "You should never lose sight the one of the other."

Just four days later, Captain Pet recorded a brief but ominous entry in his diary: "This day we met with ice." It was midsummer, and they were far to the south of the route that they would soon have to take, yet already there was ice in the sea. Pet ordered all the sails to be set, and they soon broke free of it. He concluded that these icebergs were freak leftovers from winter, having lingered in some shady spot in the White Sea.

After a further week's sailing, through thick fog, showers, and thundery squalls, the crew gave a little cheer as they sighted the shores of Vaygach Island to the south of Novaya Zemlya. This speck of land marked the boundary between the Barents Sea and the Kara Sea—a milestone in their voyage to the Far East. As they pushed their vessels into the Kara Sea, they would be leaving Europe behind. These ice-littered waters pounded the shores of Asia.

This made Vaygach Island a place of some strategic significance, and Hakluyt believed that it had been overlooked for too long. He had suggested to Pet and Jackman that they make their base there, or on one of the nearby islands, "from whence . . . we might feed those heathen nations with our commodities . . . without venturing our whole masse in the bowels of their countrey." He suggested that they build a fort and a small warehouse, and encourage the merchants of Peking to make regular visits there. Using them as middlemen, the English could establish a trade network that spread its tentacles right across the Far East.

Hakluyt's plan was flawless, except in one important respect. Vaygach Island was not quite as close to Peking as he imagined; indeed, it lay approximately 2,500 miles from China's imperial city, across a bleak Siberian wilderness of birch forest, tundra, and permafrost. There was also the Gobi Desert to be negotiated, as well as the great mountain ranges of northern Mongolia. It was most unlikely that China's merchants would be willing to make such a voyage in order to acquire English socks and gloves.

Nor, as the men discovered, was it an ideal place for a base. Vaygach was a desolate spot. There were no signs of any settlements or food supplies, and the blasts of chill wind caused the men to shiver in their jerkins. A band of them struggled ashore through a "great fogge" and promptly stumbled upon a large stone cross "and a man buried at the foote of it." The sight of this had a peculiar effect on the no-nonsense Captain Pet. He suddenly felt profoundly guilty at having sailed on without the *William* and carved his name onto the cross "to the end that if the *William* did chaunce to come thither, they might have knowledge that we had beene there."

Captain Pet seems to have realized that he was still far from China, for he ordered his men back on board so that they could continue with their onward voyage. It soon became apparent that the Kara Sea presented a formidable challenge, even to a skillful pilot like Pet. There were numerous rocky islets, powerful rip currents, and—more alarmingly—"a very great store of ice a-seaborde." The weather, too, had taken a turn for the worse. "Very much wind, raine and fogge," recorded Pet, who noted that the winds either battered their vessel relentlessly or left them becalmed. But there was good news on the horizon. On August 23, at "nine in the afternoone, we had sight of the *William*." To the weary and depressed crews of both ships, this meeting was a cause for celebration. Pet and Jackman were jubilant and any bad feelings were quickly forgotten. The men on the *George* polished up their brass instruments and proceeded to give their sister ship a lively welcome: "We sounded our trumpet, and shot off two muskets." Pet preferred to express his gratitude in prayer: "We acknowledge this our meeting to be a great benefit of God for our mutuall comfort, and so gave His Majestie thanks for it."

He quickly discovered that the *William* had made slow progress to the Kara Sea. Her sternpost had broken, her rudder was smashed, and she was having great difficulty in making headway. Mending the damaged rudder proved difficult, for the water was far too cold for the men to carry out repairs at sea. Instead, they were forced to shift all the cannon and cargo to the helm so that the stern was lifted, seesaw fashion, out of the water. The carpenters then set to work and, after a few anxious hours, completed the repairs. The *William* was at last able to steer again.

It was during the days that followed their unexpected meeting that Captains Pet and Jackman were able to consider more fully their next course of action. They had serious concerns about continuing with their voyage. The wind was blowing an icy gust from the north, and the quantity of ice in the water was increasing at an alarming rate. "Windes we have had at will," wrote Pet, "but ice and fogge too much against our willes." Another problem was caused by their lack of information. William Borough had been able to give them sailing directions as far as Vaygach, but henceforth his advice was of limited use. "It is probable you shall finde the land on your right hand," he had informed them, suggesting that Peking was about 400 miles away. But he admitted that he was not entirely sure.

There was very good reason to turn back, and yet the sheer excitement of sailing toward unknown lands drove these intrepid men forward. So much planning and hard work had been invested in their great enterprise that it seemed churlish not to make the attempt. Besides, they were looking forward to meeting the civilized folk of the East. Richard Hakluyt had handed them detailed instructions on how they were to conduct themselves, informing them that the Chinese and Japanese were not savages and could not be treated in the same brusque manner as was customary with African tribesmen or the barbarous "brutes" of South America. They were to be treated with deference and civility, and invited on board ship for a gracious welcome. "First," he advised, "the sweetest perfumes [are to be] set under the hatches, to make ye place sweet." Then, once the Japanese had been shown all due courtesy, they were to be offered the choicest dainties on board: "marmelade . . . prunes . . . almonds . . . dried peares." They were to be given sugar, oil from Zánte, cinnamon water, and biscuits in vinegar—a delicacy in Elizabethan England, which, with "a little sugar cast in it cooleth and comforteth and refresheth the spirits of man." Hakluyt also suggested that they open their phials "of good sweet waters . . . to besprinkle the guests withall, after their coming aboard." When those same guests left, they were to be given presents of jams and conserves. "With the gift of these marmelades," he wrote, ". . . you may gratifie [them]."

Hakluyt had high hopes that the English would be invited ashore, enabling them to indulge in a spot of espionage. "Take a speciall view of their navy," he wrote, "the sailes, the tackles, the ankers, the furniture of them, with ordinance, armour and munition." The English were to procure some gunpowder to test its efficacy, to note the quality of Japanese armor and to study the strengths "of the walls and bulwarks of their cities." But Hakluyt's concerns were not just military ones. He asked the captains to bring home seeds "of strange herbs and flowers" and acquire "some old printed booke" to enable someone to study the language. He even suggested that they should bring back to England "one or other young man" who could be taught English and reveal the secrets of his land.

The two captains decided to push on regardless of the risk, dodging icebergs and drifting pack ice until they found their passage blocked. "Here were pieces of ice so great," records the ship's log, "that we could not see beyond them out of the toppe." After almost a week of inactivity, the crews decided to attempt to force their way out. But it was not easy: "We were much troubled with the ice," wrote Pet. No sooner had they freed themselves than the *George* struck an iceberg with such force that her timbers shuddered and her anchor was twisted into a tangle of metal. They soon found themselves striking other icebergs, and with each collision they heard a hollow boom resonate from the deep bowels of the vessel. "Many other great blowes we had against the ice," wrote Pet, "[so] that it was marveilous that the ship was able to abide them." The damage to the *William* was considerable, while her little boat had been smashed to pieces. Worse still, both vessels were soon locked into the ice and were caught in a severe blizzard that blanketed the decks in snow. The men's safety was now in serious doubt and, as their resolve faltered, they began to scale down

Richard Hakluyt urged adventurers to gather information on Japanese weaponry. The English would later be astonished by the quality—and devastating effectiveness—of samurai swords, which were finely wrought by master craftsmen.

their expectations of reaching the Far East. Indeed, there was no longer any talk of sailing to Japan or China. Now, they prayed that they might simply escape the pack ice and return to England before their ships were crushed and they succumbed to starvation.

For once, those prayers were answered. The ice sheet parted slightly and the men seized on their advantage, hoisting their sails and slipping out through a small gap. By nine o'clock, they reached the edge of the ice that had imprisoned them and suddenly found themselves in open water, "whereof we were most glad, and not without great cause, and gave good the praise." They now had a very real chance of saving their lives and their ships, and they grasped the opportunity, racing directly to the northern cape of Norway. At Trondheim, the two captains bade farewell to each other, for Jackman—whose quest for adventure was not yet sated—was keen to sail on to Iceland. Pet had no intention of following him. He was already dreaming of candlelit taverns and Southwark strumpets. He steered his ship south for London, arriving back in the Thames on December 25, "being the Nativity of Christ." The men fell to their knees in prayer, as they gave thanks to God "for our safe returne." The crew of the *William* was not so fortunate. They were never heard of again.

Captain Pet's expedition had been a complete failure. He had singularly failed to negotiate the ice-choked waters that lapped the shores of northern Russia and could give little encouragement to any future expedition to the North. His men had hoped to return with doublets made of Chinese silks and jerkins stuffed with Japanese silver. Instead, they had arrived back in London with frostbite and missing toes. As if that were not enough, Pet's ignominious return was totally overshadowed by the triumphant return of Francis Drake, who had just completed his voyage around the world. Drake had nudged his vessel, the *Golden Hind*, into Plymouth harbor in September 1580, where he was feted as a hero, not just because he was the first Englishman to circumnavigate the globe, but because he was returning with an astonishing quantity of booty. He had rifled from the Spanish a staggering one and a half million pesos of plunder, including five huge crates of gold, twenty tons of silver, and so many coins and pearls that it would take many weeks to count them all.

Queen Elizabeth was overjoyed. When Drake finally arrived in

London, she honored him with a private audience that lasted for six hours. It was not just the vast quantity of treasure that delighted the queen. Drake's voyage had been a dazzling feat of seamanship that shattered forever the myth that the southern oceans were the exclusive preserve of the Spanish and the Portuguese. English adventurers had tried repeatedly to smash their way through the northern ice pack, believing that to sail south would be suicidal. Now, Drake had proved that the Indian and Pacific Oceans were no longer out of bounds. Indeed, he had demonstrated that English mariners could go where they chose and were more than able to play cat and mouse with their Catholic rivals. The queen would famously justify the future voyages of her sea dogs by pronouncing that "the sea and air are common to all men."

She chose to ignore Captain Pet's Arctic failure, condemning him to return to the obscurity from which he had briefly escaped. Preferring to back a winner, she prepared a lavish celebration in honor of Drake's triumph in the tropics. She decreed that the *Golden Hind* should be placed in a dock at Deptford as a lasting memorial to his historic voyage and proposed an onboard banquet. Held on April 4, 1581, it was a splendid affair—the most ostentatious celebration since the reign of old King Henry. The vessel was bedecked with flags and bunting while the shoreline at Deptford was adorned with colorful banners. The queen herself was in fine humor, aware, perhaps, that Drake's success marked a turning point for England's merchant adventurers. As she stepped aboard the newly scrubbed *Golden Hind*, she showed Drake her gilded sword and joshed that she had come to chop off his head. But he knew that she had come to do no such thing. She commanded him to kneel, then handed her sword to her guest of honor, Marquis de Marchaumont, and ordered him to knight her gallant explorer. Sir Francis repaid the honor with magnificent presents, all of which had been filched from the Spanish. There were five huge emeralds, a "baskett of silver," and a magnificent golden globe whose oceans were made from green enamel. It was those oceans that Elizabeth's adventurers now hoped to traverse.

The banquet grew raucous as night descended, and the noise of viols and tabors could be heard up and down the great river. As the evening wore on, more and more curious spectators gathered to witness the historic scene. At one point, so many people had assembled on the bridge that linked the ship to the shore that the timbers began to creak and groan. Suddenly, there was a tremendous crack and a hundred or more people were plunged into the muddy river. Wiser heads might have seen this as a warning that Elizabethan technology did not always match its enthusiasm.

Not everyone had been invited to share in Drake's triumph. Just upstream from Deptford was Limehouse, the land of the living poor, where an Elizabethan underclass was packed like herrings into squalid and unsanitary tenements. Limehouse lay outside the walls of London, a sprawl of shacks and dwellings that had been roughly built to contain a population that had already reached bursting point. The antiquary John Stowe bemoaned the fact that there had been a great deal of new building in recent years and that "shipwrights and . . . other marine men have builded many large, and strong houses for themselves, and smaller for sailers." The city was indeed growing too fast, and there were many complaints about the number of houses being erected. In the same year as Drake's return, Queen Elizabeth had issued a royal proclamation prohibiting the construction of any new buildings within three miles of the city gates. Limehouse was particularly infamous for its "dissolute, loose and insolent people," but not all its inhabitants were thieves and petty criminals. Many mariners and carpenters also lived there, as well as the navigators and shipwrights who built and manned the vessels of the great gentlemen adventurers. The Thames was "the principal storehouse and staple of all commodities within this realm," whose banks were a confusion of wharfs and jetties. This was where crews gathered to tout for work and offer their services for voyages into unknown seas.

One of these men was William Adams, a youth of seventeen years when Drake was knighted. He had been born in the Kentish town of Gillingham, a haunt of fisherfolk, and was baptized on September 24, 1564, probably a day or two after his birth. He came from humble and impoverished stock who left few traces of their existence. Young William would also have been lost to history, but the wheel of fortune raised him up and provided him with a spectacular new life on the farthest side of the globe.

His childhood would have remained a mystery, had it not been for a letter that he wrote—many years later—when he was feeling homesick and melancholic. An Elizabethan physician would have recognized his symptoms as an excess of black bile and would have prescribed a large dose of thistle to "comforteth the brain." Adams preferred to cure himself by writing to his long-lost friends, reminding them of his identity. "I am a Kentish man," he informed them, "borne in the towen called Gillingham, two English miles from Rochester [and] one mile from Chatham." He proceeded to tell them that from the age of twelve, he had been "brought up in Limehouse near London."

The letter reveals a haphazard education and a happy-go-lucky attitude to life. His spelling is folksy and phonetic, while his turn of phrase is delightfully piquant. The Elizabethans obeyed few rules when they set quill to paper; William Adams obeyed none, and both his syntax and spelling are decidedly eccentric. He speaks of "drisslling rayne" and "veri ffayr wether," of "spiss" [spice] and "ollefantes teeth."

There are no surviving portraits of Adams, unless his likeness is hidden somewhere among the European faces on the Japanese *byobu*, or picture screens. But his letters reveal a chimerical character whose recklessness and arrogance combined with a quiet charm that could weave its magic in a foreign and alien land. In later years, he would stun his compatriots by addressing Eastern princes and potentates in the same abrupt manner that he employed with the lowliest cabin boy. They were no less shocked at the adroitness with which he would shed his old skin and adopt foreign customs.

He must have been a bear of a man—tough as salt pork and bred to survive hardship. While others wilted and died, laid low by scurvy, poisoned arrows, or the "blody flux," Adams remained in rude health. He munched his way through joints of raw penguin to keep himself alive and, when he had sucked the bones until the marrow ran dry, he gnawed the salt-toughened leather that surrounded the mast ropes. Yet there was another, more complex side to William Adams. Sometimes he was aloof and detached. At other times he was disarmingly honest. His fellow countrymen would confuse his brusque manner with arrogance and accuse him of being haughty. They failed to realize that this was the very quality that had enabled him to survive—and thrive—in the most desperate circumstances.

Adams trained as a pilot and shipwright under the famous Nicholas Diggins. To have had such a tutor was a stroke of fortune, for Diggins was a skilled shipwright who built many of the vessels used by London's gentlemen adventurers. He taught Adams how to construct the small, fast, caravel-built ships that had become popular with English captains and also gave him instruction on how to shape a ship's frame and clad it with planking. These lessons would one day save his life.

However, the young Adams was less interested in building ships than in sailing them, and he spent much of his time on the river or at sea. No sooner had he completed his apprenticeship, in 1588, than he was given command of the *Richard Duffield*, a supply ship that was charged with carrying victuals and ammunition to the English fleet doing battle with the Spanish Armada. As Lord Howard and Sir Francis Drake tussled with the enemy, Adams ferried supplies to sick and dying mariners.

A few months after King Philip II's fleet had been trounced,

Adams married his sweetheart, Mary Hyn, in the parish church of St. Dunstan in Stepney, just to the east of the Tower of London. It was a marriage in which Mary was to find herself alone for long periods, for Adams had made a mistress of the sea. He gained employment with the London Company of the Barbary Merchants, and for the next ten years he sailed back and forth to the wild shores of North Africa. It was dangerous work, for the Barbary ports were controlled by unscrupulous Turkish governors or rapacious warlords who treated the English merchants with contempt. When one ship, the *Jesus*, had the misfortune to be seized by Turkish janissaries, the crew was shown no mercy. "They searched us and stript our very clothes from our backes," wrote one of the captains, "and brake open our chests and made a spoile of all that we had." Several men were hanged, while the rest were "violently shaven," then chained together and made galley slaves.

Adams had learned his trade as a pilot at a time of great change. For too long, English adventurers had dismissed "unsure science and vayne geometry," preferring to rely upon the ancient lore of the sea. They knew that storms were preceded by a "great noise or rattling" and that catastrophe was written in the waters of the deep: "The porpisses of the sea go leaping," wrote one, "[and gulls] do leave the sea and go to dry land." Many of the manuals and sea logs in use remained rooted in the past and harked back to the homespun wisdom of the sea dog. These were satisfactory for coastal-hugging voyages, whose success depended upon a detailed knowledge of coastlines, reefs, and tidal rips. But oceanic voyages into the unknown required a whole new set of skills. Drake himself had been keenly aware of this and urged trainee pilots to study the science of navigation. So, too, did John Dee, who had helped Sir Rowland and Sir George plan their voyage to the East. He said that the master pilot needed to be an expert in "hydrography, astronomy, astrology and horometry" and added that "the base and foundation of all . . . [is] arithmeticke and geometrie."

William Adams was one of the first apprentices to have access to the new science of navigation. William Bourne's *A Regiment for the Sea*, published in 1577, had broken new ground by tackling the perils of oceanic voyages. Bourne taught English pilots how to find their latitude using a cross-staff and mariner's ring, and had even designed a sophisticated half-dial which, he claimed, gave a very approximate reading of longitude. Other recently published manuals included the Dutchman Lucas Waghenaer's brilliant *Spieghel der Zeervaert*—published in English as *The Mariner's Mirror*—and the magnificent *Art of Navigation*, translated from Martin Cortes's Spanish original. This advised pilots on how to keep track of their position during the crossing of uncharted oceans, and it reached a most important conclusion. Cortes wrote that a pilot who understood astronomy and mathematics could sail his ship beyond the horizon, even in the black of night, and "by the certaintie of the arte . . . knoweth the way where she hath gone."

It was while Adams was undertaking one of his trading voyages to the shores of Barbary that he heard rumors of secret plans afoot in Rotterdam to dispatch a large fleet to the fabled Spice Islands of the East Indies. Five ships had already been acquired and reluctant crews plucked from the town's taverns and dungeons. What the expedition's financiers now needed was a skilled pilot to guide their fleet safely across both the Atlantic and Pacific Oceans. The risks were high, but the potential rewards were enormous. The returning pilot would—if all went according to plan—command a vessel stashed with spice and gold.

Adams did not hesitate. He was now thirty-four years old, and was tiring of trading English woollens with Barbary. He knew that his nationality would be no bar to service with the Dutch, for Englishmen often sailed with Dutch fleets. Nor, it would seem, was he unduly bothered by a prolonged absence from Mrs. Adams and his young daughter. Like so many Elizabethan adventurers, he was desperate to grasp the opportunities of the age and so he signed on for a voyage that held the prospect of plunder and booty.

In the spring of 1598, Adams packed his sea chest and stepped aboard a vessel bound for Rotterdam. The curve of the Thames prevented any lingering farewells and Limehouse slipped rapidly from view. The wharves receded and the tower of St. Dunstan was lost on the skyline. Soon, a new vista emerged: the open expanse of the sea. By nightfall on the following day, Adams's little ship would be approaching the low-lying coastline of Holland.

Chapter 3

ALL AT SEA

 ILLIAM ADAMS did not travel alone to Rot-
terdam. His brother Thomas also signed up
for the expedition, along with eleven other adventurers. One of these, Timothy Shotten, had
already sailed around the globe, having accompanied Thomas
Cavendish on his 1586 voyage. He provided a spur to the little
band heading to Holland, for he brought a wealth of information
about the faraway lands of the East.

The Dutch organizers of the expedition welcomed Adams and
company and were more than willing to offer them employment.
They were rather less forthcoming when it came to explaining its
purpose. Rotterdam was rife with rumors that the fleet's financiers had little interest in trade with the East and that talk of spices
was merely a cover. Instead, these hard-nosed merchants were said
to have instructed their captains to emulate Drake's spectacular
successes in the *Golden Hind*, ransacking Spanish settlements in
South America and plundering their stockpiles of gold.

The assembled fleet made a most impressive sight as it rode at anchor in Goereesche Gap, a deep channel of water that linked Rotterdam with the North Sea. There were five ships in total— the *Hoop*, *Geloof*, *Liefde*, *Trouw*, and *Blijde Boodschop*—which an English chronicler of the expedition would later translate (not altogether accurately) as the *Hope*, *Faith*, *Love*, *Fidelity*, and *Merry Messenger*. They were singularly inappropriate names: hope and faith were in short supply, love was nonexistent, and ‘fidelity proved elusive. When the surviving crew of the *Merry Messenger* eventually returned home, they brought tales that would provoke tears and sighs rather than chuckles of laughter.

The admiral of the fleet was Jacques Mahu, a bright young bachelor who was noted for his polite manners. He warmed to Adams and asked him to serve as pilot on his flagship, the *Hoop*. Adams's brother, meanwhile, was placed on the *Trouw* and the other Englishmen were divided among the vessels.

Adams boarded his ship at the end of June 1598, carrying his prized world map, his brass globe, and his astrolabe and compass. These instruments, together with his knowledge of the night sky, were all he would have to pilot the *Hoop* halfway around the world.

The five ships of the Dutch trading fleet were bristling with weaponry; many suspected their real mission was plunder and pillage.

Adams was fortunate that Timothy Shotten was able to give him a firsthand account of each of the two possible routes to the East. Both were fraught with danger. The westerly route, around the southernmost tip of America, involved a long and lonely crossing of the Pacific Ocean. The easterly alternative, around Africa's southern cape, was scarcely more appealing, as it was notorious for its unpredictable weather. When the English adventurer James Lancaster had attempted this route seven years earlier, his ship had been battered by hurricanes and struck by lightning, with devastating consequences for his crew. "Some were striken blind, others were bruised in their legs and armes, and others in their breasts so that they voided blood two dayes after."

The expedition's financiers plumped for the first option, reinforcing speculation that their real goal was Spanish treasure. But reaching that treasure was not going to be easy, as Shotten had discovered in 1586. He and his men had suffered terrible hardships as they entered the southern seas, with the worst of the dangers concentrated in the Straits of Magellan, which linked the Atlantic and Pacific Oceans. They had been buffeted with "contrary windes and most vile and filthie fowle weather, with such raine and vehement stormie windes . . . that hazarded the best cables and anchors that we had." Revictualing in this barren land had proved almost impossible. The crew had leaped ashore in search of edible plants, but had instead found themselves face to face with a "great store of savages." It quickly became apparent that these barbarians were looking at the newcomers with hungry eyes. "They were men-eaters," reads the account of the voyage, "and fed altogether upon rawe flesh and other filthie foode."

The primitive condition of the hunter-gatherer tribes of Patagonia had appalled Shotten and company. They fought with stone axes, ate rotting fish, and were "as wilde [as] any wilde beast." Some were giants with lopsided bones, while others had abnormally shaped limbs and feet. "We took the measure of one of their feet," wrote one, "and it was eighteen inches long."

Such wonders lay in the distant future for Adams and his men, and there were many dangers between Rotterdam and Patagonia. The Dutch fleet set sail on the morning of June 24, 1598, slipping westward along the English Channel. "We set saile with five ships . . . ," wrote a laconic Adams, "and departed from the coast of England the fifth of July." The fleet was blessed with fair winds, making rapid progress as it entered the Atlantic Ocean and headed southward toward the Bay of Biscay.

The fleet's vice admiral, Simon de Cordes, had lured his crews aboard by promising that they would be "furnished with all necessarie provision," and he was true to his word. His captains proved so extraordinarily generous with food supplies that the crews could scarcely believe their good fortune when they saw the size of the portions. They were given "so large stores of bisket . . . that they could not eat it, but filled their chests and casks with it." As the ships approached the shores of North Africa, Simon de Cordes realized that he had been far too generous in the early weeks of the voyage. To rectify matters, he instituted a "bread policy"—which meant that rations were decreased when fresh supplies were available. But the amount of food in the ships' holds was still woefully inadequate. In mid-August—less than two months after setting sail—rations were slashed to a minimum. Henceforth the men were to receive daily just half a pound of bread, three cups of wine, and a little cooked fish when the weather was calm enough to light the stones. It was a poor diet for hungry men.

Adams, who had been transferred to the *Liefde*, knew it would be impossible to reach the Straits of Magellan without pausing somewhere in Africa to stock up on water, fruit, and salt. He also knew that this would be extremely dangerous, since Portuguese coastal forts posed a serious obstacle to acquiring victuals. But fresh fruit and clean water were increasingly necessary as the equatorial heat beat down on the hungry and dehydrated crew. "Many of our men fell sicke through the unwholsomenesse of the aire,"

wrote Adams, who had learned from Shotten of the perils of tropical waters. Scurvy and dysentery—the dreaded "blody flux"—
became life-threatening when they struck men already weakened
by poor diet.

The Cape Verde Islands were a frequent stopping point for
vessels heading farther south—the last place to replenish victuals
before making for the southern Atlantic. But although these "flor-
ishing green" islands were blessed with wild lemon groves and orange trees, they were also infamous for their stagnant and
malodorous air. The slave trader Sir Richard Hawkins said they
were situated "in one of the most unhealthiest climates of the
world." He added that "in two times that I have been in them . . .
[they] cost us the one halff of our people, with fevers and fluxes of
sundry kinds; some shaking, some burning, some partaking of
both."

The islands also happened to be under the control of the Portuguese, who were most unlikely to welcome men who, to their
eyes, were *piratas*—and Protestant ones at that. When Jacques
Mahu sent a message ashore saying that he came in peace, he was
curtly informed by the Portuguese that "they could not believe
what the fleet said." They refused to supply him with water and
victuals until the governor—who was away—gave them the order
to do so.

Captain van Beuningen of the *Liefde* was incensed and rashly
suggested an all-out assault on Praya Island. The other captains
concurred with his bold proposal and landed 150 soldiers, ordering them to scale the cliffs and capture the castle. "They marched
to the fort . . . with two flying colours." It was a dangerous operation, for the bastion was situated on a high bluff of rock with an
entrance "so steep that six resolute men might defend it against a
thousand." In the event, the battle was over after just nine or ten
shots. The Portuguese garrison ran away and van Beuningen's
men entered the fort in triumph. The victorious Dutchmen fortified the place with "benches, trunks, chairs and pieces of wood."

Then, confident that they were masters of all they surveyed, they wondered what to do next.

It slowly dawned on them that capturing the fort had not been such a good idea after all. They were now holed up on a desolate mountaintop and were still no closer to acquiring any desperately needed supplies. Indeed, all they had achieved was to further antagonize the Portuguese. Van Beuningen began to realize that he had won a hollow victory and that he had little option but to abandon his hilltop position. Sheepishly, and with considerable embarrassment, his men dismantled their barricades and packed up their cannon. According to an expedition journal, "they thought it was better to capitulate and to obtain by fair means what they wanted."

The crew of the Liefde *captured Praya's clifftop fort (top right) after firing just nine or ten shots. But they lacked food and water, and quickly realized it was a hollow victory.*

The Portuguese governor was incensed when he learned about the Dutchmen's conduct and admonished them for acting like enemies. He said that "if they had behaved themselves as friends, they might have easily obtained what they descried." Now, in the heat of his anger, he ordered them to leave the Cape Verde Islands immediately and he moved all his cannon to the shoreline in preparation for an attack. With great reluctance, the Dutch accepted they had no option but to continue their voyage with minimal supplies of food and water.

Adams was furious at the turn of events and was clear in his own mind where the blame lay. "We abode foure and twentie dayes," he later wrote, "[and] the reason that we abode so long at these islands was that one of the captaines of the fleet made our generall beleeve that at these islands we should find great store of refreshing, as goats and other things." The failure to revictual was a bitter blow to these sick and hungry men, and their morale was soon to be dealt an even greater blow. On September 22, the *Hoop* raised a flag to summon all the captains on board. The news was indeed grim. The expedition commander, Jacques Mahu, had died of a raging fever, leaving the great fleet leaderless. Captains and sea dogs alike were devastated, for Mahu had been extremely popular. "He was of a mild and sweet temper," wrote one, "honest, careful, diligent and very kind to the seamen." His funeral was a solemn affair. "The dead body was laid in a coffin half-filled with rocks, covered with a mourning cloth, carried by the captains from the stern of the ship to the bow, and let into the water with the sad sound of drums, trumpets and the wailing of the bagpipes." His successor—named in sealed papers—was the vice admiral, Simon de Cordes.

Adams was alarmed that the fleet was in such a sorry predicament. There was no question of turning back, for both the current and the wind would have been against them. But to head into the unknown with empty holds and bellies was to court disaster. They had to find food as a matter of priority and with scurvy "infecting and infesting every ship," they hoisted their sails "with intent to refresh their men and make better provision of water and other necessaries at the Isle of Anno-Bueno."

It was a dangerous choice, but it was the best option in the circumstances. Off the coast of equatorial Guinea lay the rugged yet fertile isle of Annabon, an isolated chunk of tropical greenery whose rearing, smoking volcano made it an easy landmark. The safest—but longest—route to Annabon was to hug the African coastline until the fleet reached the headland of Cape Lopez. From here, it was just a few days' sailing to the volcanic island. But the advantages of following the coastline, which would enable the men to fill their water casks, were countered by the savage tribesmen said to live on shore. When Shotten had sailed this route with Cavendish, their vessel had come under sustained attack from the native tribes. One of Shotten's crewmates had been "shot into the thigh, who, plunking the arrow out, broke it, and left the head behind." It was a fatal error, for "the poison wrought so that night that he was marveilously swollen, and all his belly and privie parts were as blacke as inke, and the next morning he died."

In the event, a landfall on this coastline was not possible. Each time the Dutch fleet approached the shore they were met with a violent undertow and hazardous surf, and the fleet was forced to continue all the way to Cape Lopez before it was able to drop anchor and "set our sick men a-lande." The men were now in the heart of equatorial Africa and the shoreline was a mass of tangled greenery. Giant laurels and myrtles, flowering acacias, and monstrous tropical ferns—all trailed their brilliant green tentacles in the soupy water. The stench of rotting vegetation permeated the vessels and the men complained of being "subject to many blaming and smothering heats, with infections and contagious aires." Worse still, the wet season had arrived with a vengeance and the jungle was steaming in the heat. Few of the men had seen anything like it.

Yet there was a feeling of cautious optimism at their arrival at Cape Lopez, for the cape itself was known to be inhabited by friendly tribes. When the English adventurer William Towerson had visited these shores, he had been entranced by the native tribes—especially their voluptuous womenfolk, who were a feast for the eyes after long months at sea. "[They] have exceeding long breasts," he wrote. So long, indeed, that "some of them wil lay the same upon the ground and lie downe by them." His fellow sea dogs had been pleased to note that the women were "given to lust and uncleannesse" and enjoyed enticing mariners back to their thatched huts. If this was music to the ears of the English, it was even more welcome to the Dutch, who discovered that these tribal maidens "esteeme it to be good fortune for them to have carnall copulation with a Netherlander, and among themselves, brag and boast thereof."

The men were even more handsomely endowed than their womenfolk, and took great delight in a public display of their wares. "[They] have a great privie member," wrote the Dutch adventurer Pieter de Marees, "whereof they make great account." They became "very lecherous" after their habitual drinking bouts, but there was a high price to be paid for their debauchery. Many of the men were riddled with worms, which lived "in their privie members and, which is more, in their cods [testicles]." Although these tribesmen were "wilde" and "barbarous," they showed peculiar sensitivity when it came to breaking wind. "They are very careful not to let [out] a fart if anybodie be by them," recorded de Marees and "wonder at our Netherlanders that use it [farting] so commonly, for they cannot abide that a man should fart before them, esteeming it to be a great shame and contempt done unto them."

The vice admiral, Simon de Cordes, knew that his most urgent task was to acquire food and water. Accordingly, he sent Captain Sebald de Weert of the *Geloof* ashore to make contact with the local chieftain. The captain was not impressed with what he found. The chieftain was a diminutive fellow whose "throne" resembled a shoemaker's chair "scarsly one foot high." He had a furry lambskin tied to his feet and wore "a garment of violet-coloured cloth with gilded lace, attired like a rower." He was "without shirt, shoes, or stockings, having a partly-coloured cloth on his head and many glasse beades about his necke." His hat was decidedly eccentric—a conical-shaped jester's horn—while his face was powdered with white makeup. His courtiers, not wishing to be outdone, had painted themselves bright red and wore equally outlandish hats "adorned with cockes feathers."

Sebald de Weert was even less impressed when he poked his nose into the chieftain's mud-walled dwelling. "The palace," he wrote contemptuously, "was not comparable to a stable." Captain de Weert decided upon a little extravaganza to impress the chieftain. He ordered his trumpeters to blast their brass and, when si-

The African chieftain at Cape Lopez sat on a throne "scarsly one foot high" and wore an eccentric conical hat that resembled a jester's horn. The Dutch blew their trumpets (right) in order to impress him.

lence had once again returned to the jungle clearing, he explained that he had come "to seeke refreshing for our men." The chieftain nodded and mumbled something to his wives, who scurried back to their cooking pots. After a long interval, they finally returned, bearing earthenware dishes. Captain de Weert was hoping for fresh meat and fruit, and waited excitedly for the women to serve the meal. His expectations were quickly dashed. One of the pots contained a stew made from smoked hippopotamus, which he found not at all to his taste, while the other contained "a few roasted plantans."

More disappointment was in store. The chieftain now expected the Dutchmen to reciprocate his kindness and began to call for food from the ship. Captain de Weert was less than happy to oblige but asked his men to bring a few supplies in order to "satisfy his [the chieftain's] barking." These included a bottle of Spanish wine, which the chief glugged in one gigantic gulp: "In the Spanish wine, the Guinean forgot his temperance and was carried to his rest." As the chieftain fell into a deep slumber, the crew were left listening to their rumbling bellies.

The captains of the fleet realized that Cape Lopez was not going to supply them with the necessary quantity of supplies and were increasingly alarmed by the unhealthy tropical climate: "Many that were well fell sick because the air of that country was very unwholsome." Sixteen men expired and were buried in the African jungle, while de Weert himself fell sick of "a violent fever." The captain decided to press on toward Annabon, but no sooner had they arrived at the island than they discovered that it was swarming with Portuguese musketeers. Worse still, the air was "worse than that of Guinea, [and so] the diseases amongst the seamen encreased every day." A nighttime raid yielded paltry supplies—biscuits, a few cheeses, and some bottles of wine—but it was not enough to feed hundreds of starving men. Many of the crew members were suffering from severe dysentery, and fever was taking its toll. One of those who died was Thomas Spring, "an English young man of great towardnesse."

On January 2, 1599, the fleet once again weighed anchor and set course for South America, praying that their ships would survive the passage. The tropical African waters had severely weakened the timbers, and when a sharp squall battered the fleet shortly after sailing from Annabon, it caused severe damage. The mainmast of the *Geloff* snapped into three pieces, revealing the wood to be as soft as a sponge and riddled with wormholes. The vessel was towed by the *Liefde* while a new mast was made by carpenters. They need not have bothered, for the breezes soon died and left the fleet in becalmed waters. The little fleet had now entered the doldrums, or windless zone, of the southern Atlantic, where a ship could "lie half a yeare without wind or water . . . [for] there is not a breth of air stirring." With the prospect of many weeks at sea before reaching South America, Vice Admiral Simon de Cordes was left with no alternative but to slash the already meager daily rations. "Our general commanded," wrote Adams, "that a man, for four dayes, should have but one pound of bread, that was a quarter of a pound a day, with the like proportion of wine and water." One of the *Liefde*'s crew was so hungry that he crept into the ship's kitchen and stole some bread. His punishment was swift and merciless. He was hanged and his body hurled into the sea as a warning to others.

Adams knew that the reduction in rations would quickly increase the rate of death and disease. "[This] scarcitie of victuals brought such feeblenesse," he wrote, "that our men fell into so great weaknesse and sicknesse for hunger that they did eate the calves' skinnes wherewith our ropes were covered." Salty leather was no diet for sick men and scurvy began to tighten its deadly grip on the fleet.

This terrible sickness was the scourge of every long sea voyage, and all were familiar with its symptoms. "It bringeth with it a great desire to drinke," wrote Sir Richard Hawkins, "and causeth a generall swelling of all parts of the body; especially of the legs and gums, and many times the teeth fall out of the jawes." The men's skins turned sallow and blotchy and their breath became rank. As their condition worsened, they became breathless, fatigued, and depressed. The second stage of the illness was accompanied by bruising, swellings, and excruciating pain. The afflicted became lethargic and were stricken with kidney problems and acute diarrhea—an unpleasant condition on a vessel where each trip to the latrine involved a precarious balancing act at the stern of the ship.

Opinions varied as to the cause of scurvy. "Some attribute [it] to sloath," wrote Hawkins, "[and] some to conceite." Others argued that it was caused by dirty ships and said that "the best prevention for this disease is to keepe cleane the shippe; to besprinkle her ordinarily with vinegar, or to burne tarre." What none on this expedition realized was that the English adventurer James Lancaster had discovered a cure for scurvy seven years earlier. He "had brought to sea with him certaine bottles of the juice of limons, which he gave to each one as long as it would last, three spoonfuls every morning." It had had a quite remarkable effect, and "by this meanes, the generall cured many of his men and preserved the rest." Unfortunately, Lancaster's cure was quickly forgotten and scurvy was to remain a blight among seamen for another 161 years.

As the winds at long last freshened, the ships began to pick up speed. They had by now left the tropics behind and the weather changed dramatically as they headed into a freezing South Atlantic winter. The sudden drop in temperature caused some spectacular deaths. One of the English sailors on the *Trouw* was chewing some bread when his limbs locked rigidly. The fleet's doctor, Barent Potgeiter, was astonished at what he saw. "He was sitting on a bench . . . when he suddenly dropped backwards looking terribly ill, foaming at the mouth. He never spoke, and died a few hours later." Two days later, a second crew member, Jonghman von Utrecht, suffered a similar attack: "He screamed, foamed at the mouth, scratched, kicked and pushed." He was carried belowdecks and denied food and water. He began muttering to himself, became delirious, and lost control of his bowels. His end was quite horrible: "he was so senseless that he could not clean himself or void his excrements in a regular way, and it being then very cold, the moisture that was about him freezed and benumbed his flesh, insomuch that they were forced to cut off his legs." He died a few days after this painful operation.

At the end of March, the men awoke to a sight they would never forget. "We sawe the land," wrote Adams, "in lattetude of 50 degrees, having the windes a two or three days contrary." They had reached the coast of what is now Argentina. The crew wanted to drop anchor immediately, but with a brisk northerly filling their sails, the captains decided to press on toward the relative safety of the Straits of Magellan. It was a wise decision, for they entered the straits not a moment too soon. "At which time," wrote Adams, "winter came, so that at that time there was much snowe."

The Straits of Magellan presented a formidable challenge to Elizabethan pilots. There were hidden shallows and underwater rocks, and in places the waterway was so narrow that ships had to be maneuvered with extreme caution. Drake's men had been overawed by the monumental scale of the landscape. "The mountains arise with such tops and spires into the air," wrote one, "and of so rare a height, as they may well be accounted amongst the wonders of the world; environed, as it were, with many regions of congealed clouds and frozen meteors." The forces of nature had wreaked havoc on Drake's fleet, and his ships were battered by "the violent force of the winds, intollerable workeing of the wrathful seas, and the grisely beholding of the cragged rocks."

It was Adams's job, as pilot of the *Liefde*, to navigate a safe passage through these hazardous waters. He was anxious to negotiate the straits immediately, for winter was advancing with alarming speed and it was only a matter of time before the waters would freeze solid. But the sight of thousands of penguins, "which are fowles greater than a ducke," proved too great a temptation for the hungry crews. The fleet dropped anchor and the men clambered ashore; within minutes, they had clubbed to death more than 1,400 of the unfortunate birds.

Adams had been right to show concern for the weather, for over the coming days there was "wonderful much snow and ice." One of the ships lost her anchor when the cable snapped in a storm; shortly afterward, a thick sea mist descended on the fleet and hindered its progress. When the mist lifted, the winds had changed direction, now blowing from the south and bringing hail and snow. De Weert retired to his cabin and noted in his journal that he and his men were trapped in "a perpetual stormie winter

Adams's ship had almost run out of food when a lookout sighted penguins on an island in the Magellan Straits. Within minutes of landing, the crew had clubbed to death more than 1,400 of the birds.

. . . always the storme found them worke, and miserable was their toile without any furtherance to their intended voyage." Soon, he was too cold to continue his diary and simply wrote a list of his grievances: "raine, winde, snow, haile, hunger, losses of anchors, spoiles of ship and tackling, sicknesse, death, savages, want of store and store of wants conspired a fulnesse of miseries."

Adams remained confident that he could negotiate a passage through the ice-choked waters, recording that "many times in the winter we had the wind good to go through the straights." But with several anchors lost and an inaccurate chart of the seabed, it was deemed too dangerous to press on to the Pacific.

Food supplies soon ran short and so did the stockpile of firewood. The severe frost made life a misery, for it "increased their appetite and this decreased their provision." Simon de Cordes ordered six tons of dried beans to be distributed, but it was not enough to stave off hunger. Some of the crew tried to profiteer from the desperation of the sick, selling their portions and living off raw mussels. Two men on the *Blijde Boodschop* were sentenced to death for stealing oil. A gallows was constructed on the shore and one of them was hanged. The other escaped death by showing deep remorse, but a few days later he was once again found stealing oil. This time, he was whipped until his flesh was raw. The captains were obliged to stand guard at mealtimes, wielding sticks and beating the riotous and unruly.

The crews' first encounter with the native "savages" occurred at the beginning of May when a group of tribesmen rowed toward the fleet. The crews were astonished to note that "[they] were ten or eleven foot high . . . of a reddish colour, and with long hair." These "wilde men" hurled rocks at the mariners, shouted abuse, and then rowed away. Some three weeks later, a small group of sailors stumbled upon "a company of savages" while they were ashore. These "savages" managed to capture five of the Dutchmen and "tore in pieces the first three," ripping them apart limb by limb. The other two were rescued by Simon de Cordes, who

The tribesmen of southern America were gigantic. "[They] were ten or eleven foot high . . . of a reddish colour, and with long hair." They proved formidable adversaries in combat.

landed with a platoon of guards. The men were horrified by the indigenous tribes of southern America: "these savages were all naked, except one, who had a sea-dog [sea lion] skin about his shoulders." They carried wooden spears with a deadly arrowhead, which "would run so far into the flesh that it was almost impossible to draw out." In one attack, these harpoons passed "through four layers of clothing and ended deep inside the chest." Others sank so deep into the flesh "that they had to be pushed through."

With the straits choked with ice and the shoreline thick with hostile savages, the men had little option but to remain on board their ships. Simon de Cordes attempted to raise morale with a little pageantry. He formed a guild "to perpetuate the memory of so dangerous and extraordinary a voyage" and made his captains knights of this guild, which he called the Order of the Furious Lion. They swore oaths of loyalty, and then the entire company was armed and rowed ashore to a fanfare of trumpets. The tribesmen melted away and, with a great cheer, the men promised to use all their endeavor "to conquer the Spanish dominions." De Cordes then ordered a pillar to be erected in memory of the occasion, with a plaque bearing the names of his knights. He ordered that the dead be buried at the foot of this pillar.

It was a splendid monument and the ceremonies proved a tremendous boost to morale. But the men's spirits were not raised for long. The monument was smashed to pieces "by the savages, who also plucked out the corpses from the graves and dismembered them and carried one away." The body of Simon de Cordes's barber was particularly badly mutilated; his head was smashed with clubs, his heart lay on some rocks and his genitals had been hacked off. The men hastily reburied his body along with all the other pieces they could find.

Winter began to slacken in the last week of August, as the snow turned to sleet and then to rain. At the beginning of September the fleet at last raised its anchors and continued through the straits, toward the Pacific Ocean. Although there is no exact record of the death toll during their enforced stay in the straits, it must have been well into three figures. The "snow and ice" had claimed many victims, and Adams recalled that "many of our men died with hunger." De Weert added that his own ship, the *Geloof*, had lost "by diseases and otherwise, so many of his men that of an hundred and ten, there were left but eight and thirtie."

Just a few days after weighing anchor, the lookouts caught their first glimpse of the Pacific Ocean. This was the moment of which they had long dreamed, and it should have been a cause for congratulation. But there was no time for festivities. "We came into the South Sea," wrote Adams, "[and] were, sixe or seven dayes after, in a greater storme." The fleet was scattered "one from another" and blown in separate directions. One ship was flung far into the Pacific; others were driven back into the straits. After more than a year in each other's company, each vessel found itself on its own.

Simon de Cordes had anticipated this event and had arranged a rendezvous on the shores of Peru. But after all the hardship and suffering, this enforced separation broke the spirit of many of the mariners and very nearly broke the ships as well. The *Blijde Boodschop* was hit by an enormous wave that smashed her bowsprit, together with her foremast and sails. Helpless and alone, she drifted for many weeks until eventually she was captured by the Spanish. Her crew was imprisoned, interrogated, and chastised for sailing into waters claimed by Spain. Only a handful of her crew would ever make it home.

The crew of the *Geloof* decided that they had experienced more than enough suffering and elected to abandon their voyage. They reentered the straits and eventually reached Rotterdam in July 1600, by which time only thirty-six of the original one hundred and nine crew members were left alive.

The *Trouw*'s crew were made of sterner stuff. Throwing caution to the winds, they pointed their vessel west and headed for the East Indies. This proved an unwise decision, for the ship was captured by the Portuguese on her arrival in the Spice Islands. Her crew, reduced from eighty-six to twenty-four men, were either shackled and imprisoned or executed. Six eventually escaped their dungeons and reached their families in the Netherlands. The one Scot who sailed with the fleet, William Lyon, was still a prisoner in 1606.

The *Liefde* was driven wildly off course by the tempest. "We had many hard stormes," wrote Adams, "being driven to the southward in 54 degrees." It took the crew almost three weeks to regain their position, only to find themselves once again pushed southward. "Eight or ten dayes after, in the night, having very much wind, our fore-saile flew away." The storm eventually ended, and "we fownde reasonable windes and weather, with which we followed on our pretended voyage towardes the coast of Peru."

The fleet's captains had agreed to wait at the rendezvous for thirty days. Adams hoped to use the intervening weeks to stock up on fresh victuals, exchanging food for trinkets with native tribesmen. After briefly calling at the offshore islands of Mocha and Santa Maria, in November 1599 the *Liefde* dropped anchor in "a faire sandy bay" and the men rowed ashore "to parley with the people of the lande."

When a few of Drake's men had attempted this two decades earlier, they had met with a particularly nasty end. They were captured by savages, who worked "with knives upon their bodies, [and] cutt the flesh away by gubbets." These chunks of flesh were tossed into the air while the tribesmen danced themselves into a frenzy. Then, "like doggs, [they] devoured it in most monstrous and unnatural manner."

On this occasion, the natives were no more happy to see the arrival of the *Liefde* than they had been the *Golden Hind*. "They would not suffer us to come a-land," wrote Adams, "shooting a great store of arrows at us." The crew were deterred by this hostility but quickly realized that they must either fight for their food or starve. "Having no victualles in our shipp, and hoping to finde refreshing, by force we landed twenty-seven or thirty of our men and drove the wilde people from the waterside." Many of the crew sustained injuries in the landing, and their wounds made them even more determined to return to their ship with food. "So we made them signes [that] our desire was for victualles, showing them iron, silver and clothe, which we would give them in exchaunge for the same."

When the natives saw the beads and trinkets aboard the *Liefde*, they threw down their bows and decided to trade: "They gave our people wine, with potatoes, to eate and drincke, with other fruit." It was not enough to fill the men's empty bellies, but the tribesmen "bid our men by signes and tokens to go aboard and the next day to returne againe, and that they would bring good store of refreshing."

For the first time in months, there was a feeling of optimism aboard the *Liefde*. The crew now believed that these Indians had enough food to fill the hold of their ship and were relieved that they had not encountered any Spaniards. Captain van Beuningen decided to row ashore the following morning, along with his officers, in order to gather as many supplies as possible. "The capten himself did go in one of the boates," wrote Adams, "with all the force that we could make." Van Beuningen hoped the natives would bring their wares to the foreshore where he could easily load them onto his boat, but they seemed not to understand his sign language and signaled that he should land. The captain was wary. He was an experienced soldier and his instinct led him to be naturally cautious. To step ashore would expose him and his men to real danger and he had no wish to enter a trap. But the Indians repeatedly refused to come to the shoreline, leaving him with little option. He "resolved to lande, contrary to that which was concluded abord our shipp."

Van Beuningen took no chances. He landed with twenty-three of his finest foot soldiers, including Adams's brother, Thomas, and instructed the men to make a great show of strength. What none of them realized was that "about a muskett-shott from the boates, the Indians lay in ambush, more than 1,000." They were waiting with their bows drawn; when the pre-arranged signal for the attack was sounded, they "immediately fell upon our men with such weapons as they had and slewe all our men, to our knowledge."

So sudden was the onslaught, and of such ferocity, that it was over in seconds. Captain van Beuningen was dead—as were the cream of his crew—and the only survivors were those who had remained in the boat. They could scarcely believe what they had just witnessed and were so fearful for their lives that they made a dash back to the *Liefde* to break the terrible news. "[They] did long waite to see if any of our men did come agein," wrote Adams, "but being all slaine, our boates returned [with] . . . sorrowfull newes of all our men's deathes."

Adams was distraught. He had lost his closest friends in the ambush, "among which was my brother Thomas." For more than seventeen months these men had lived together as companions in the confined quarters of their vessel. Now, at a single stroke, they had suffered a devastating blow to their confidence, as well as to their ability to continue with their voyage. The *Liefde* was now seriously undermanned and morale had never been lower. "[It] was very much lamented of us all," wrote Adams, "so that we had skarce so many men left as could wind up our anker."

When it was clear that there were no more survivors, the crew sailed "in great distresse" toward the offshore island of Santa Maria. Here, at last there was good news awaiting them. "We found our Admiral [the *Hoop*]," wrote Adams, "whom, when we saw, our hearts were somewhat comforted." But she, too, had

The Dutch fleet was attacked in the Magellan Straits (above) and on South America's Pacific coast. The Liefde's *crew suffered a particularly brutal attack; twenty-three men were slaughtered within a few seconds.*

been attacked by natives. "[We] found them in as great distrese as we, having lost their general, with seven and twenty of their men slaine at the island of Mocha."

It was time to make a decision. Everyone now sensed that they were not going to be reunited with the rest of their fleet. They also knew that they could not contemplate striking out across the Pacific without filling their holds with victuals. But they no longer had enough healthy men to risk another landing on this coast.

It was while they pondered their predicament that they were able to seize the initiative. Two Spaniards—possibly coastal guards—rowed across to the *Liefde* in order to discover where she was heading. They quizzed Adams and inspected the ship before declaring their intention of returning ashore. "But we would not let them," wrote Adams, ". . . whereat they were greatly offended." Adams informed them that they would have to earn their freedom. "We showed them that we had extreame neede of victuals, and that if they would give us so many sheepe and so many beefes, they should goe on land." The Spaniards were incensed but had little alternative but to comply. They arranged for large quantities of food to be brought to the vessels; so much, in fact, that the crew of the *Liefde* and *Hoop* were "for the most part recovered of their sicknesse." At long last, the ships were in a position to continue with their voyage.

Simon de Cordes's first task was to find a replacement for Captain van Beuningen. He chose the able Jacob Quackernaek to take command of the *Liefde*, then summoned a more general meeting—attended by Adams and Shotten—in order to decide "what we should doe to make our voyage for the best profit of our merchants." There were several possibilities. The most obvious was to head to the Spice Islands, the "spiceries" of the East Indies, where nutmeg and mace could be had for a song. This would please the financiers of the trip, since there was a huge profit to be reaped from spices, and it had the advantage that many of the small islands and atolls were as yet uncontrolled by either Portuguese or Spanish. The Philippines was another option, although here they were likely to clash with the forces of Spain. The *Liefde*'s cargo finally settled the matter. Her hold was crammed with broadcloth, which was unlikely to find a market in the tropical climes of the Spice Islands. "We gathered . . . that the Mollucas and the most part of the East Indies were hot countreyes," wrote Adams, "where woolen cloth would not be much accepted."

Such material would be of far greater value to people in more northerly climes, where the weather was colder and the winters were harsh. The more the men pondered their destination, the more they realized that there was an obvious answer. It lay to the northeast of China—a kingdom of fabled riches. "At last it was resolved to go for Japan," wrote Adams, who added that "woollen cloth was in great estimation in that island." The proposal was put to the sea-battered crew, who had no desire to return home through the Straits of Magellan, "wherefore we all agreed to go for Japan."

The men might have thought twice about such a voyage if they had had any notion of the distances involved. It had taken them more than a year to traverse the Atlantic and their passage had been aided by favorable trade winds. The voyage to Japan involved crossing the world's largest ocean, whose currents and winds remained a total mystery. When Ferdinand Magellan had crossed the Pacific, he and his crew had survived only by eating stewed mice and sawdust. The chronicler of the voyage had concluded his account with a stark warning: "I do not think that anyone for the future will venture upon a similar voyage."

The *Liefde* and the *Hoop* set sail into the unknown at the end of November 1599. The weather was kind at first and they made better progress than anyone had dared hope. "[We] passed the line equinoctiall with a faire wind," wrote Adams, "which continued good for diverse months." This enabled the two vessels to keep together until they reached "certaine islands"—lost somewhere in the mid-Pacific—where the inhabitants were said to be "men-eaters."

The sight of land proved too much for one group of sea-weary men. Broken by their experiences of the voyage and fearful of the empty ocean, they made a secret vow to chance their luck on this remote island rather than sailing any farther on the rotting *Liefde*. "Coming neare these islands . . . eight of our men, being in the pinnesse, ranne from us." Their flight caught Adams and his crew by surprise. They were too weak to chase after them and so they abandoned the men to their fate. Adams recorded that they were, "as we suppose, . . . eaten of the wild men." The place of their landfall has long remained a mystery, for neither Adams nor his captain had any idea of their position, but it is possible that the *Liefde* had unknowingly reached (and discovered) Hawaii, more than 179 years before Captain Cook. When the English missionary William Ellis landed in Hawaii in 1822, he was told that a boatload of sailors had pitched up at those shores long before Cook's arrival. These men had been kindly received by the native islanders, had married Hawaiian maidens, and had been made honorary chieftains.

The loss of eight men was a serious blow to the morale of the *Liefde*'s remaining crew. Soon after, the weather grew tempestuous and brought to an end their run of good luck. "We had a wounderous storme of winde as ever I was in," wrote Adams, "with much raine." As the wind screeched through the rigging and the waves formed huge peaks and troughs, the men grew fearful for their safety. Their vessels were in a poor state of repair and were not built to withstand such a ferocious battering from the sea. The gale blew even harder, pitching the ships into precarious angles. Suddenly, there was a cry from the lookout on the *Liefde*. The *Hoop* had keeled over and her lights had gone out. Within seconds, her silhouette had disappeared beneath the surface. She had vanished, swallowed in one almighty gulp of the sea. She was never seen again, and no survivors were ever found.

Adams was too preoccupied to dwell upon the loss of the *Hoop*. In typically stoic, understated fashion, he wrote just four words about the disaster: "We were," he said, "very sorry." His crew was rather more distraught, for they feared the same fate. Their only hope was that Adams could steer them through the storm.

The *Liefde* was now alone on an empty ocean and the men had absolutely no idea of their position. Their maps and charts were hopelessly inadequate, rendering their equipment useless, and they continued to sail in what they believed to be a north-westerly direction. "We proceeded on our former intention for Japan," wrote Adams, ". . . but founde it not, by reason that it lieth false in all the cardes and mappes and globes." The men were by now suffering the most terrible deprivations. They were half starved, sick with scurvy, and many were troubled by acute dysentery. "Great was the misery we were in," wrote Adams, "having no more but nine or ten able men to go or creepe upon their knees." Sickness hit indiscriminate of rank or status, "our captain and all the rest looking every hour to die."

Adams stopped writing any notes, and the rest of his crew also fell silent. They were too debilitated—or too ill—to put quill to paper. Toward the end of March they came within sight of an island called Una Colonna, possibly one of the desolate Bonin Islands, "at which time many of our men were sick again." The effort of manning the ship's boat and rowing ashore to this barren speck of land was now beyond them; after four months and twenty-two days spent crossing the Pacific, even Adams was approaching despair. He was convinced that if they did not reach land within a few days they would surely die.

On April 12, 1600, more than twenty months after setting sail from Rotterdam, Adams awoke to an almost mystical sight. There was a mauve smudge on the horizon that grew more and more distinct as the day progressed. Adams called to his men; he stirred the sick and carried them on deck. At first he scarcely dared to believe his eyes, but he soon became convinced that they were nearing their goal.

The breezes that had been against them for so long suddenly shifted and nudged them toward land. The coastline grew closer, until the men could discern cliffs, trees, and a large cluster of temples. "So we, in safety, let fall our ancker, about a league from a place called Bungo." Almost sixty years after Pinto, but in the very same harbor, William Adams had reached Japan.

Chapter 4

IN THE NAME OF THE FATHER

 THE *LIEFDE*'S CREW was too weak to row ashore. They were racked with scurvy and dysentery and their bones ached from the lack of food. Of the twenty-four men still alive, most were unable to stand and some were on the verge of death. "There was no more but six," wrote Adams, "besides myselfe, that could stand upon his feet." When he saw a band of fearsome-looking Japanese heading toward the *Liefde*, he knew that resistance was hopeless, for none of the men had the strength to load a musket. "We suffered them to come abord of us," he wrote, "not being able to resist them."

The Japanese boarding party was quite unlike the "savages" and "wilde men" that Adams and his crew had met elsewhere on their voyage. These fearsome warriors were small but stocky, yet were elegantly attired and immaculately coiffured. They cut quite a dash as they clambered aboard the *Liefde*. Adams himself had no opportunity to record his first impressions, but most newcomers to Japan were left feeling that they were distinctly underdressed in comparison with the Japanese. This strange-looking race wore their hair neatly plucked at the front, revealing shiny pates, but tied into a long bushy lock at the back. This was smeared with scented oil and tucked into a bun. They wore exquisite silken robes, "after the fashion of a nightgown," and were armed with terrifying curved swords so sharp that they could slice through bone. Fortunately for the crew of the *Liefde*, on this occasion they kept them firmly in their scabbards. Indeed, they showed no interest in Adams and his crew and ignored the groaning men on deck. "The people offered us no hurt," recalled Adams, "but stole all things that they could steal." Their pillaging was carried out systematically and with considerable care. The *Liefde* was turned inside out and the choicest items were pilfered by the raiders. "All thinges was taken out," wrote Adams, ". . . what was good or worth the taking was carried away." What grieved him most was the loss of all his sea charts and navigational equipment—the tools of his trade. Only his prized world map, secreted in the *Liefde*'s great cabin, remained undiscovered.

He was desperate to speak with the raiders in order to beg them for food and fresh water. He attempted to converse in Dutch and Portuguese, both of which he spoke tolerably well, but the men looked at him with blank eyes and barked something in Japanese. Adams gave up trying to communicate, "neither of us both understanding the one the other." The only word he could make out was "Bungo"—the fiefdom in which he and his men had ended their harrowing voyage.

Much had changed in Bungo since Pinto's arrival almost sixty years earlier. Otomo Yoshiaki was long dead and his family had suffered a string of calamities and military setbacks. The fiefdom was no longer intact, for the Otomo lands had been partitioned between quarreling minor princelets. War had become endemic and violence a way of life. But luck—for once—was on Adams's side. The local brigand who controlled this particular stretch of coast was intrigued to learn of the arrival of the *Liefde*. When he heard that the ship had been ransacked, he ordered discipline to be restored and, belatedly, "sent soldiers aboard to see that none of the marchants' goods were stolen." Some of the pilfered cargo was returned and the perpetrators were punished for their crime.

The brigand also recognized that the near-derelict vessel was in no condition to remain offshore, where her rotten timbers were at the mercy of the winds and tide. Three days after arriving in Japan, "our shippe was brought into a good harbour, there to abide till the principall king of the whole island had news of us, and untill it was knowne what his will was to doe with us." Adams and his men suddenly found themselves treated with great friendship. They were given the use of a little house on the fore-shore, "where we landed all our sick men and had all refreshing that was needfull." For some, the fresh fruit and clean water came too late. Three of the weakest men died shortly after being landed and several more were so seriously ill that they were unable to eat. "[They] lay for a long time sick," wrote Adams, "and in the end also died." The eighteen remaining crew members made a sur-prisingly rapid recovery and were soon congratulating themselves on having survived their terrible ordeal. After a voyage of un-speakable hardship, they had met with friendship on the farthest side of the world.

Or so they thought. What they did not realize was that they had landed in a stronghold of Portuguese Jesuits who had spent half a century propagating their faith in this part of Japan. These fanatical monks were led by the aristocratic Alessandro Valignano, a charming yet ruthless individual who had supreme authority over every Jesuit mission, and every monk, from the Cape of Good Hope to Nagasaki Bay. He harbored a passionate hatred for "hereticke" Protestants and had spent more than twenty years en-suring that Catholicism was the only outside faith to gain a foothold in Japan.

Valignano had first arrived in Japan in 1579, bringing with him deep-seated prejudices that he had picked up elsewhere in the East. His previous attitude toward native populations had been one of contempt. He opined that "dusky races are very stupid and vicious, and of the basest spirits," and claimed that most were "bestial" and scarcely human. But Valignano found himself swallowing his words when he landed in this distant country. He was stunned by the sophistication of the Japanese and found himself admitting that this strange race surpassed the Portuguese in both learning and manners. "We who come from Europe find ourselves as veritable children . . . [and] have to learn how to eat, sit, converse, dress, act politely and so on." He was no less amazed by

The Jesuits made Nagasaki their center of operations (above) and spent years learning Japanese customs and manners. By 1600, they had made numerous converts and even infiltrated the court.

the complex etiquette of the Japanese and described the land as "another world, another way of life, other customs and other laws." In his most extraordinary admission, he confessed that "the fact that there are contradictions and differences between Japanese and European customs does not mean . . . that they are in any sense barbarians, for barbarians—truly—they are not."

Valignano discovered that the Jesuit mission was in a poor state and had made very few converts. He was quick to recognize that its greatest problem lay in the attitude of its monks toward the Japanese. Most were a great deal less cultured than those they were trying to convert, and were incapable of explaining their doctrine and faith. The Japanese were particularly bemused by the monks' interest in the poor and sick, and could not understand why anyone would wish to care for the lowliest stratum of society. When the Jesuits founded a leper hospital in Bungo, the local nobility recoiled in disgust. Lepers were *yeta*, or outcasts—"the most base, low and vile people in Japan." Charity played no part in Japanese society, and many concluded that the monks had some ulterior motive for devoting themselves to caring for its jetsam. It later became a commonplace that "beggars were given a meal if they expressed the desire to become members of their religion," while nobles were "tricked with new-fangled bric-à-brac . . . and flattered with gifts of baubles and beads."

Valignano understood that such misunderstandings were causing immense damage to the Jesuit cause. He also realized that if the monks wanted to convert the people and influence the rulers, there was only one solution—one that was as simple as it was shocking. The Jesuits must go native. They must wear Japanese clothes, eat Japanese food, and adopt the highly complex rules of etiquette in this hierarchical community. In short, they must learn to comport themselves with polish and finesse, and adopt the Japanese virtues of moderation, composure, and cleanliness.

Valignano knew that this would require great willpower on the part of his monks and would demand that they forgo many pleasures that they took for granted. To help them in their task, he wrote a handbook of decorum, his *Advertimentos*, which set out their social behavior. This was followed by more practical advice in his *Sumario* and *Historia del Principio*. "I prohibited whatever damaged the credit and authority of the fathers," he wrote, ". . . [and] things which would be considered grossly unsuited to their dignity." His first rule was to forbid the raising of pigs and goats and the slaughtering of cows, noting that "the Japanese have a great revulsion from eating any kind of meat." Roasted pork and braised beef no longer filled the cooking pots in the monastic refectory attached to the Santa Casa da Misericordia in Nagasaki. Henceforth, the Jesuits were to eat a Japanese diet that consisted of "salted or raw fish, limes, sea snails and such bitter or salty things." The monks were disgusted by raw fish, finding it "no less abhorrent to us Europeans than our food . . . to the Japanese." But Valignano was in no mood for compromise. He advised his monks to intone the Te Deum while crunching their sea snails, reminding them that "they must not weaken and be easily overcome by initial repugnance of these [foods]."

Valignano also ordered that kitchens and refectories were to be cleaned on a regular basis. Dishes were to be scrubbed and table coverings put in to soak. The monks, moreover, were to improve their appalling table manners. The fastidious way in which the Japanese ate their meals had fascinated the Portuguese ever since Pinto had dined with the lord of Bungo. Now, the Jesuits were also forced to eat with chopsticks, a torture for the older generation, who complained bitterly. "You must first take the sticks in one hand and tap the table with their points in order to adjust them properly," wrote one disgruntled padre. "Then you must raise the *goki* [large bowl] and take three morsels of rice, and then you must put the bowl on the table. Back on the table, I say, and nowhere else." And so the meal slowly progressed, mouthful after painstaking mouthful, until all the food was consumed. Valignano also ordered the monks to replace their tin crockery with elegant Japanese tableware: black or vermilion lacquered bowls "made of wood and fashioned on a lathe."

The Jesuits were also urged to adopt the Japanese mode of squatting on their heels while eating, which must have been physical torment for the statuesque Valignano. But he did not complain, nor did he expect to hear dissenting voices from his monks. "I request and require," he wrote, "[that] all my dearest padres . . . should win control over themselves in everything to the foods in Japan." Only when the Japanese servants had left for the night were the monks allowed to eat meat, and even then they were to be careful "that scraps of bones are not let fall upon the table." Valignano warned his monks that the Japanese had extremely sensitive noses and that "soup made of beef is to be put in plates, and not in [lacquer] bowls, so that the cups and soup-bowls be free of smell when Japanese afterward eat in our residences."

Valignano was not content that his monks adopted merely the outward observances of the Japanese. He persuaded them to think and behave as if they were Japanese, to act with dignity and stoic decorum. "[They] must take great care not to show impatience, anger or irritation, nor to give any sign of any other passion in their speech or countenance, because in the eyes of the Japanese, such things greatly detract from the credit and respect in which they are wont to hold the fathers."

Aware of the opprobrium that had followed the opening of the Jesuit leper hospital, Valignano now decreed that hospitals should accept only those from the highest levels of society. And, since Japanese society was strictly hierarchical, Valignano took the startling decision to form his own monks into Japanese-style ranks, with each individual aware of his place in the hierarchy and the manner in which he should speak to his superiors. Slowly, painfully, and often against their will, the Jesuits learned to imitate their hosts. When a newly arrived monk entered the Nagasaki seminary in 1596, he was shocked at the extent to which the Jesuits had adapted to their adopted homeland. "They so imitate the Japanese," he wrote, "that they wear their clothes, speak their language [and] eat like them on the floor." He was even more startled to see them "eat with a small stick, observing the same ceremonies as the Japanese do themselves," and added that "they have compiled a book entitled *The Customs and Ceremonies of Japan*, to be read to the pupils in the seminary."

Valignano's work had not been in vain; the Jesuits had reaped rich dividends and, by the time that Adams and his men stepped ashore, they had made upwards of 150,000 converts. Their influence was felt in the highest levels of courtly society and they were granted frequent audiences at court. They also maintained good relations with the feudal nobility and town governors, while their padres—who were posted throughout Japan—kept their superiors in Nagasaki informed of matters of local concern.

It was not long before news reached Nagasaki that a strange, sea-battered ship had been washed up in Kyushu. Two fathers of the Church had first sighted her when she was still far out to sea and had been surprised to see such a large ship making her way toward Bungo. "It was not the monsoon for ships to come from China," wrote Diogo do Couto in his account of the vessel's arrival. The monks concluded that she was a Spanish vessel sailing from the Philippines and that "through some storm, [she] had been driven out of her course."

Assuming that the crew were fellow Catholics and in danger of being cast away by the rough seas, they had pleaded with the local lord to help the mariners ashore and had even gone "with some boats to assist her." They had been appalled to discover that the vessel belonged to the Dutch—a nation of heretic Protestants—and had rowed straight back to shore in order to send an urgent message to the Portuguese settlement at Nagasaki. The arrival of heretics was the worst possible development; it was imperative that they should be silenced—killed—immediately.

The Jesuits had good reason for wanting the *Liefde*'s crew slaughtered and an even more pressing desire for the executions to be carried out as quickly as possible. These enemies of Catholicism were carrying a theological tinderbox that threatened to undermine everything that Valignano had achieved. For the Jesuits had always presented the Church as united in faith and doctrine, with the Pope as its universal head. They had never revealed to the Japanese that Christendom in Western Europe had been riven in two by the emergence of Protestantism.

The monks' unwelcome news was delivered directly to the Santa Casa da Misericordia, where it was greeted with consternation by the Jesuit fathers. They informed the local Japanese authorities that the arrival of an unauthorized ship was a grave matter and began scheming for the destruction of both the vessel and her crew. "The ship," they told one lord, "was one of Lutheran corsairs, enemies of the Portuguese and all Christians."

The Japanese took their warning very seriously—especially Lord Terasawa, "the governor-general of those realms," who "hastened to the kingdom of Bungo . . . and laid hold of the Hollanders and their goods." He was bewildered by the assortment of cheap cloths and trinkets aboard the *Liefde*, which were quite unlike the silks and rarities that the Portuguese were accustomed to bring from China. The ship was carrying eleven great chests of coarse woollen cloth and a box containing 400 branches of coral. There was a trunkful of amber and some parcels of scarlet material, as well as "a great chest of glass beads of divers colours, some mirrors and spectacles, many children's pipes [and] two thousand cruzados." More surprising was the "great quantity of nails, iron, hammers, scythes and mattocks . . . with which it would seem they were coming to conquer and inhabit." But by far the most alarming item of cargo was the weaponry. The vessel was laden with guns and armor, including 19 large bronze cannon, 500 muskets, 5,000 cannonballs, 300 chain-shot, three chests filled with coats of mail, and 355 arrowheads. Such hardware reinforced the impression that the ship's crew were in fact warriors, while their disheveled appearance confirmed, in the governor's mind, that they were not honest traders. "Nor did they come well dressed, and splendid with the pomp of servants and attendants, as the other merchants were accustomed to come, but only as soldiers and sailors." It took little persuasion on the part of the Portuguese to assure the governor that they were "people not of good title."

Lord Terasawa wanted to know more about their voyage and the purpose of their mission, and asked the Jesuit monks to interpret for him. Adams was chosen as the ship's spokesman and acquitted himself well, explaining how he and his men had come to arrive in Japan. One of the Portuguese accounts displays a grudging respect for Adams, stating that he was "a good cosmographer and with some knowledge of astrology." A second account is less charitable. It reports that Adams "gave no satisfactory account whatever" of the voyage and implies that their lengthy crossing of the Pacific was a result of poor seamanship: "They disembarked all so enfeebled that they looked like dead men."

Adams was concerned that the Jesuits were manipulating his words. He called these interpreters "our deadly ennemies" and said that their report "caused the governours and common people to thinke evill of us in such manner that we looked always when we should be set upon crosses, which is the execution in this land for theevery and other crimes." He was even more troubled to learn that the Jesuits were describing his men as *wako*, or pirates. Such an accusation was certain to awaken the wrath of the Japanese authorities, for many of Bungo's merchants had suffered at the hands of pirates. Indeed, piracy was a terrible crime in Japan and was punished with even greater severity than in England. In London, Adams must have been accustomed to seeing buccaneers hanged on the waterside gallows at Wapping. In Japan, the customary punishment was crucifixion, which ensured a slow and painful death. The victim was strapped to the cross before being slowly speared to death, and it was said that the most expert torturers could insert sixteen spears in a body without piercing a single organ. "They use a sort of iron manacles," observed the Florentine adventurer Francesco Carletti, "which are fixed to the wood of the cross and then wound round the wrists, the neck and the legs." Once the victim was securely fastened, the cross was raised and the executioner ordered to commence his delicate work. "He pierces the sufferer's body with a spear, thrusting it into the right side upwards . . . and out above the left shoulder, thus passing through the whole body." This was repeated on the other side of the body, so that the spears crossed internally. Sometimes, so many spears were employed that the condemned man looked like a giant hedgehog.

The *Liefde*'s crew were by now seriously alarmed at the way in which their words were being manipulated by the Jesuits. "Thus daily," wrote Adams, "more and more, the Portugalls incensed the

Japanese crucifixions ensured a slow and painful death. The victim was strapped to a cross, and spears were inserted with great care to ensure that internal organs remained undamaged.

justices and people against us." To these desperate survivors, stranded on the shores of a strange and potentially hostile land, these were frightening times. The fear began to prey on their minds, troubling their sleep and filling them with dread. Eventually, two of the company broke under the pressure. Gisbert de Coning and Jan Abelszoon van Oudewater hatched a plot to defect to the Jesuits and save their own skins by betraying their comrades. Coning slipped unnoticed out of the house, made contact with the Jesuits, "and gave himselfe out to be marchant of all the goods in the shippe." Oudewater soon followed suit. "These traitours sought all manner of ways to get the goods into their hands," wrote Adams, "and made knowne unto them [the Jesuits] all things that had passed in our voyage." But although these turncoats had placed their erstwhile companions in even graver danger, Lord Terasawa hesitated from issuing the order to have the *Liefde*'s crew executed. The ship's arrival was so strange and her cargo so unorthodox that he felt it necessary to take advice from a higher authority. A message was sent to the court in Osaka, asking for advice on how to deal with these unexpected arrivals.

An answer was received almost immediately. "Nine days after our arrival," wrote Adams, "the great king of the land sent for me to come unto him." Five galleys were dispatched from Osaka, "to bring me to the court where his Highnes was." Adams had no idea as to the identity of this "Highnes," nor did he know how long it would take to reach Osaka, but he was aware that his voyage would decide his fate and that of his men.

Osaka was an impressive city. It was huge—as big as if not bigger than London—and was divided by a river "as wide as the Thames." But unlike London, which had only one ancient bridge to serve its inhabitants, Osaka had dozens, "all of them richly ornamented with carved work" and decorated with beaten copper. One Englishman who later passed through the city after a tremendous siege noted that "in the whole course of my life, I never saw anything equal to the ruins of these bridges." But the real draw of

Osaka was its rambling, elegant castle, whose scale and elegance far surpassed the Tower of London. It was one of the marvels of Japan, a building of such immensity that all who saw it were impressed. It had a mass of "bulwarks and battlements, with loopholes for small shot and arrowes, and divers passages for to cast stones upon the assailants." It was held to be impregnable, for the walls were almost impossible to scale. A massive drawbridge led into the interior.

The castle's monumental exterior walls had been built for military strength. Once inside, visitors found themselves in an enchanted world of follies and pleasure gardens, ornamental ponds and miniature waterfalls. When the Jesuit padre Luis Frois had been invited here some years earlier, he had been astonished to discover that there were entire landscapes in miniature within the walls, "wherein the four seasons of the year are reproduced with its unhewn rocks, trees, shrubs, greenery and many other natural things." Vast sums of money had been spent on creating exquisite gardens whose rambling paths and crooked trees were a world away from the formal landscapes so beloved by the Elizabethan gentry. "[The Japanese] take much delight and pleasure in lonely and nostalgic spots," wrote the Jesuit João Rodrigues, "[such as] woods with shady groves, cliffs and rocky places, solitary birds . . . and in every kind of solitary thing." Osaka Castle had little follies, ornamental tea pavilions, and "sumptuous and lovely *zashiki* [parlors] decorated with gold, which look down on the many green fields and pleasant rivers below."

Padre Luis Frois had been even more astonished when he came to view the interior of the castle. One room sparkled with gold, another with silver, while many of the chambers were bedecked with silks and damasks. "And although it is not customary to sleep either in beds or on couches in Japan, we saw two furnished beds decorated with gold and all the rich trappings which are to be found on luxurious beds in Europe." Japanese nobles lavished fortunes upon the decoration of their palaces, which were a

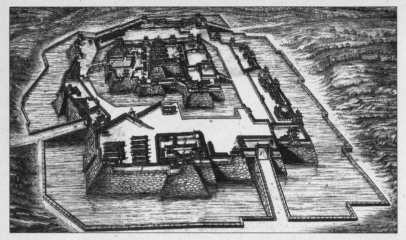

Osaka Castle was one of the marvels of Japan. Its battlements were built for military strength but once inside, visitors found themselves in an enchanted pleasure garden.

curious mixture of the opulent and the spartan. There was very little furniture, yet doors and framework glittered with gold leaf, while walls were lined with handmade paper decorated with trees, springs, birds, and lakes. There were depictions of leafless trees in winter snowscapes, clusters of juicy fruits hinted at autumn, and brightly colored blossoms suggested spring.

Adams was led deep inside Osaka Castle until he reached the audience chamber—"a wonderfull costly house," he later recalled, "[and] gilded with gold in abundance." The sliding doors were opened, the guards dropped to the floor in obeisance, and William Adams of Limehouse found himself face to face with an enormously plump man with long eyelashes and a wispy beard. His name was Tokugawa Ieyasu.

Ieyasu was not king of Japan, as Adams thought, but he did wield enormous power. His extraordinary rise had been achieved through a mixture of ruthlessness and guile. Born into a family of provincial warriors, he had formed a small but highly efficient army, which pushed back the boundaries of his feudal territories until he became a force to be reckoned with. His enhanced status was achieved at an opportune moment. Japan's most truculent warlords had slowly been crushed by the brilliant general Toyatomi Hideyoshi, who had risen to become chief minister to the impotent emperor. Hideyoshi harbored dreams of founding a dynasty, but when he died in 1598 his son, Hideyori, was just five years old. Central power fell to a regency of five elders who were sworn to hold the peace until the young successor came of age. One of these elders was Ieyasu, who was supposed to be equal in status to the other four. But Ieyasu was very different from his fellow elders. Fearless, sharp-witted, and worldly, he inspired awe in all who met him. Portraits depict him as a veritable mountain of a man, his vast bulk wrapped in delicately patterned silks. He could

Ieyasu was wily and worldly, inspiring awe in all who met him. In later life, he grew so fat that he found it impossible to mount his horse.

be a dandy when occasion demanded, and men marveled at his splendid costumes. "He wore a blue satin robe embroidered with many silver stars and half-moons," wrote one visitor to the court, "and he carried a sword girded at his waist." He had a venerable countenance, yet his enormous gut provoked much mirth when he was out of earshot. "No one cuts such an odd figure as the Lord Tokugawa," wrote one of his contemporaries. "He has such a fat belly that he can't tie his own girdle." In later life, Ieyasu was sadly forced to agree. "The fact is," he said, ". . . [I] have a fat belly [and] can't mount and dismount my horse with armour on." He was a passionate devotee of falconry and enjoyed military exercises. Indeed, some said that warfare, archery, and armor were his only interests.

A brilliant strategist in battle, he would mastermind his troops' maneuvers from the saddle of his horse. Although his peers found him cold and humorless, there was passion beneath the dull exterior. As the battle grew fierce, he would hammer the pommel of his saddle until the blood gushed from his hand. He did this so often that "in the end, the middle joints of his fingers got calloused and stiff, and in his old age he found it difficult to bend them."

Ieyasu was fascinated by the world beyond Japan. An official chronicle of his reign stresses his desire to meet people from other realms: "according to his judgment, there could be no other way to govern the country than by a constant and deep faith in the sages and scholars." The same chronicle records that, "whatever the subject, he was interested." Just over a year before the *Liefde*'s arrival, he had summoned the Franciscan monk Jeronimo de Jesus to an audience and asked him to persuade the Spanish in the Philippines to come to his land. "I have a keen desire for them to visit . . . ," he said, "to refresh themselves and to take what they wish." However, friendship was not his prime motive. He wanted their master shipwrights to help him build vessels that would carry his countrymen in safety as far as Mexico and the East Indies. The

Spanish refused, telling themselves that to build ships for the Japanese "would be equivalent to giving them the very weapons they needed to destroy the Philippines."

To be granted an audience with Ieyasu was the greatest honor for Adams. Only the richest and most powerful officials were received; all lesser mortals had to speak with his advisers. The pomp and pageantry of his courtly retinue was designed to strike fear into all who visited. Servants were treated like animals: "[they] entered and left on their hands and knees in the greatest reverence and silence." The court secretaries, of whom there were many, were bedecked in the most extraordinary costumes. "All of them," wrote one, ". . . wore long pantaloons which trailed two spans behind them on the floor, so that it was quite impossible to see their feet."

On the rare occasion when lords were granted an audience, they were expected to bring a large quantity of presents. One *daimyo* brought gifts worth 20,000 ducats; then, "at over a hundred paces from where his Highness was seated . . . [he] prostrated himself, bowing his head so low that it looked as if he wanted to kiss the ground." Despite this elaborate show of deference, the lord did not even get to speak with Ieyasu: "He turned and withdrew with his large retinue."

Adams had no knowledge of courtly etiquette, yet he was received with great warmth by Ieyasu. "He viewed me well," wrote Adams, "and seemed to be wonderfull favourable." Ieyasu was delighted to find himself in the company of a stranger from an unknown land and was particularly interested to meet a foreigner who was said to be a sworn enemy of the Portuguese and Spanish. He was also impressed by Adams's aloof and laconic manner, and felt sure that this shipwrecked mariner held many secrets. But the lack of a common language hindered any conversation. "He made many signes unto me," wrote Adams, "some of which I understood, and some I did not." In his frustration, Ieyasu called for "one that could speake Portuguese"—either a Jesuit monk or a Japanese novice—and began quizzing Adams on his homeland and his voyage.

"The king demanded of me what land I was," wrote Adams, "and what moved us to come to his land, being so farre off." Adams informed him that his country was on the other side of the globe and explained that "our land had long sought out the East Indies, and desired friendship with all kings and potentates in way of marchandize." He added that England and the Low Countries produced many commodities that would prove indispensable to the Japanese, while Japan appeared to produce many things that would be useful back in Europe.

Ieyasu, a shrewd observer of men, was quick to grasp that the antagonism between Adams and the Portuguese was real and deeply felt. This surprised him, for the Jesuits had always stressed that Europe was united in both faith and rule. When he realized that this was not the case, he probed Adams on the matter, asking "whether our countrey had warres." Adams paused for a moment before deciding that the truth would do him no harm. "I answered him, yea, with the Spaniards and Portuguese, being in peace with all other nations." Ieyasu was intrigued and asked about the cause of these wars. Adams obliged and "gave him to understand of all thinges, which he was glad to hear of it as it seemed unto me." Ieyasu was particularly interested to learn about the yawning religious rift between the Jesuits and the crew of the *Liefde*, and "asked me divers other questions of things of religion." His questions were so detailed that Adams left off recording them all, for "the perticulers here to write would be too tedeous."

Ieyasu was equally fascinated when Adams described the route that had brought the *Liefde* to Japan. The Portuguese were accustomed to sail by way of the Cape of Good Hope, and Ieyasu was surprised to learn that Adams and company had come the other way around the globe. "Having a chart of the whole world," wrote Adams, "I shewed him." When he pointed at the fragmented Straits of Magellan and said that he had piloted the *Liefde* through this channel, Ieyasu was unsure whether Adams was to be trusted. "He wondred," wrote Adams, "and thought me to lie."

Adams's audience continued until midnight, at which point Ieyasu was weary. His final question was to ask what trading goods the *Liefde* was carrying. Adams informed him of her cargo and asked if he and his men could be granted the same trading privileges that had long been granted to the Portuguese. "To which he made me an answer, but what it was I did not understand." Adams was none the wiser as Ieyasu swept out of the chamber.

It seemed to him that his audience could scarcely have gone better, for the venerable warlord had appeared to be spellbound by his English guest and no less delighted with his answers. But Adams had misread the inscrutable face of Ieyasu, and his hopes of clemency soon proved vain. Ieyasu was still deeply suspicious of the arrival of the *Liefde* and remained unconvinced by Adams's answers. Without further ado, he "commanded me to be carried to prison."

This was the worst possible news, for conditions in Japanese prisons were appalling. Inmates were commonly held in enclosed cells with neither windows nor light. Prisoners were stripped naked—although some wore a *fundoshi*, or breechcloth—and were forbidden to wash. Remand prisoners were treated with much the same contempt. There was a bucket for the men to perform their bodily functions, but many were so weak with dysentery that they were unable to move, and lay in their own filth.

Adams left no account of his time in prison, for all his possessions were taken from him and he had no writing materials. Others who survived their ordeal committed their harrowing stories to paper. "The stench was unbearable," wrote a Franciscan friar who had the misfortune to be incarcerated. "What with the great heat and fire which came from the multitude of living prisoners, a dead body would corrupt within seven hours and became so swollen and hideous that the very sight of it caused horror."

Adams's plight was made worse by the fact that he was powerless to counter the Jesuits, who were busy scheming against him and his men, urging Ieyasu to have them condemned to death. "In which long time of imprissonment," wrote Adams later, "the Jesuits and the Portuguese gave many evidences ageinst me and the rest, . . . [saying] that we were theeves and robbers of all nations." They told Ieyasu that if Adams and his men "were suffered to live, it should be ageinst the profitt of His Highness and of his countrey."

Adams's confinement was a terrifying experience; he spent each day awaiting the call from the executioner. "I looked every day to die," he wrote, "to be crost [crucified] as [is] the custome of justice in Japan." But Ieyasu resisted the Jesuits' pleading, for he had been enthralled by his meeting with Adams and was inclined to keep the shipwrecked mariners alive. He told the monks that Adams and his men had not done "his lande any harme nor dammage, [and] therefore [it was] ageinst reason and justice to put us to death."

As a further snub to the Jesuits, he asked for another meeting with Adams, and this time he asked many more questions "of the qualities and conditions of our countreys, of warres and peace, of beasts and cattell of all sortes, of the heavens." He was satisfied with what he learned and released Adams from prison, lodging him in a secure house in Osaka.

Ieyasu had made two important decisions in the weeks since he first met Adams. He would keep the *Liefde*'s crew alive but he would also forbid these foreigners from leaving Japan. Ieyasu still dreamed of developing Japan's shipbuilding and improving the skills of her pilots, and it was clear that these intrepid adventurers could be of great use. He was also keen to develop technology in the country's silver mines, and the crew of the *Liefde* seemed to possess the very skills that were needed.

Adams was held under house arrest for a further six weeks before being once again called into Ieyasu's presence. This time, there was good news. "He asked me if I was desirous to go abord the shipp and see my countreymen. I answered, 'very gladly,' the which he bad me doe." In this way, wrote a relieved Adams, "I was freed from imprissonment."

Adams had heard no news of his shipmates in all the time he had been in detention, but he soon learned that they were alive and much recovered from the trials of the voyage. During his period of incarceration, they had sailed the *Liefde* to Osaka port—on Ieyasu's orders—and it was there that Adams was reunited with the men. "I found the capten and the rest recovered of their sicknes," wrote a joyful Adams. As he stepped aboard the vessel, there were "weeping eyes on both sides . . . for it was given them to understand that I was executed long since." The Jesuits had told the crew that Ieyasu had ordered Adams's death and that the rest of them would soon be killed as well.

Although the men were reunited, they were none the wiser as to their eventual fate. Helpless and destitute, they did not even have enough money to buy victuals. In desperation, they appealed to Ieyasu for help. His response was swift and generous. He ordered that all of the *Liefde*'s stolen goods should be returned immediately and gave the men 50,000 *reals* in compensation —enough to restock their hold with fresh victuals. After another month spent aboard the *Liefde*, the men received a new message from Ieyasu. "The emperor commaunded that our shipp should be carried to the eastermost part of the lande"—to Edo—where Ieyasu had his permanent residence.

It was a terrible voyage, "by reason of contrary winds we had," and it took them several weeks to reach their destination. Adams's principal concern was to gain permission to sell their remaining cargo, for he intended to use the money to buy victuals and supplies for their ship. Once her hold was filled, the men hoped to set sail from Japan. In the meantime, they began lobbying for the necessary permission to depart. "I sought by all meanes . . . to get our shipp clear," wrote Adams, but his pleas fell on deaf ears.

Next, he resorted to bribery, proffering large sums of money to members of Ieyasu's retinue. But it was a fruitless exercise, which drained their limited resources. Within a few weeks, "we spent much of the monney that was given us."

Ieyasu was in fact far too preoccupied to deal with the *Liefde*. The council of elders had suddenly turned against him, with the other four members forming an unholy alliance. Led by Ishida Mitsunari, they began to engineer a military showdown, hoping to crush Ieyasu's forces once and for all. Ieyasu monitored developments with cool detachment. He commanded the loyalty of a huge number of troops, and his confidence was boosted by the *Liefde*'s quantity of weaponry, which had been promptly confiscated on the ship's arrival. If events turned to war, as seemed likely, the ship's nineteen cannon would prove invaluable.

Battles in Japan were fought on an epic scale and often involved tens of thousands of men. The crack troops in all armies were samurai, whose great curved swords were wielded with deadly effect. These elite forces—highly trained and disciplined—could wreak havoc on the field of battle. Adams would later see them in action and, stunned by their ruthlessness, would describe them as being "valliant in warres." He said that they rarely took hostages and noted that "justice is severely executed upon the transgressor of the lawe."

The strategy of the samurai was to cut a swath through the ranks of their enemies, slicing to pieces anyone who dared to stand in their way. This was intended to cause confusion and disarray, as well as to test the mettle of the opposing forces. Although these warriors fought with clinical efficiency, battles endured for many hours and sometimes even days. Treachery was rife, and it was not uncommon for entire regiments to switch allegiance in mid-battle. Men were trained to fight to the death, and surrender was extremely rare. Vanquished troops would rather commit ritual suicide than allow themselves to be captured.

Ieyasu had been in receipt of good intelligence about the

movements of his enemies and realized that they were intent on luring him into combat. He relished the fight and, a few days after his third meeting with Adams, he left Osaka and headed for Edo to begin preparations for war. The forces opposing him numbered almost 80,000 men, while Ieyasu himself could count upon about 70,000. All were in a high state of readiness, yet for six weeks there was an uneasy standoff as the two armies monitored each other's weaknesses and movements.

It was Ishida's army that made the first move. In mid-October, his men started to converge on the little village of Sekigahara, some fifty miles from Osaka. Ieyasu's troops soon followed, entrenching themselves on the hillsides outside the village. The appalling weather guaranteed that the battle would be messy and confused. The first skirmish broke out in the early hours of October 21, when Ishida's forces found themselves unexpectedly under attack. They fought back fiercely, prompting a much larger engagement than either side had planned. As the gilded banners of war were unfurled and the samurai warriors unsheathed their swords, the heavy drizzle developed into a spectacular rainstorm. A westerly gale screamed through the Sekigahara defile, creating havoc and confusion. Then, a thick fog descended on the field of battle and the two armies found themselves locked in combat. Almost without warning—and certainly without planning—the troops began to fight all along the battlefront, sinking to their knees in the muddy morass.

It is not clear how much damage was being caused by the *Liefde*'s great guns. One Spanish report suggests that they were fired continually into the enemy ranks. If this is true, the cannon would have inflicted severe casualties on the mass of sword-wielding foot soldiers. More certain is the fact that Ishida was determined to seize the initiative by launching a surprise attack on the rear of Ieyasu's great army. His master plan was to lead the initial engagement, then summon his fearsome allies to smash their way through Ieyasu's left and right flanks. But these crack troops

Japanese troops were ruthlessly efficient. The soldier (right) was in charge of a gunner squadron—his bamboo cane contained a spare ramrod. Horsemen (below) cooked food in their battle helmets, and also used them to water their horses.

refused to yield and, when they did at last counterattack, they swooped down upon Ishida's own forces and hacked them to pieces. Two divisions, each more than 10,000 strong, were totally routed and the tide of battle was dramatically turned. Ieyasu's forces scented victory and redoubled their offensive when they realized that the panicking enemy army was in full flight, led by their ignominious commander. Ishida was later captured and decapitated, and the triumphant Ieyasu was left as the undisputed master of Japan.

His victory was a turning point in Japanese history. Although the infant Hideyori was still alive—and still the ruler-in-waiting—no one doubted that Ieyasu now called the shots. In the aftermath of the great battle, he reorganized fiefdoms and confiscated land from many of the lords who had opposed him. He also strengthened his grip on power and, within three years, would take the ancient title of shogun, which at long last gave him the legitimacy he craved.

It is unclear when Adams and his men learned the welcome news of Ieyasu's victory. They were still on board the *Liefde*, which remained at anchor in Edo Bay, and were preoccupied with their own troubles. "Four or five of our men rebelled against the capten and myself," wrote Adams, "and made a muteney amongst the rest of our men, so that we had much trouble with them." Some of the men vowed to chance their luck on shore, while the rest elected to remain on the *Liefde*. But even they soon tired of the endless waiting game and joined the mutinous rebels. "Everyone would doe what he thought best," wrote Adams, who agreed to the crew's suggestion that the remaining money given by Ieyasu should be divided among them. "The monney was delivered according to every man's place . . . [and] everyone tooke his way where he thought best."

When Ieyasu learned of events on the *Liefde*, he must have been secretly pleased. He now knew that the crew had given up all hope of setting sail from Japan and decided to reward them with a most generous settlement. Every man was given an allowance of two pounds in weight of rice a day, which was more than enough to ensure survival. But Ieyasu's generosity came at a price. He wished to give the men employment and he had a particularly important job for William Adams.

Chapter 5

SAMURAI WILLIAM

THE *LIEFDE* was the men's only link with the world beyond Japan. As long as she was still afloat, she offered the possibility of escaping from the Land of the Rising Sun and attempting the long voyage back to their family and friends. But they were only too aware that the vessel was in a pitiful state. Her timbers were rotten and her mullioned windows, set deep into the stern, were falling apart. Storms, tropical rains, and a severe winter had all contributed to her decline. After more than two years without repairs, she was scarcely seaworthy.

The crew knew that their chances of fleeing in the *Liefde* were slight. Even if they could get permission to leave Japan, which was unlikely, the chances of their surviving a voyage across the East China Sea in such a wreck were minimal. At some point, one of the men clambered aboard and hacked off the figurehead of Erasmus that adorned her prow. It was the only keepsake that they would have of their journey, for shortly afterward the *Liefde* broke apart and slipped beneath the waves. Her loss was a distress to the seamen, who now knew that they were doomed to a lengthy stay in Japan. Unless or until an English or Dutch rescue vessel arrived, they were stranded in one of the remotest spots on earth.

The *Liefde*'s disappearance was also a blow to Ieyasu, who had marveled at her passage through the Straits of Magellan and across the Pacific. Aware that Adams and his men were not just skilled seafarers but also knew how to keep a craft afloat in the most hostile conditions, he decided to commission them to build a replica of the ship in which they had made their great expedition.

Shipbuilding expertise had long been lacking in the wharves and shipyards that dotted the coastline of Japan. Although the Japanese were daring sailors who pushed their barques into distant oceans and had regular traffic with the East Indies, their ships were of poor construction and handled badly in high seas. The Chinese expert Mao Yuan had dismissed them with contempt in his 1600 book on warfare, *We Pei Chih* (*On Preparations for War*), describing Japanese vessels as "wretchedly small . . . and easily sunk." He ridiculed the use of a grass called *tanbokuso* to caulk the ships, claiming it was "very extravagant in labour and costly for materials." Ieyasu agreed and decided to put Adams's talents to good use.

"The emperour called me," wrote Adams, "as divers times he hath formerly done." But on this occasion he did not wish to discuss geography or mathematics. "He would have me make him a small shipp"—a trading craft—that would be capable of sailing as far afield as the Philippines and Mexico.

Adams was alarmed by the request. Although his former tutor, Nicholas Diggins, had taught him the basic principles of shipbuilding, he had never actually constructed a vessel. Nor did he have any experience of cutting and shaping timber for the ship's frame. This was a highly complex process, fraught with difficulty. If its skeleton was not correctly shaped and aligned, the vessel would be at risk of capsizing in the high seas that surrounded

Japan. Adams explained some of the problems to Ieyasu and mumbled some excuses as to why he could not undertake such a task: "[I] answered him that I was no carpenter and had no knowledge thereof." Ieyasu frowned when he heard Adams's protests and commanded him to build the ship nonetheless. " 'Well doe your endeavour,' saith he. 'If it be not good, it is no matter.' "

Adams realized that the task ahead presented him with a rare opportunity to demonstrate that he could be of great service to Ieyasu. He threw himself into the work, acquiring timber and giving orders to his men. He was almost certainly aided by Pieter Janszoon, the *Liefde*'s carpenter, who had many of the necessary tools and most of the skills. The men used the now-lost *Liefde* as their template, building the new ship's frame in much the same manner. For month after month they cut timbers and planking and slowly assembled the ship. When she was at last finished and the men stood back to review their work, they were rather pleased with the result. She was indeed a miniature replica of the *Liefde*— "made in all respectes as our manner is"—and had a displacement of some eighty tons.

When the last rope was attached and the pennants put in place, Ieyasu was invited to the quayside to view the vessel. "He came abord to see it," wrote Adams, "[and] the sight whereof gave him great content." It did indeed. Ieyasu was delighted with the ship, telling Adams that, henceforth, he was welcome to visit the court whenever he wished and "that allways I must come in his presence."

Ieyasu was even more impressed when he had seen the majestic vessel under full sail, "[and] commaunded me to make another"—one that was capable of making ocean voyages. This second craft was to be on a much grander scale—about 120 tons—and took many months to build. When it was finally finished, Adams was extremely proud of his handicraft. "I have made a voyage in [her] from Kyoto to Edo," he recorded, "being as farr

*The Japanese constructed magnificent pleasure craft (above) but lacked the
expertise to make ocean-going vessels. Ieyasu decided to utilize
William Adams's talents.*

as from London to the Lizard or the Lande's End of England."
The ship would eventually prove her seaworthiness by surviving a
treacherous crossing of the Pacific, for Ieyasu lent it to the Spanish
governor of the Philippines, whose own vessel was shipwrecked
off the shores of Japan.

Ieyasu now saw how wise he had been not to execute Adams
and regularly summoned him to meetings, "giving me from time
to time presentes, and, in the end, a yearly stipend to live upon."
This provided Adams with a considerable sum of money—some
seventy ducats of silver and more than two pounds of rice each
day.

The Jesuits were horrified by the rise of this heretic sea dog.
They had been infuriated by their failure to have Adams crucified;
now, they realized that he posed a serious threat to their relation-

ship with the shogun. "After he had learned the language," wrote Padre Valentim Carvalho, "he had access to Ieyasu and entered the palace at any time. In his character of heretic, he constantly endeavoured to discredit our church as well as its ministers." The Jesuit fathers knew that it would be dangerous to murder Adams, so they tried a different approach. They redoubled their efforts to convert him and his men to Catholicism, aware that any success would be a spectacular coup for their mission.

They recognized that this would not be easy and laid down contingency plans in the event of failure. These included an extraordinary offer "to procure for him and his companions a safe conduct permitting them to leave Japan." They were so alarmed that Adams and his men would "contaminate, with their conversation and perverse doctrines, the souls of the Christians still fresh and tender in the Catholic faith" that they were prepared to risk Ieyasu's wrath by smuggling them out of the country.

In 1605, one of the Jesuit monks—almost certainly Padre João Rodrigues—met Adams at court and, somewhat clumsily, attempted to convert him: "[He] took advantage of the occasion to demonstrate to him the falsity of his sect, and the truth of the Catholic religion, by arguments and obvious reasons, drawn from the Holy Bible." Adams scoffed at the monk and gave a bold defense of his Protestant faith. "[He] had a lively intelligence," reads the Jesuit account, "and, though he had not studied, tried to justify his errors by citing the authority of the same holy scriptures."

When the padre perceived his failure, he announced his willingness to secure passage for the *Liefde*'s survivors on the next vessel to depart from Nagasaki. But although Adams was desperate to leave Japan, he had no desire to place his life in the hands of his bitterest enemies. He declined their offer and angered them further by mocking their waning influence at court.

The small Franciscan community also tried to convert Adams and his men, but they chose an altogether more original approach. A fanatical but decidedly crazy friar called Juan de Madrid con-

ceded that debate was wasted on such stubborn heretics and offered instead to perform a miracle. He summoned the men to
Uraga Bay near Edo and gave them one of two options. Pointing
to two mountains, one on either side of the bay, he offered "[to]
remove a greate tree, over the water, from the top of one mountaine to another." His second proposal was to "remove the whole
mountaine itselfe."

The men sniggered into their beards and joshed that the local
landowner would be less than happy if his mountain were to disappear. The friar was nonplussed by their jocularity and proceeded to offer them two further choices: "to make the sun to
stand still in the fermament, as it did in the time of Joshua . . . [or]
walke on the water, as St Peter did." The men declined his offer
to stop the sun, saying that it would burn their sensitive skins, but
were very taken with the last option. They all agreed that they
would like nothing better than to see Friar Juan walk on water.

Adams was as skeptical as the rest of the men. He said that "he
firmly beleeved that all miracles ceased longe since, and that those
of late time were but fictions and nothinge to be respected." Such
skepticism only encouraged the friar, who was determined to
demonstrate the vigor of his faith. Indeed, he was so convinced of
success that he traipsed around the local town of Uraga, publiciz-
ing the forthcoming miracle, "so that thousands of people came to
behould and see the event."

The crew of the *Liefde* watched impatiently for the spectacle to
begin. No one believed that the friar could perform a miracle and
they were delighted that he was going to make a fool of himself in
front of the vast crowds that had gathered. But as Friar Juan began
to prepare himself, the men suddenly became alarmed. The friar
was known to be a strong swimmer, and it dawned on them that
he was about to perform some sort of illusion or trick. "The frire
. . . [was] well provided of a greate piece of wood made in forme
of a crosse," wrote one, "which wrought from above his girdell to
his feete." The men were unsure as to exactly how this wooden

contraption would keep Friar Juan afloat, yet it appeared to have been constructed in such a way "as to have kept up any reasonable swimer above water, as this man was well knowne to be."

But it was by now too late to warn the crowds that Friar Juan was a charlatan. He had already walked down to the water's edge with great show, playing to the enormous crowd. He prayed, crossed himself fervently, and gingerly placed his foot onto the water's surface. It sank to the bottom. So did his other foot. He continued edging forward, but his body refused to become weightless and his "greate peece of wood" appeared not to work. He was soon plowing through the water, which shelved down steeply from the shoreline, until he was up to his neck. The cross, far from providing him with buoyancy, was dragging him down and it would be only a matter of seconds before his head disappeared beneath the waves. Suddenly, the men from the *Liefde* took pity on the friar. Melchior van Santvoort rushed across to a little skiff on the beach and pushed off into the water to rescue the foolish padre: "For all his cunninge and holinesse, he had been drowned." Wet, bedraggled, and mortified, he was plucked from the sea. His bold attempt had failed, "to the utter scandall of all the papists and other Christians."

On the following morning, Adams went to visit Friar Juan in order to quiz him about his miracle. But the poor man was not in a good state. Adams "fownd him sicke in his bed," although as plucky as ever when asked about his supposed miraculous powers. " 'For,' said he, 'had you beleeved that I could have done it, I had assuredly accomplished it.' " Adams could not stop himself from ribbing the padre, saying, "I told you before that I did not beleeve you could doe it, and now I have better occasion to be of the same opineon still." The friar, broken and humiliated, realized that he was defeated and "got him[self] packinge out of this cuntry." He took passage to Manila, where he found that his reputation had preceded him. He was feted for his attempt, and the admiring crowds gave him the nickname *O Milagreiro*, "the miracle-monger." But the local bishop proved rather less charitable toward his fellow Franciscan "[and] put him into prison for his rash attempt." It was indeed rash; news of his failed walk on water soon spread through Japan, and it was said that even many years after, the people "canot forget so notable a miracle-monger."

When the Jesuits and Franciscans came to terms with the impossibility of converting the Liefde's crew, they redoubled their efforts to monitor their whereabouts and track their movements. The Jesuits had monks in many Japanese towns and a system of communication that allowed messages to be relayed quickly back to Nagasaki. Yet it was not always easy to keep an eye on the men, for once Ieyasu's gifts of money had been distributed, the eighteen survivors split into groups and went their own ways. Some stayed close to the court, hoping to benefit from Ieyasu's patronage. Others despaired of their ill fortune and drank themselves into oblivion. Within a few years of being washed up in Japan, only thirteen were left alive.

A few of these prospered in their new homeland. Jan Joosten van Lodensteijn found favor with Ieyasu and was granted a stipend like Adams. The Liefde's enterprising purser, Melchior van Santvoort, was even more successful. He rented junks from the Japanese and established a flourishing little trade between Japan and Indo-China. But none was as adept as Adams in proving himself indispensable to the shogun. He became Ieyasu's protégé and, to the horror of the Jesuits, began to be treated as an oracle: "What I said," wrote Adams, "he would not contrary it." He taught Ieyasu geometry and mathematics, acted as an interpreter, and gave advice on the world beyond Japan. For many years, Ieyasu had consulted Padre João Rodrigues on such matters and had used Rodrigues's services as his court interpreter. Now, he became increasingly reliant on William Adams, and the Jesuits found themselves in the unenviable position of having to employ an Englishman as their intermediary. "My former ennemies did wonder," wrote Adams, "and at this time must entreat me to doe them a friendshipp." He was at first reluctant to pass on their messages, since these were the very men who had tried to have him crucified, but eventually he decided to dispense "good for evill . . . [and] God hath blessed my labours."

He hoped that his position at court would eventually reap rich dividends—that the shogun would grant him permission to leave Japan. He had received no news of his wife and daughter since his arrival as a virtual castaway and was growing increasingly desperate to set sail for home. Hopeful of a fair hearing, he made an emotional appeal to Ieyasu: "I made supplication to the king to depart his lande, desiring to see my poore wife and children according to conscience and nature." But Ieyasu frowned at the request and refused; "[he] was not well pleased withall," wrote Adams, "and would not let me go away more for my countrey."

The shogun was concerned by Adams's repeated demands to leave Japan, for he was only too aware that his English servant was in possession of many useful skills. He decided to reward him for his services by showering him with honors, land, and property, hoping to encourage him to settle permanently in Japan. Adams had already bought a town house in Edo; now, he unexpectedly found himself in possession of a far larger property. "For the servis that I have done and doe daily, being employed in the emperor's service, the emperor hath given me a living."

This "living" was actually a rambling country estate, situated at Hemi on the Miura Peninsula near Edo. Like most Japanese manor houses, it would have been constructed from cedar and was raised from the ground on wooden stilts. Sliding bamboo doors provided access to a veranda, with a vista that stretched across woods and thickets toward the snow-capped peak of distant Mount Fuji. For Adams—who had spent much of his life in the squalid poverty of Limehouse—this country estate provided him with respect and authority. He was now a lord of the manor, with duties, responsibilities, and very real power over his retainers. The estate had several villages within its borders, and these were inhabited by "eighty or ninety husbandmen"—serfs—"that be my slaves or servauntes." Whenever Adams returned to his estate from Edo, these "husbandmen" would line the roads to greet him and his guests.

His English counterpart would have been astonished. The Jacobean lord of the manor owned vast tracts of land, as well as deer and hawks, spaniels and terriers. But his influence over tenants was limited by the manorial court and parish officials. Adams had no such restraints. "Each man enjoys absolute power over his family and servants," wrote Valignano in his *Historia del Principio.* "[He] may cut them down or kill them, justly or otherwise, as he pleases, without having to give an account to anybody." Fear of punishment ensured that Adams was treated with the greatest respect by his retainers and serfs. They ran alongside his horse

William Adams cultivated rice on his country estate at Hemi. This was planted (above) and harvested by serfs "that be my slaves or servauntes."

whenever he returned to Hemi and made extravagant displays of obeisance. The stoic manner in which Japanese peasants accepted their fate was a source of constant surprise to Europeans. "[They] live quietly and contentedly in their misery and poverty," wrote Valignano, adding, "changes in station are common and frequent in Japan, for in no other country in the world does the wheel of fortune turn so often as here."

It was not long before the shogun proved even more generous to William Adams. In gratitude for his services to his court—and as a mark of his respect for the Englishman—he took the startling decision to bestow upon him "a lordshipp . . . [which was] never before given to a straunger." This "lordshipp" was indeed a great privilege and was quite without precedent in Japanese history. Adams was honored with the title of *hatamoto*, or bannerman, a prestigious position that made him a direct retainer of the shogun's court. This linked him to the great warrior class that had dominated Japanese history for centuries, for his fellow *hatamoto* were all samurai—battle-hardened fighters—whose role was akin to that of an elite officer corps, or a military bureaucracy. They were chosen for their unwavering loyalty and prowess on the field of battle and spent a large part of their time practicing martial arts. Adams's rise to the status of a samurai bucked this trend. He had not fought under Ieyasu, nor was he an expert in the martial arts. His contribution had been more prosaic although no less useful. As adviser and translator, he had brought news from a world of which Ieyasu had been kept in total ignorance.

At some point after being made a *hatamoto*, Adams appears to have abandoned his English garb and attired himself according to the fashion of the Japanese. He later recalled with pride his two great scimitars—worn by all samurai—and made frequent mention of acquiring silks and satins. These were the favored materials for making courtly kimonos, with their traditional drooping sleeves, adorned with exquisite decorations. Foreigners found it frustratingly difficult to fasten these giant sheets of cloth, and it took a great deal of practice to wear them in the correct fashion. "They fold the right-hand side over the body," wrote one Spanish novice, "and then over this they wrap the left-hand side." The material was held in place with a smart silk sash, which was wrapped around the belly and knotted at the hips. If it was not tied tightly enough, the whole kimono was in danger of falling to the ground.

Adams evidently mastered Japanese clothing, just as he managed to attain fluency in the highly complex language. He was happy to be called by his Japanese name—Anjin Sama, or Mr. Pilot—and was soon so at ease with his adopted homeland that he took to using the Japanese calendar in his diary: "the eighth daye of the moon called Shemo."

For years, Adams had petitioned to leave Japan; now, the lordship and the gift of land convinced him that his future was more assured here than in England. He owned a country estate and a town house in Edo, and had attained a rank in the courtly hierarchy that would have been unthinkable in the land of his birth. He still thought about Mary and his daughter, and wrote letters in which he pondered their fate: "hoping that, by one meanes or other, in proces of time, I shall have news from one good friend or other of my good acquaintance, wife and children, the which with patience I doe wait the pleasure of Allmighty God." But he knew that it might take many years for his letters to reach England, via the Dutch ships that came to Japan, and that it was even more unlikely that he would ever be reunited with his family.

He had long been attracted to the daughter of a highway official called Magome Kageyu, who was in charge of a packhorse exchange on one of the great imperial roads that led out of Edo. Although Magome's position was important, he was not of noble birth, nor did he have a high social standing. Adams's choice of his daughter, Oyuki, for a lover is unlikely to have been made for financial reasons and certainly not for any connections that might have been gained by having Magome as a father-in-law. Probably

It took much practice before foreigners mastered the art of wearing a kimono. The material was held in place with a wide sash and was often decorated with exquisite patterns.

he was genuinely in love; after the customary courtship, the couple were married. There were now two Mrs. Adamses, each ignorant of the other and living on opposite sides of the globe.

Adams was delighted with his good fortune, aware that everything had turned out for the best. "God," he wrote, "hath provided for me after my great misery." He was soon to receive even better news. In 1609 the Jesuits, who for so long had been his implacable enemies, suddenly found themselves caught in an unexpected crisis, which would lead to a showdown in the secluded and tranquil bay of Nagasaki.

Nagasaki was invisible from the sea. Flanked by vertiginous mountains and enveloped in cedars, her maze of streets was obscured from shipboard view until vessels had entered the fine natural harbor. The village had thrived since the Jesuits had taken possession of its farms and wooden shacks in 1580. Nagasaki was now a prosperous port that had reaped rich rewards from the trade in Chinese silks, and her streets were endowed with a colorful array of churches, religious colleges, and dwellings. But newcomers expecting to find a Portuguese colonial town were surprised to discover that the town resembled many other settlements up and down the Kyushu coastline. The merchants' mansions were crowned with decorative concave roofs in the Japanese fashion, while even the humble dwellings had sliding bamboo doors with translucent paper screens. The Jesuit church was the most extraordinary sight of all. With its hexagonal ground plan and pagoda-style stack of layered roofs, it looked more like a Buddhist temple than a place of Christian prayer.

The shade-dappled streets were often thronged with crowds, especially when the annual ship from Macao was in port. Sailors searched out whores and drinking dens, while bewhiskered Portuguese *fidalgos*, or noblemen, swaggered around in their puffed pantaloons, buckled shoes, and floppy hats. The richest of the merchants came with their own retinue of slaves and servants, and were shaded by palanquins made of silk. Many belonged to the Misericordia fraternity—a brotherhood for monks and laymen who shared high ideals and a common Catholic faith.

The arrival of the annual Portuguese ship from Macao was heralded by feasting and celebration. In 1609, there was even more cause for celebration than usual, for the *Nossa Senhora de Graça* (*Our Lady of Grace*) was the richest vessel to call at Nagasaki for many a year. She was carrying a staggering 200 tons of silk— worth 600,000 cruzados—and a huge stockpile of silver bullion. The Jesuit fathers were delighted, for, as middlemen, they stood to reap glittering rewards from the sale of the merchants' cargo.

It quickly became apparent that the arrival of such a richly laden ship was arousing jealousy and greed. The Japanese governor of Nagasaki sent armed guards to inspect the cargo—as was his right—but the captain of the vessel haughtily refused to allow them aboard. The governor was infuriated and announced that he was coming aboard in person. But he, too, was denied permission. His outrage quickly turned to fury when he learned the captain's identity. André Pessoa, former governor of Macao, had made himself extremely unpopular by his actions in that colony just a few months earlier. A band of Japanese sailors had gone on the rampage, and Pessoa had responded by storming their lodgings and killing a large number of them. Those who were captured alive were forced to sign an affidavit declaring their responsibility for the bloodshed. Once they had been released, they made their way back to Japan with tales of woe and suffering.

News of Captain Pessoa's behavior in Macao had quickly reached Ieyasu, whose initial reaction had been to fine the Portuguese for their actions. But when he heard that Pessoa had also slighted Nagasaki's governor, he settled on a more extreme policy, deciding "to kill the captain with all the Portuguese, and to seize the ship with all its cargo." Captain Pessoa was summoned to attend Ieyasu at his court, with the assurance that he was to receive a full pardon for his role in the Japanese deaths. Sensing treachery, he wisely refused to go ashore, preferring the safety of his heavily armed vessel. Ieyasu was so infuriated by such disobedience that he ordered the local lord, Arima Harunobu, to seize the captain-major and his vessel.

Arima relished the task, for some of his men had been involved in the Macao debacle and he was thirsting for revenge. He assembled a band of some 1,200 samurai warriors and, in the first week of January 1610, prepared for a nocturnal assault. The samurai rowed across Nagasaki Bay in thirty boats and were so confident of success that they screamed insults at Pessoa and blasted their muskets into the night sky. Pessoa held his fire until they were dangerously close, then shot two successive broadsides that smashed through the flotilla, causing carnage. To add insult to injury, "each shot was accompanied by a concert of flutes [trumpets]."

Arima's men were forced to retreat and regroup, but although they repeatedly rowed out into the bay, they found it impossible to get near the *Nossa Senhora de Graça*. For three nights in succession they were beaten off by Pessoa's great guns. On January 6, the Portuguese captain succeeded in edging his carrack out of the harbor and toward the safety of the open sea. Arima now grew desperate and launched one final attempt on the Portuguese vessel. To enable his men to board the craft, he constructed a wooden tower "which was carried by two big boats." It was the same height as the Portuguese ship's mastheads and was covered in wet hides as a protection against fire. Arima also hired an extra 1,800 mercenaries—samurai—to swing the odds of success firmly in his favor. The attack began at about nine o'clock at night and met with far greater success than the previous attempts. A few of the boldest Japanese fighters even managed to board the carrack, but before they could wield their great curved swords, they were cut to pieces by the Portuguese defenders. Pessoa himself killed two Japanese samurai with his own hands.

The sailors on board were jubilant and were already proclaiming victory when events took a most unexpected turn. A chance musket shot, fired by one of the samurai, struck a grenade that one of Pessoa's defenders was about to hurl at the Japanese. The burning shrapnel set fire to gunpowder on deck, and the mizzen sail suddenly burst into flames. Within seconds, the entire upper works of the ship were ablaze. Pessoa immediately realized that all was lost and that the great ship was doomed. High on excitement and half deranged by the heat, he now decided on a spectacular finale. "With an intrepid heart, [he] put down his sword and shield in a cabin without saying another word and, taking a crucifix in one hand and a firebrand in another, he went below and set fire to the powder magazine." The resulting explosion was immediate and catastrophic. The *Nossa Senhora de Graça* rose slightly in the water, split in two in a wall of flame and sank in thirty-two fathoms of water. Of Pessoa himself, nothing whatsoever remained.

Ieyasu was furious when he learned what had happened. He threatened to kill every Portuguese trader in Nagasaki and exile every Jesuit in the land. In the event, wiser counsel prevailed and Ieyasu retracted his threats. But he refused to recant on one expulsion. Padre João Rodrigues, his onetime court interpreter, was told to pack his belongings and leave. He was simply not needed anymore, for Ieyasu had a new interpreter—William Adams—who was more agreeable company.

The sinking of the *Nossa Senhora de Graça* dealt a severe blow to the prestige of the Jesuits. They lost some 30,000 cruzados, leaving them "in the most miserable condition that can be imagined." It was a setback, too, for the Portuguese merchants, who lost an entire year's revenue because of the sinking of the vessel. Their difficulties were compounded when they discovered that two Dutch vessels had recently made landfall at the little island of Hirado, just a few hours' sailing from Nagasaki. One of these ships was carrying an industrious merchant called Jacques Specx, an employee of the Dutch East India Company who had been given the unenviable task of establishing a "factory," or trading base, in Japan.

The merchants and burghers of Rotterdam had long toyed with the idea of sending traders to Japan. News of the *Liefde*'s extraordinary voyage had reached them more than eight years earlier, when it was carried home by the Dutch adventurer Oliver van Noort. He had encountered some Japanese traders in the East Indies who told him that "a great Holland ship, by tempests shaken . . . [had] put in at Japan." This had intrigued the Dutch merchants, but they were far too preoccupied in trying to establish themselves elsewhere in the East. The nearest Dutch outpost to Japan was in Pattani, on the Malay Peninsula, where the factors were led by the lethargic Victor Sprinckel. He had shown little interest in attempting to cross the East China Sea and even less enthusiasm in going to the aid of his erstwhile compatriots. When, in 1605, two of the *Liefde*'s crew had made contact with Sprinckel, he had resisted their calls to open trading links with Japan. Instead, he berated the men for allowing William Adams, the *Liefde*'s sole surviving Englishman, to become Ieyasu's most trusted confidant.

Jacques Specx was a more dynamic individual than Sprinckel, yet he quickly realized the difficulties of his mission. He had just three assistants, none of whom spoke the language and all of whom knew almost nothing about Japan. But when, with Adams's help, he approached Ieyasu to beg for trade privileges, he was given a warm welcome. Ieyasu immediately expressed his desire for trade and wrote an enthusiastic letter to Prince Maurice, "lord of Holland," to tell him of his delight at the prospect of Dutchmen visiting his land. "If countries are alike animated," he mused, "what objection is there to annual visits, although they are separated by a thousand, nay ten thousand, leagues of sea and land?"

Ieyasu's enthusiasm met with a cool response in the Netherlands. The merchants could not spare any vessels to send to Japan, and Specx spent long hours staring forlornly at the horizon in the hope of sighting a friendly sail. Fearful that Ieyasu would rescind his trade privileges, he made contact with Adams and asked for help in procuring a second audience with the shogun. "Because this Mr Adams had introduced himself so well to the monarch," records a contemporary Dutch journal, "there was neither lord nor prince in this country who was in a better position."

The two men headed for the court in February 1611 and, on arrival, met with Ieyasu's president of the council, as well as dozens of other courtly officials. Adams offered Specx advice on how the Dutchman should behave and Specx followed it to the letter. "We tried to answer in the Japanese manner," wrote a bemused Specx, "which meant exchanging lots of compliments." As noon approached, the hour for the audience with Ieyasu drew near. The door was opened by an elaborately dressed courtier. Specx was called into the presence chamber and ordered to leave his gifts of carpets and tusks on a little display table. He was then ushered before Ieyasu to pay his respects. "Once we had saluted the emperor," records the Dutch journal, "he asked us how many soldiers we had on the Moluccas; if we were trading in Borneo; if it was true that it was from there that one found the best camphor?" Next, Ieyasu quizzed Specx about products found in northern Europe and asked "which scented wood we had in our country and which ones we valued most." Adams translated the Dutchman's answers, to Ieyasu's evident delight, for Specx was later told that the shogun was not accustomed "to speak in such familiar tones to anybody, not even to the great lords of the country."

The meeting had only just come to an end when Adams found himself called back into the chamber for a private audience. Ieyasu, with all the Dutch gifts laid out before him, "had looked at all the cloth, the trinkets, the velvets and the guns, one after the other, and said: 'When the Dutch ships will come, will they bring lots of curiosities and beautiful merchandises?'" Adams assured Ieyasu that this would be the case, "promising his majesty that the vessels which would come from Holland would bring several beautiful things. The emperor answered, 'Yes, yes, I can see that the Dutch are masters in the manufacturing trades as well as in the war.' "

Adams's role as intermediary won the Dutch their renewed trading rights. "The Hollanders be now settled," he wrote, "and I have got them that [trading] priviledge as the Spaniard and Portuguese could never get in this fifty or sixty yeers in Japan." He was in the process of relaying this information back to Specx when he was brought the disconcerting news that a large Spanish embassy had arrived at court in order to request the immediate expulsion of the Dutch from Japan—something that neither Adams nor Specx had foreseen. The embassy was headed by Sebastian Vizciano, the ambassador from New Spain, who presented himself with all possible pomp. He was dressed in the finest robes, including "a doublet, a jacket, breeches, a ruff, a cape [and] a plumed cap with fine gold trimmings." On his feet were white shoes with dainty buttons and to complete the effect he wore a golden sword and dagger. He brought with him a retinue of twenty-four musketeers who blasted their guns with such relish "that they used up a barrel of gunpowder in the hour."

Vizciano's mission was not simply to expel the Dutch from Japan; he also came with a series of other demands, the principal of which was to ask permission to map the island coastline. Ieyasu granted this request with his customary good grace, but soon found himself insulted by Vizciano's overweening hubris. The Spaniard refused to prostrate himself in front of Ieyasu—on the grounds that the Spanish monarch was the greatest ruler on earth—and he demanded that Spanish friars be granted free admission to Japan. Ieyasu had hitherto remained calm, but now his anger began to show. "The doctrine followed in your country differs entirely from ours," he said, ". . . it is best, therefore, to put an end to the preaching of your doctrine on our soil."

Vizciano was outraged and now made his demand that the

Dutch—together with Adams—be expelled from Japanese shores. This proved too much for Ieyasu, who was shocked by Vizciano's arrogance. He informed the Spaniard that even the "devils of hell" would be treated like "angels from heaven" so long as they obeyed Japanese law. He further warned Vizciano that "the lands of His Majesty, being open to all foreigners, none ought to be excluded from them."

Specx and Adams were delighted when they learned of Captain Vizciano's offensive behavior. He had openly bragged that the king of Spain "did not care about trade with Japan" and told one Japanese lord that the Spanish king's only desire was to save the pagan Japanese from the eternal fires of hell. "His Christian majesty," he said, "[had] a pious desire that all nations should be taught the Holy Catholic Faith and thus be saved." Ieyasu was disgusted by Vizciano's arrogance and returned his presents, "as he was custom to do with foreigners when he did not want to gratify their demands." He had never before experienced such a raw display of pride and expressed deep misgivings about allowing the Spaniard to map Japan's fractured coastline.

When Ieyasu turned to Adams for advice, the Englishman's reply was carefully calculated to cause maximum damage to the Spanish cause. He said that the king of Spain's goal was to conquer the whole world and that in pursuit of this policy he had a cunning plan: he sent friars and Jesuits into the lands he hoped to conquer, in order to convert as many people as possible. When his troops later arrived in force, they found it easy to establish a beachhead from which to attack. Adams told Ieyasu that no English ruler would ever have agreed to such a petition, since it was clear that the Spanish were interested only in finding a suitable landfall for their invading troops.

Soon after the visit of Sebastian Vizciano, Adams's thoughts turned once again to England. He feared that information about his survival had still not reached London and that his family and friends had received "no certen newes, as I thinke . . . [of]

whether I be dead or livinge." He was desperate to inform them that he was still alive and "doe pray and entreat, in the name of Jesus Christ, to doe so much as to make my being here in Japan knowen to my poor wife." But his problem was that he could never be sure that his letters had actually reached England. The few Dutch vessels that called at Japan took several years to reach home, and there was no guarantee that those on board would forward his correspondence.

What Adams did not realize was that the Dutch had been deliberately withholding the letters he had written. Selfish, ruthless, and thoroughly deceitful, these hard-nosed traders would do anything to deny the English information about Japan. They had even managed to keep Adams in ignorance of the fact that English ships had been sailing to the East Indies for almost a decade and that a small band of adventurers had established a permanent base in Java as long ago as 1603. Throughout Adams's long years in Japan, he had been separated from his compatriots by a journey of less than two months.

When this finally became clear to him and he realized the scale of the Dutch betrayal, he was furious. "Had I known that our English shippes hath trade in the Indies," he later wrote to a friend, "I had long a-troubled you with writing, but the Hollanders have kept it most secret from me till the year 1611, which was the first newes that I heard."

Adams now wrote a frantic letter to the small band of Englishmen based in the Javanese port of Bantam, informing them of all the adventures he had experienced during his eleven years in Japan. Since he had no idea to whom he was writing, he addressed his missive, rather forlornly, to his "unknown friends and countrymen."

"I have emboldned myselfe to write these fewe lines," he wrote, "desiringe the worshepfull company . . . to pardon my stoutness." Aware that these traders would have no idea as to his identity, he informed them that his name was William Adams and added, with more than a hint of pride, "I am a man not unknowen in Radcliffe and Limehouse." He prayed that his countrymen would do their utmost to convey his letter back to England and provided them with a list of his old friends. "I doe know," he wrote, "that compassion and mercy is so that my friendes and kindred shall have newes that I doe as yet live in this veil of my sorrowfull pilgremage."

Adams also urged his countrymen to sail to Japan, informing them that this was one of the best countries in the world with which to do trade. "The people of the lande [are] good of nature, courteous out of measure and valliant in warres." He added that there was little problem of crime and cheating, and that there was "not a lande better governed in the worlde by civil pollecy." Aware that jealousy of the Dutch always provided a spur, he also informed them "that the Hollanders have here an Indies of monney."

With the Portuguese and Spanish in disgrace, and the Dutch trading post seriously understaffed, Adams knew that there was never a better time for the English in Bantam to try their luck in Japan.

Chapter 6

INTO UNKNOWN LANDS

NIGHT ARRIVED SUDDENLY in Bantam. As soon as the fearsome equatorial sun slipped beneath the Java Sea, the sky melted into an inky black. For the next eight hours, the handful of Englishmen living in this treacherous port were in constant fear of coming under attack from native headhunters and cutthroats. Augustine Spalding, the head of the factory, was accustomed to bolt the fortified gate as dusk fell and pray that no fire-tipped arrows would be shot over the palisade fence in the middle of the night.

Bantam was England's principal toehold in the Indies, a bustling port on the north coast of Java that attracted large flotillas of junks, dhows, and native prahus from as far afield as India, China, and Japan. It was one of the principal entrepôts of the East Indies—a place where hawkers and traders dealt in Moluccan nutmegs, Indian calicoes, Chinese porcelain, and—just occasionally—Japanese lacquerware.

A small English factory had been established in Bantam in 1603, when the veteran Captain James Lancaster, commander of the East India Company's first voyage, left eleven men with orders to stockpile spices. Those men had been surprised to find themselves living among a cosmopolitan community. Bantam's souks and spice markets, thronging with merchants, made for a colorful spectacle. The native Javanese dressed in pintado loincloths and velvet mandilions, while the wealthier merchants—who donned taffeta caps and calico cummerbunds—looked as if they were on their way to a courtly soirée. The Chinese merchants attired themselves with even greater panache. They sported long robes and gowns and often wore silken cauls on their heads, which only partially concealed their immensely long ponytails, bound into a greasy knot. The town's governors wore menacing hooded cloaks, while the local priests had a strange habit of kissing the ground. Even more alarming were the bands of deranged soothsayers who, according to the English factor Edmund Scott, ran "up and downe the streetes like madmen, having swords drawne in their hands, tearing their haire and throwing themselves against the ground." To make the local color complete, the town's infant ruler liked to be drawn through the streets in a chariot pulled by a team of gleaming white buffalo.

Bantam was a good place to buy spices, but the worst possible place to settle men who were already suffering from acute dysentery after more than twelve months aboard a leaky and unsanitary vessel. Scarcely had those first English factors built their lodgings than they began to expire. The factory's chief and deputy both died within a few months, while the other men were struck down with violent sicknesses and raging fevers. They quickly discovered that rotting, disease-ridden Bantam was one of the least hygienic places in the East. Typhoid and cholera were rife, while malaria was a constant fear, for the mudflats and swamplands provided a fertile breeding ground for mosquitoes. One captain labeled Ban-

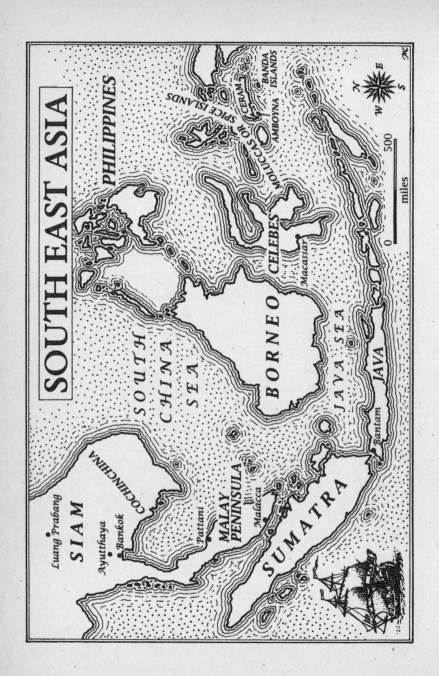

SOUTH EAST ASIA

PHILIPPINES

SPICE ISLANDS

MOLUCCAS OR CERAM

BANDA ISLANDS

AMBOYNA

CELEBES

Macassar

SOUTH CHINA SEA

BORNEO

JAVA SEA

JAVA

Bantam

SUMATRA

MALAY PENINSULA

Malacca

Pattani

COCHIN CHINA

SIAM

Luang Prabang

Ayutthaya

Bankok

N
E
W
S

0   500
miles

tam "that stinking stew." Another noted wryly that "Bantam is not a place to recover men that are sick, but to kill men that come thither in health."

The English factory—a two-story wood and cane structure— was extremely flimsy and "all the upper-workes of our houses, by reason of the heat, are open." It was frequently flooded by the monsoon rains, which cascaded through the roughly thatched roof and dripped all the way to the ground floor. In the heat of mid-day, the sun beat down on the men inside, while in the evening, clouds of mosquitoes descended on the place. Night was the worst time of all: the men hung flaming torches all around the perimeter fence, "otherwise, in the dark nights, they [the Javanese] being so blacke as they are, might have entred suddenly upon us as before we should descry them."

It was impossible for the factors to get any sleep, for a criminal Javanese underclass terrorized them from dusk till dawn. "They began to practise the firing of our principall house," wrote Scott, "with fiery darts and arrowes in the night." On several occasions the cane roof crackled into flames and was doused only just in time. The men were constantly terrified by the thought of being burned alive in their warehouse. "O this word fire," wrote Scott, "had it beene spoken near me, either in English, Mallayes, Javanese, or Chinese; although I had been sound a-sleepe, yet I shoulde have leaped out of my bed." There was constant treachery and plots "to have us slaine in the night," and continual fear of being tortured or killed by native headhunters. There were good reasons for moving the Bantam factory elsewhere, but the merchants lacked both the will and the motivation. After more than nine years in the same place, there was an air of semipermanence to the little trading post, and it had become the center of operations for all English merchants trading in the East.

On April 26, 1612, Bantam's chief factor, Augustine Spalding, was overjoyed to spot an English vessel entering the bay. "There had been no English shipps heere," he recorded, having dreamed

Bantam was home to a cosmopolitan community. Native merchants (top) wore krises, or curved daggers, in their belts. Foreign traders (bottom) wore colorful robes and looked even more exotic. These three—possibly spice dealers—are from Pegu (in Burma/Myanmar), Persia, and Arabia.

of this moment for more than a year. Now—fearful that his eyes were playing tricks—he ran to the shoreline to check that it was true. It was indeed. The aptly named *Globe* had arrived in Bantam on the fourth stage of what was fast proving an extraordinary odyssey through the ports of Southeast Asia.

The *Globe*'s voyage had been the brainchild of two bold entrepreneurs, Peter Floris and Lucas Antheunis. These shadowy and dubious figures had turned up in London two years previously and headed straight to Philpot Lane, the home of Sir Thomas Smythe, governor of the East India Company. Smythe was immediately suspicious. The men admitted to being Dutch, but their backgrounds were mysterious and they appeared to have adopted pseudonyms in order to conceal their identities. Yet both had considerable experience of trade with the East, and the silken-tongued Floris was impressively eloquent when he spoke of how best to exploit the riches of the Orient. One of his compatriots later remarked that Floris knew "all secrets and designs, which would be exceedingly important for them [the English]."

Floris's idea was daring in the extreme. He had grown increasingly concerned at the glut of spices on the markets of London and Amsterdam, and was aware that there were enormous and as yet untapped profits to be made in the East. His master plan was to shun the conventional spice trade and involve himself instead in the highly profitable internal trade of Southeast Asia, trafficking in luxury goods between Java, Indo-China, and Japan. Floris knew that only the rarest commodities fetched the highest prices, and his project would require a small band of adventurers to push deep into territories never before visited by Englishmen—the monsoon forests of Indo-China, the uncharted hinterland of Siam (modern Thailand), and the still-unknown land of Japan. Floris and Antheunis hoped to establish little warehouses throughout the East—from Java to Japan—and intended to settle men wherever possible.

Thomas Smythe had a passion for adventure—so long as it entailed profit—and was intrigued by Floris's proposed voyage. He, too, had long been concerned that the glut of spices had caused prices to tumble and had suggested that merchants branch out into other commodities such as silk, "wherewith these parts of Christendome have not been glutted." He was even more enthusiastic when he learned that Floris and Antheunis were prepared to invest £1,500 of their own money in the enterprise, and he willingly gave the men permission to sail under the auspices of the East India Company.

King James I also gave his backing to the voyage, aware that the revenue from increased customs duties would help to fill his empty coffers. He wrote letters of introduction to a number of Eastern princelets and chieftains, one of which was addressed to the "greate king of Japan." Its tone was flattering and obsequious. He told the Japanese "king" how impressed he had been to learn of his "princlie and favourable disposition" and explained that his reason for writing was his desire to "solicitt your freindshipp and amity." He was diplomatic in concealing his desire to tap the country's rumored riches, although he did inform the king that he was hoping for "interchange [of] such comodities as may be of most use to each other's countreys." He remained vague about these "comodities," but few in England would have doubted his meaning. The king wanted the Japanese to buy English broadcloth and hoped that they would pay for it with large quantities of silver.

King James envisaged the establishment of a permanent trading post in Japan and asked the shogun for "your royall proteccion for the setllinge of their trade." He said that he had ordered Floris and his men "to demeane themselves with all respects of courtesie and friendshipp towards your people" and prayed that they would remain on their best behavior during their stay in Japan. King James promised the Japanese "king" that any of his subjects who traveled to England would be provided with all "neede and necessities." His letter ended with a prayer: "[that] Almightie God . . . preserve and prosper you, and . . . make you victorious against your enemies."

Although both the king and Sir Thomas Smythe had high

hopes for the success of this mission, both men continued to express misgivings about the wisdom of sending two Dutchmen on what was, in part, an English diplomatic mission. Smythe took particular care when he came to choose a suitable captain for the expedition. Anthony Hippon was a man of "integritie [and] wisdome" whose leadership qualities were so impressive that he had earned himself the nickname "good shepherd." Smythe also appointed a merchant—Robert Browne—who was known to him personally. Browne would have been a fine choice had it not been his misfortune to suffer from acute seasickness. After each hearty luncheon of salt pork and stale beer, he would vomit violently over the side of the vessel. Traveling ashore in the ship's pinnace caused him even greater distress; it made him so nauseous that before long he had to "tarry aboarde."

The rest of the merchants and mariners were healthy but unhelpful. Second-in-command, Thomas Essington, was quarrelsome and inexperienced. John Johnson, the master, was usually "so drunke that he coulde not well stande," while John Skinner, the mate, was an inveterate gambler. Crew members Job Palmer and Richard Bishop would grow to hate each other with such passion that they would fight a duel, while many of the rest of the crew would mutiny at one point or another.

The *Globe* set sail from England's south coast in the first week of February 1611 and made rapid progress toward the Cape of Good Hope, where the men dropped anchor and rowed ashore. Although Floris bemoaned the fact that "much refreshing was not here to be had at this time of the yeare," the men managed to lade the *Globe* with eighty sheep and twenty cattle. This was more than enough to enable them to continue with their onward voyage to India, where they hoped to buy the cottons and chintzes that were so prized in Java and Siam.

Floris and Antheunis had already visited the subcontinent and knew that there were three principal entrepôts on India's eastern coastline—Pulicat, Petapoli, and Masulipatnam. Their attempt to land in Pulicat, the most southerly port, almost ended in catastrophe when a ferocious storm blew up as they rowed ashore. "We were in greate distresse," wrote Floris, "especially Mr. Browne, in regard of his sicknesse." As Browne retched into the warm waters of the Bay of Bengal, the rest pulled on the oars and finally reached land, only to discover that trading prospects were poor. A band of Dutch adventurers had already staked out their claim on these shores, while the local governess—a testy lady of the court—refused to grant the men an interview. As the temperature soared and tempers frayed, Robert Browne took a turn for the worse. He was now vomiting so badly that Captain Hippon had to be brought ashore to care for him, but it was clear that his seasickness was compounded by some nasty tropical disease. Floris grew increasingly disgruntled with the way in which he was being treated and decided to set sail. After petulantly calling the governess an "olde whore," he led his men back to the *Globe* and headed up the coast for Petapoli.

Trade here proved even less fruitful and Floris ordered the vessel to continue onward to Masulipatnam. Robert Browne was by now so wretched that he asked if he could be landed ashore and make for Masulipatnam overland. But he was too weak to climb into the ship's pinnace and was therefore obliged to endure yet more pitching and tossing. After a further week of acute sickness, his pallid and mournful features suggested that the end was near. According to the ship's journal, at "about nine of the clock, at night, deceased Mr Robt Browne . . . the nexte daye in the morning he was buried on shoare and, for a remembrance to suche as may come after, we erected a tombe for him."

Masulipatnam presented the last opportunity for trade on this coastline, and Floris was determined to succeed. Although the local governor was a "villaine" and a "knave," Floris managed to acquire chintzes, wraps, and painted cloth for extremely low prices. He was delighted that he had bought a considerable cargo "withoute having made any penny in badde debts" and was pleased to note that "our estate is at present in very good being." He could now steer the *Globe* in the direction of Bantam, where he was assured of acquiring yet more goods that would have a ready market in Pattani, on the Malay Peninsula.

Floris's arrival in Bantam was greeted with great cheer by the dwindling band of Englishmen who had the misfortune to be based there. Augustine Spalding bemoaned the dearth of English shipping and told Floris of his difficulties in making money. The paucity of good men was his chief cause for concern; those that had been keenest to search out new markets had proved suspiciously inept at returning a profit. Spalding had only recently dispatched men to the swampy port of Sukadana on Borneo's west coast, where diamonds were to be had for a song. But although these traders had been given generous supplies of silver, the factory soon found itself threatened with bankruptcy. "Our witts are not able to conceive to whose profite this is done," wrote a sarcastic Floris, who knew all too well that the traders themselves had stolen the money.

Floris's stay in Bantam gave him time to sell some of his cottons and plan the next stage of his voyage. Augustine Spalding encouraged him to sail to Japan, informing him that a Dutch ship had recently delivered the letter that William Adams had written the previous year to his "unknown friends and countrymen."

"Havinge so good occasion by hearinge that certaine English marchauntes do lie in the island of Java . . . ," it began, "I have emboldened myselfe to write these few lines." Floris had already heard rumors that a lone Englishman was living in Japan, but he had no idea of the heights to which Adams had been raised. Spalding's letter revealed that Adams was an influential member of the shogun's inner circle, spoke fluent Japanese, and was the lord of a country estate that was close to Ieyasu's court. It also contained the tantalizing news that Japan was a land of rich natural resources—and that the Japanese had an insatiable demand for imported goods. Floris was keen to head for the Land of the Rising Sun and told Spalding that he would deliver any correspondence to Adams. But it was not feasible to sail directly to Japan. He first needed to dispose of the cottons that he had bought in India—and that meant heading to Pattani on the Malay Peninsula.

The *Globe* left Bantam in May 1612 on the next leg of a voyage that had already lasted fifteen months. So far, only seven men had been lost to sickness, but the curse of Bantam struck soon after they set sail, and the death toll rose alarmingly as they crossed the Java Sea and followed the eastern coastline of Sumatra. "It was the corruption of Bantam which now broke forth dailye," wrote Floris, as he watched crew weaken and die. "This daye, we loste two men with the fluxe"—amoebic dysentery—while two days later "died Arthur Smith of the fluxe." Many others were too weak to man the sails and rigging. Men were still falling sick when they arrived in the Gulf of Siam and dropped anchor at the dank and humid port of Pattani.

Situated on the Malay Peninsula, Pattani was still the base for a small group of Dutch traders—led by Victor Sprinckel—who had first turned up there in 1605. Like Bantam, it was a vibrant and cosmopolitan port. Exotically attired merchants from Siam used it as a depot and trading post, and ships irregularly plied their trade between Pattani and Japan. The quayside wharves were often stacked with Siamese sappanwood, which fetched a high price in Japan, while another important commodity was bezoar, a stone that was said to be efficacious against poison.

The Dutch merchants had found that life in Pattani was not altogether disagreeable. "Women are commonly offered to strangers to do household service by day," wrote one, "and other offices at night." This could prove a most agreeable way to spend the sultry tropical nights, so long as the lady in question was not married. "Adultery is punished with death, inflicted by their parents in what kind themselves choose."

The Dutch might have been expected to show friendship to Floris and Antheunis, but they did not approve of them working

for the English and offered only "disgust and distaste." The elderly
"queen" of Pattani proved to be a great deal more welcoming.
Tall, flamboyant, and as lithe as a young damsel, she made a deep
impression on Floris: "[She was] a comely olde woman, now
about the age of threescore years." Her favorite (and energetic)
pastime was the "hunting of wilde buffes [buffaloes]" and she was
also a keen dancer. She particularly enjoyed watching her courtiers
make buffoons of themselves, and when she noticed that Floris
and his men were also amused by the native dancing, she hectored
them into performing their own little dance, "wherewith the olde
queene was muche rejoyced." She was usually extremely gregari-
ous, but when she wished to terminate a conversation she simply
pulled down a curtain between herself and her guests. Floris said
that "in all the Indies, [I have] not seene many like unto her."

Floris was carrying a letter from King James I to this comely
queen and made great play of delivering it with all the pomp and
pageantry he could muster. It was "laide in a bason of golde . . .
[and] carried uppon an elephant with minstrells and a good many

*The queen of Pattani (extreme right, astride an elephant) was a colorful
character whose favorite pastime was hunting wild buffalo. "In all the Indies,"
wrote Peter Floris, "[I have] not seene many like unto her."*

lances and little flaggs." The queen was enchanted, giving Floris permission to build a factory there and to begin trade. This was a welcome development, but first he needed to cure his men. Fresh mangoes and pineapples proved of little help to those still suffering from dysentery, "which were in great number, seeming as if the plague had been in the shippe." The sickness had first afflicted the humble sea dogs, but by the time the *Globe* arrived in Pattani, it had also struck the highest ranks. Captain Hippon was taken ill soon after their arrival and he continued to weaken until it was clear he would not recover. His death was a great loss, both in "the gouvernment of the shippe, as in matters touching the seas." Next to succumb was the master's mate, Thomas Smith, "an excellent astronomer and seaman," who had safely guided the *Globe* through storms and shallows. More losses followed, until a total of nineteen men had perished.

News of this disaster spread quickly through Pattani. The town's criminal underclass decided it was time to strike at the English, breaking into their warehouse and stealing their precious Indian cottons. "We had theeves in the howse," wrote Floris, "and [it] was the strangest robbery." There were no fewer than fifteen men sleeping in the warehouse, with "Mr Lucas and I in a bedde aparte, lying close together, having a great blacke dogge lying under my cabin." The gold and the most valuable cottons had been stowed in a huge coffer, and there was "no greater space betweene the bedde and coffer, butt that only the lidde might shutte and open." Yet the feather-footed thieves managed to enter the room without waking the dog, smash the coffer's padlock, and steal the money, cottons, and Floris's rapier. "It is to be wondered that neither I nor nobody else in the house did see or heare anything," wrote Floris, especially as there was "a burninge lampe hanging in the howse and watche kept in the yarde."

Despite the setbacks, the men endeavored to sell their remaining cottons and acquire goods for Japan. Floris continued to be shunned by the other Dutchmen in the town, although he managed to strike up a friendship with one adventurer, Peter Johnsoon, who announced that he was on the point of departing for Japan. When Floris realized that Johnsoon could be trusted, he asked if he would be so kind as to deliver a letter to Adams. Johnsoon said he would be "verye glad" to assist, "having an occasion to do a kindnesse to Mr Adam, to whom he was beholding."

The men on the *Globe* quickly discovered that trade in Pattani had been affected by wars in the surrounding region, and the once-prosperous merchants showed no desire to risk their money on Floris's Indian luxuries. It was clear to all that they would have to look elsewhere for trade before they could strike out across the East China Sea. This decision was greeted with mixed feelings by the men. Some were more than ready to return home, having seen enough of death and disease, but others were thriving on hardship. One small band of adventurers, led by Lucas Antheunis, proposed an extraordinary expedition into the forested hinterland of Siam, where they believed they would be able to acquire the perfumed woods and exotic skins that were necessary for trade with Japan. Floris agreed to their proposal and helped them build a boat that could carry them to Siam. He promised to follow in the *Globe* as soon as he had exhausted all possibility of trade in Pattani.

Antheunis and his men set off in the third week of July 1612 and reached the Siamese coast just over a week later. They were welcomed by local governors, who informed them that they must travel to inland Ayutthaya, the principal city in this steaming hot land, in order "to carry the newes of our arrivall [to the king]." Such a voyage would lead them into uncharted territory. There were no maps of Siam's interior, and the English had very little idea as to what kind of people they would meet en route. Only one Englishman had ever visited Siam—an Elizabethan adventurer called Ralph Fitch, who had traveled overland from India almost thirty years earlier. When he eventually returned to England, his overriding memory was not of the trading possibilities, but of the weird sexual customs of Siamese men. "[They] wear bunches, or little round balles, in their privy members," he later recalled. "They cut the skin and so put them in, one into one side and another into the other side." Fitch had been told that this painful custom was devised so "they should not abuse the male sexe," but his interpreter had added with a wink that "the women do desire them."

Antheunis and his men had little time to dwell upon such sexual customs; they were too busy trying to negotiate a passage up the mighty Chao Phraya River. Helped by a team of musket-wielding "blacks," they rowed against the rippling current of this mud-filled river, passing through a sleepy little town called Bangkok. Here, they picked up the governor and his sidekick, "[who] received me with all kindness," and continued their journey toward Ayutthaya. The voyage proved more and more difficult as they headed north, for the country was in an unsettled state and landing was dangerous. It also became increasingly hard to maneuver the heavily laden craft upstream. They passed mildewed temples and dank villages, and cursed the tropical humidity. The weather was atrocious, "now being in the time of raining," and the men were constantly soaked to the skin. The current of the great river began to quicken and rapidly broke its low-lying banks, spilling muddy water into the thick vegetation. "The countrye being covered with water," wrote one, "the tide came very fiercely downewards." It took them more than four weeks to reach Ayutthaya, the ancient royal city that was the principal residence of King Intharaja and his court.

The king was delighted—if a little surprised—by the arrival of his uninvited guests, asking "how long we had been from home, and, after that, bidde us welcome and promised us free trade." He listened attentively to their explanation of how they wished to acquire supplies for Japan and, marveling at the bravado of these Englishmen, presented everyone with "a little golden cuppe and a little piece of clothing." He soon proved even more generous, providing the English with a "faire howse"—made of brick—"which may yett serve many yeares." The "howse" proved too comfortable for a few of Antheunis's adventurers, who began to harbor wild and foolhardy dreams of pushing even farther north, into Siam's tropical hinterland. They hoped to reach the fabled city of Luang Prabang, which was deep in the wooded mountains of what is today the northernmost province of Laos. This oriental backwater was accessible only by rowing for many weeks up steaming, fast-flowing rivers whose dripping banks were lined with dense monsoon forests. These concealed any number of dangers, as well as an array of weird animals: langurs, gibbons, monkeys, and flying squirrels. The inhabitants were said to be ferocious and savage. The Dutchman John Huyghen van Lindschoten, who had spent many years in Goa gathering information on the East, said they "live like wild men and eat men's flesh, and marke all their bodies with hot iron, which they esteeme a freedome."

Undaunted by the prospect of being eaten, a few men headed north in early 1613, hoping "to discover the trade of that country." They took with them a large quantity of red gingham, cotton yarn, and painted linen, and began rowing up the Chao Phraya River, passing mighty teak trees and huge jungles of bamboo. It soon became apparent that trade was impossible, for war had displaced many of the merchants, and they returned with a small quantity of "gold, badly conditioned."

Antheunis had not been idle while his men ventured into northern Siam. Learning from Ayutthaya's merchants that the Japanese had an insatiable appetite for sappanwood, he watched in amazement as two Japanese junks moored at the city's riverside quay and filled their holds with a huge and expensive cargo. He was even more surprised to discover a Dutchman among their crew. His name was Jan Joosten van Lodensteijn, one of the survivors of the *Liefde*, who told Antheunis how he had begun trading with Indo-China and expected to reap "good profite." Soon after, Antheunis encountered another of the *Liefde*'s survivors,

Melchior van Santvoort, who had already made himself a fortune from the Indo-China trade. Antheunis quizzed Santvoort about William Adams and asked if he would deliver King James I's letter to the shogun. Santvoort graciously agreed, paving the way for the *Globe*'s arrival in Japan.

While Antheunis and his men were busy in Ayutthaya, Floris had sailed the *Globe* from Pattani to Siam. As he anchored the vessel at the mouth of the Chao Phraya River, a huge bank of black clouds announced the imminent arrival of a tremendous tropical storm. Inland Ayutthaya was its first victim. Severe winds struck the town on October 24, 1612, and caused instant and devastating destruction. "[There] arose suche a suddayne storme and running aire," wrote one of the Englishmen, "that olde folkes had never seen the like in that country; the trees were blowne oute of the grounde."

It was not long before the storm slammed into the *Globe*. Two of her anchor cables snapped and she began to drift toward "very sharpe rockes," which threatened to crush her to splinters. It was fortunate that the crew on board were able to maneuver her into deeper water. Eight of their companions were not so lucky. They had the misfortune to be manning the pinnace when the storm struck. "Before they could gette aboard, they sawe the shippe go away"—blown beyond their reach by the hurricane-force wind. They rowed toward her with all their strength, but monstrous waves were now racing in from the sea, engulfing their fragile craft. "The boate was beate to the grounde," wrote Floris later, "and four men drowned." The boatswain, George Ponder, had a most unpleasant death. He was "devoured of a whale"—swallowed whole like Jonah—which circled the ship as it slowly digested its meal.

The accident had a profound effect on the survivors. Alone in tropical waters and stricken with fear, they bickered with each other and made "injurious speeches to the captain." Drink was the easiest way for them to forget their predicament. John Johnson, the master, was so drunk and disorderly that he attacked his captain "very scornefull and injuriously, calling him rogue, rascall, dogge, and other such-like vile woords." He shouted, screamed, and, "rising at laste, stroke at him." Floris fought back and the two "were wrestling together till some came to parte them." Johnson was locked in a cabin to calm down, but he proved so uncontrollable that Floris "caused him to be nailed up." Even this precaution was inadequate. Johnson smashed down the door and stumbled on deck with "a naked dagger in his codpisse." This time he was seized and locked up in a more secure cabin from which he was unable to break free.

The men's appalling behavior broke Floris's adventurous spirit. He was still toying with the idea of sailing the *Globe* over to Japan, but Pattani's merchants warned him that "those of Japan are at enimitie with this place, and have burned Pattani twice in these five or six yeares." He was also faced with an increasingly unruly crew, who were in no mood for any more adventure. The oppressive climate of Pattani sapped their spirits and tropical diseases broke their bodies. Many were "inclined to druncke drincking" and refused to be parted from their beloved liquor. "It is hard," concluded a weary Floris, "for a leopard to alter his spots." He continued in his attempt to sell cottons, but even his enthusiasm was dented when Pattani caught fire and was largely destroyed. In October 1613, he weighed anchor and set sail for India, leaving a handful of men in the charred remains of Pattani. A few more chose to stay in their lonely Siamese outpost at Ayutthaya, where they were led by the dauntless Lucas Antheunis. Isolated from the outside world, yet hopeful that English shipping would return to Siam, Antheunis began stockpiling the sappanwood that commanded such high prices in Japan.

While Floris and his crew were suffering in Pattani, Bantam was hosting a new band of English adventurers. These were led by the irrepressible Captain John Saris, who had already visited the port more than three years earlier. Now, in October 1612, he sighted Bantam for a second time and nudged his ship, the *Clove*, into the harbor. He was not pleased to be back. The weather was insufferably hot and the plague of mosquitoes made the twilight hours a misery. "The place here is so unhealthfull," he wrote, and bemoaned the fact that his men were "dangerously disordering themselves with drinke and whores ashoare." Whoring in Bantam was indeed a dangerous pastime, for the town's prostitutes were riddled with syphilis. The boatswain's mate, John Scott, was the first to die, "his gutts eaten with the pox." Saris added: "God help the rest; many of them [are] infected, by the report of the surgion."

Saris had long dreamed of sailing to Japan. On his previous voyage to Bantam, he had researched the possibilities of trade with this unknown realm and concluded that luxury goods could reap spectacular profits. He envisaged making his fortune from silks and satins, "sugar-candie," and sandalwood, and he learned from Bantam's merchants that the Japanese had a passion for "lascivious stories [paintings] of warres, by sea and land." He took his report back to Sir Thomas Smythe in London, who was more than willing to let Saris pursue his dream. Although the captain was reminded that India was "the maine and principall scope of this our voyadge," Saris was given free rein to push even farther east. "We wishe you, Captain John Saris, to proceed with the *Clove* and, with all possible speede that you may, endevor your course for Japan."

John Saris was a curious choice of commander for such a delicate mission. He was both a martinet and an eccentric—a tough disciplinarian who had an unusually colorful streak. He had a passion for pornography and erotica, and his cabin was decorated with an array of plump and buxom nudes. The glory of his collection was a large canvas of a naked and plump-breasted Venus, "very lasiviously set out," but he had many other items—he coyly

Captain Saris's research into Eastern trade had revealed that the Japanese were avid consumers, as this Kyoto street scene suggests. Saris hoped to make his fortune from silks, satins, "sugar-candie," and sandalwood.

referred to them as his "bookes and pictures"—which he would show to honored guests in the privacy of his own cabin.

Saris's pornographic peccadilloes were unknown to the directors of the East India Company in the spring of 1611. In their eyes, this straight-talking young man was the perfect choice of commander. He was a younger son, like so many company servants, who had turned to the sea when he realized that he stood to inherit none of the family patrimony. His flamboyant streak suited Smythe admirably; he could play the English ambassador with some skill—and would have to, for he was carrying yet more letters written by King James I—but he could also be the gruff, sharp-talking sea dog. His men would later complain that he had an "ill carriage" and a "tyrannicall manner," but they probably accepted that tongue-lashings and floggings were necessary for discipline.

Under Saris's capable command, the *Clove* made swift progress around the Cape of Good Hope and on to the Comoros Islands, off the coast of Madagascar, where the captain had his first opportunity to practice his ambassadorial charms on a native ruler. He ordered his men to give a fanfare of trumpets for the exotic King Booboocaree, then invited His Majesty to a banquet. Apart from the fact that it was Ramadan and the king was fasting, the meeting was a triumph. Saris performed even better when he reached the dusty shores of Arabia and so charmed the governor of Mocha with his pleasantries and frothy chat that, before he knew it, he had been whisked into a private chamber, where the governor kept "his buggering boyes." Saris was horrified, quickly made his excuses, and left, but not before the governor had helped him slip into a smart new costume—his present—which included a vest of gold, a sash, and a flamboyantly striped turban.

Saris finally reached Bantam at the end of October 1612 and began preparing for the onward voyage to Japan. He knew that he would be totally dependent on William Adams when it came to establishing relations with the Japanese court and hoped that he would be able to make contact with him soon after arriving. Aware that language was going to be his greatest problem—especially when he first stepped ashore—he hired an interpreter, nicknamed John Japan, who was fluent in Japanese and Malay. His next task was to find a Malay speaker who also knew English. This proved surprisingly easy. Saris was told of a Spaniard called Harnando Ximenes who spoke the "Mallay tongue very perfect." Ximenes agreed to his terms of employment and boarded the

Clove. By the first week of January 1613, Saris was able to make the final preparations for his voyage. He bought victuals and some spices, and purloined a viol, tabor, and pipe in order to provide some merriment for his men. Then, on January 14, he ordered his pox-ridden crew aboard and let off a spectacular blast of cannon-fire. As the noise echoed around the bay, the *Clove* slipped away from the shore and headed into unknown waters.

The voyage to Japan got off to a poor start. Scarcely had the vessel left Bantam than she sprang a leak and for twelve hours everyone on board had to man the pumps. Soon after, the curse of Bantam struck again. Two of the crew dropped dead of a tropical sickness. One was Saris's favorite trumpeter, David Usher, who could blast out any tune that was requested, and Saris bemoaned the loss of "a most excellent man in his profession."

Saris had intended to follow a route that would take him through the watery heart of the "spiceries," halting at the clove-rich Spice Islands of Tidore and Ternate. But local Dutch traders were most unhappy at his arrival in waters that they claimed for themselves. They asked who was piloting his ship and, when Saris refused to tell them, they threatened to "cut him in peeces before our faces." The native chieftains proved even more cause for alarm. The *Clove*'s crew were appalled to watch the king of Tidore return from battle with a hundred severed heads, and trembled with fear when they learned that he was keen to acquire some English heads as well. "I ordered double-watch to be kept," wrote Saris, "match in cock, and all things in readines, douting trechery." These precautions deterred the native king and the men set sail with heads intact. They soon proved rather more adept at killing themselves. John Meridith "beate out his braines" by standing in the path of a falling tree, whilst his fellow shipmate James Miles was also "dangerouslye wounded" by a tree. But there were a few light-hearted moments. One island chieftain gave the crew 200 coconuts in exchange for a few loincloths, and when the *Clove* dropped anchor at Butung Island on the southeastern tip of

Celebes, they were amazed to discover that the headhunting king's ambassador was an Englishman—Mr. Welden—who had fallen in love with a local girl. Saris offered to take him on board, but Welden was happy with his lot and said that to head for Japan "would be his undoing."

Almost six months after leaving Bantam, Saris spied land on the horizon—"a most plesent and fruitefull land as any we have seen since we came out of England." The *Clove* had reached Miyako-jima, the most outlying of the Ryukyu Islands, which lay some 500 miles to the south of Japan. They attempted to land, but the strong winds blew them straight past the island and they were forced to continue northward across the East China Sea. After five days of struggling with ropes and sails, the men once again caught sight of land. This time it was Kyushu.

As they neared the entrance to Nagasaki Bay, the *Clove* met with four Japanese fishing skiffs. Two of the skippers were hired to guide the *Clove* toward the offshore island of Hirado, which Saris knew to be home to a small band of Dutch traders. The *Clove* was edged through a narrow channel between the mainland of Kyushu and the rocky shoreline of Hirado. On the left side—at the point where the two coasts appeared to touch—a small opening led into a deep bay. In the center of the bay, rising abruptly from the shimmering water, was a small island forested with pines. The brilliant red archway of a Shinto temple shone out against the dark green background.

At three o'clock in the afternoon of June 10, 1613, the *Clove* came to anchor in Hirado Bay. After more than two years at sea, Captain Saris had at last reached Japan.

Chapter 7

GREETING MR. ADAMS

 THE SIGHT of the *Clove* caused quite a stir on shore. The townsfolk of Hirado were not used to unexpected visitors, and word of the ship's arrival soon reached the local lord. He made his way directly to the harbor and ordered his boats to be made ready. He was going to visit the *Clove*.

Captain Saris watched with interest as the flotilla approached, admiring the flamboyant costumes of his lordship and the young lad who was accompanying him. "Both of them [were] in silk gowns," he wrote, "girt to them with a skirt and a pair of breeches." At their sides hung two huge swords with fearsome-looking blades. Their manner of greeting Saris when they finally clambered aboard was quite extraordinary. They removed their shoes and proceeded to bow, over and over, while Saris and his men watched in bemusement. "Clapping their right hand within their left," wrote Saris, "they put them downe towards their knees, and so wagging or moving of their hands . . . [they] crie,

'Augh, augh.' " As they continued to bow, the captain led them to his cabin, "where I had prepared a banquet for them, and a good consort of musicke."

Saris was concerned to treat his guests with all due decorum. He was fortunate to have on board a copy of Richard Hakluyt's *Principal Navigations*, which contained the advice given to Captains Pet and Jackman more than thirty years earlier. Now, it finally proved its use, and Saris followed it to the letter: "I entertained his majestie with a banquet of severall sorts [of] conserves furnished all in glasse, which gave him great content . . ." As the visitors got their first taste of salt pork and dried peas, Saris made polite conversation, using his interpreters to discover more about his noble guests. Both were from the ruling Matsura family, which had controlled the little fiefdom of Hirado since the thirteenth century. The older of the two was called Shigenobu and had been lord of Hirado until 1589, when he had ostensibly retired from public life. He had been officially succeeded by his youthful grandson, but the old man kept a firm grip on the reins of power and clearly remained in control. Saris found it almost impossible to pronounce their names and was even more confused by their honorary titles. Brushing aside Japanese etiquette, he called the elderly ruler King Foyne and the young one King Figen.

Their fiefdom was tiny—Hirado Island was just twenty miles long and five miles wide—but it occupied a strategic position just off the northwest coast of Kyushu. The Portuguese had first arrived here in 1550, when the island was locked in combat with one of Kyushu's lords, and they had quickly made converts to Christianity. Although the then ruler had declared himself to be an "astute abhorrer of the Christian religion," he was prepared to tolerate the Jesuits in the hope that their presence would bring commerce to Hirado. This policy of openness had been continued by King Foyne, who was delighted that the English captain had chosen his fiefdom in which to drop anchor.

When the meal was over, Saris reached into his doublet and

plucked out a letter from King James I, "which he received with great joye, saying he would not open it till Ange [had] come, who could interpret it." Saris was puzzled as to the identity of Ange, until his interpreter told him that it was a Japanese word—*anjin*—that translated as pilot, "and ment Mr Adams, who is here so called."

Saris, who had been on the point of inquiring about William Adams, was delighted to learn that he was still alive and that his fame stretched across the length and breadth of Japan. He now realized that Sir Thomas Smythe had been absolutely correct in describing Adams as being "in greate favour with the kinge." Smythe had told Captain Saris that Adams was to be questioned on every detail of trade and etiquette: "[We] desire his opinion [on] what course should be held . . . for the delivery of His Majestie's letter now sent." He was also to be asked for advice on what gifts should be given to the shogun and the manner in which they should be presented. Saris was ordered to give Adams passage home if he so desired. "If, at your departure from Japan, the said William Adams shall importune you to transporte him into his native countrie, . . . we pray you then to accommodate him with as convenient a cabben as you may." He was to be treated with dignity and respect, and given "all other necessaries which your shipp may afford him."

Saris informed King Foyne that he was extremely anxious to make contact with Ange—who held the key to the Japanese court—and his lordship offered to assist by providing boats and messengers. These were immediately dispatched to Edo, where Adams was currently residing, with a request that he travel to Hirado with all possible speed.

It was growing dark by the time Saris's little banquet was over, and King Foyne was anxious to return to shore. As he said his farewells, he thanked the captain for his hospitality and promised much "kinde and free entertainement." This arrived rather sooner than anyone expected. Scarcely had the "king" and his grandson pushed off in their boats than a new troupe of visitors rowed over to the *Clove*. They included a large retinue of nobles, as well as dozens of soldiers, who clambered aboard clutching gifts of venison, wildfowl, and wild boar, along with baskets of fruit and fish. Saris suspected treachery, but their smiles and gifts were genuine enough. They greeted the English crew, deposited their gifts, then rowed back ashore.

On the day that followed the *Clove*'s arrival, King Foyne came aboard once again, bringing with him a retinue of noblemen, as well as their curious wives and daughters. Saris was keen to show the girls his collection of erotica and at one point managed to draw them to one side. They entered "into my cabbin, where the picture of Venus hung, very lasiviously set out . . . [and] fell down and worshipped it, [mistaking it] for Our Lady, with shows of great devotion." Saris watched in bemused disbelief. The women, it transpired, had secretly converted to Christianity and were unaware that this painting was the pride and joy of Saris's pornography collection.

Saris was embarrassed but not deterred. He had taken quite a shine to the Japanese ladies and found their pretty features much to his liking. "They were well faced, handed and footed," he wrote, "cleare skinned and white, but wanting colour, which they amend by arte." They adorned themselves in the most exquisite silk kimonos, and on their delicate little feet they wore "halfe buskins [boots] bound with silk ribbon." Saris was delighted to see that they were bare-legged and particularly liked their hair, which was "tied up in a knot . . . in a comely manner." Not all newcomers to Japan were quite so smitten. One Jesuit expressed his horror at discovering the women's habit of dyeing their teeth black, noting that it "gives their mouths a most extraordinary appearance of a cavernous darkness."

Old King Foyne quickly noted Saris's interest and, anxious to avoid an awkward incident, "requested that none might stay in the cabbin." Saris reluctantly complied, but was pleased that the king's restriction did nothing to dampen the increasingly convivial atmosphere. Indeed, the king himself began to join in the merriment and appeared to contradict his earlier request by urging the ladies to enjoy themselves. "The king's women seemed to be somewhat bashfull," wrote Saris, "but he willed them to be frollicke." And frolic they were. They sang for the English sea dogs and gave a recital on the shamisen—an instrument which, Saris noted, "did much resemble our lute, being bellied like it, but longer in the neck." After much jollity on all sides, Saris invited them to a great feast.

A few days later, King Foyne brought yet more women aboard. These were rather less bashful, and soon proved so "frollicke" that Saris began to wonder if they were prostitutes. "[They] were actors of comedies," he wrote, ". . . [and] are as the slaves of one man." The owner, or pimp, treated the women as commodities and "puts a price what every man shall pay that to doe with any of them." They could be used for any service that was required, and the Japanese saw nothing immoral in hiring them. Indeed, "the greatest of their nobilitie, [when] travelling, hold it no disgrace to send for these panders to their inn." The girls were often highly cultivated—being well versed in the arts of acting and singing—and knew the exact etiquette of pouring drinks. They were accorded the greatest respect by those who had hired them, even by lusty men who intended "to have the use of them," yet were treated like animals when they died. "Unworthy to rest amongst the worst, they are bridled with a bridle made of straw . . . [and] dragged through the streetes into the fields, and there cast upon a dunghill for dogges and fowls to devoure."

The more unruly members of Saris's crew soon grew jealous of the flirtatious antics of their captain and decided they wanted their own share of the fun. Thomas Jones, the ship's baker, decided to swim ashore under the cover of darkness, but was caught in the water and hauled back to the Clove. Others were more successful. Christopher Evans, who had a long history of outlandish

Captain Saris found Japanese ladies much to his liking. "They were well faced, handed and footed," he later wrote. They were also very "frollicke," and knew exactly how to entertain Saris and his men.

behavior, was fortunate to be a faster swimmer than Jones. He managed to get ashore on several occasions "and in most lewd fashion spending his time in base bawdy places, denying to come aboard." When Evans was finally caught, Saris made an example of him by putting him in the bilboes, or onboard shackles. Evans was furious. "He did more deeplye sweare to be the distruction of Jack Saris, for so it pleased him to calle me."

Saris might have had more success had he employed Japanese punishment, which, he soon discovered, was as brutal as it was severe. When three local men started a street brawl, King Foyne ordered their summary execution. When this had been carried out, all the able-bodied men of the town "came to try the sharpenesse of their *katanas* [scimitars] upon the corps[es], so that before they left off they had hewn them all three into pieces as small as a man's hand."

The casual violence of the Japanese never ceased to amaze newcomers. It was common practice for samurai to test their swords on criminals, hacking at their corpses "until the wretched body is chopped into mincemeat." They were also in the habit of stitching the bodies together so that the same exercise could be repeated again and again. "They often sew up bodies which have been cut up by swords," observed the Jesuit João Rodrigues, who said that "the delight and pleasure which they feel in cutting up bodies is astonishing."

Saris's principal purpose for sailing to Japan was to oversee the establishment of an English factory. This required the assistance of William Adams, for the English could not begin to trade without permission from the ruling shogun. But Saris soon discovered that, in provincial Hirado, the mere mention of Adams's name was enough to open doors. When he asked King Foyne if he could have "a convenient howse ashoare," the old man readily agreed and suggested that a couple of the crewmen should go with him in order to view some properties.

Hirado was a bustling little town with a small harbor and a long waterfront. A couple of stone staircases led down to the shoreline, and an old bridge spanned the narrow creek. The better dwellings were constructed of sweet-smelling camphor wood and were protected from the worst of the storms by the mountainous backdrop that encircled the town. Although Hirado was not a prosperous place, it was built upon ancient foundations and its few monasteries had accrued considerable riches over the centuries. The great Zen monastery of Yasumadake was already 400 years old when Saris and his men set foot in Japan. It was surrounded by lush greenery, and its fine wooden buildings housed about a hundred monks.

King Foyne's retainers enjoyed a particularly comfortable existence in Hirado, whose streets were often crowded with finely attired courtiers, merchants, and soldiers. "This Hirado lieth close by the water," wrote one Englishman who arrived a few years later. "The common people go clad in armour, but your gentry go very well and richly clad with short cloakes, and are carried in palinquins, having a pike of eight or ten foot long carried before them."

It did not take long for Saris's men to find a property that was suitable for their needs. It was owned by the head of the local Chinese community, Li Tan, and provided handsome living quarters and a spacious warehouse in which to store supplies. Li agreed to undertake essential repair works and "furnish all convenient roomes with matts according to the fashion of the countery." The English, in return, agreed to pay six months' rent in advance.

Saris struck an additional deal with Li, in which the Chinese man would also supply the men with food and drink. This arrangement was not at all to the liking of the men who had been temporarily landed in Hirado. Jasper, one of the ship's carpenters, was so unhappy at the quality of the food that he abused the Chinese man "very grocely" and said "that his wine was not good, and [began] throwing his dishes about the howse." Li had never witnessed such petulant behavior and was shaken by the experience. So was Captain Saris, who ordered the boatswain's mate to flog the truculent Jasper. But the boatswain's mate was too drunk to comply, so Saris himself gave both men a thrashing. Just a few hours later—perhaps repenting of his severity—he sent ashore two hogsheads of wine and one of cider.

He also sent gifts for the Japanese, having learned that it was the custom in Japan. King Foyne was given more than seventy presents and, as each one was ceremoniously opened in sight of the Clove, Saris ordered his cannon to be fired, "[it] being the fashion so to doe." A further boatload of gifts was sent to other members of the royal household, while various notables were given cloths and cottons. When the young King Figen told Saris how much he liked his gold-fringed parasol, the captain reluctantly took the hint and presented it to him. King Figen was delighted and "most kindlye accepted, requiting me with a million of compliment."

Saris had yet to make contact with the small group of Dutchmen in Hirado. Jacques Specx was temporarily absent and his place had been filled by Captain Hendrick Brouwer, a duplicitous individual who had watched the *Clove*'s arrival with considerable alarm. Saris hunted high and low for something suitable to present to Captain Brouwer before finally selecting "a pott of English butter," which, after more than two years at sea, must have been distinctly rancid. It was clear to both men that the close proximity of the Dutch and English factories could lead to rivalries. Saris tried to preempt any difficulties by striking a trade agreement, which forbade each party from undercutting the other. But scarcely twelve hours had passed before the Dutch captain had broken the agreement, "excusing himselfe that he had no warrant from his masters."

When the two men next met, Captain Brouwer proved even less amenable. He informed Saris that a richly laden junk had recently arrived from Siam with a cargo of sappanwood that had been procured by Lucas Antheunis. Saris's initial reaction was one of satisfaction, for the wood could be sold for an enormous profit and would be a great boon for the newly founded factory. He was rather less pleased—and more than a little suspicious—to be told that the Dutch had already bought the cargo and intended to sell it for their own account. Captain Brouwer showed Saris a scrap of paper as proof of purchase, but the English captain was not convinced and told the Dutchman, "I would not be jested with." He said that if he was not given more reliable evidence of the deal, he would "take that course as should not be pleasing to him." It was an ominous beginning to the relationship between the English and the Dutch in Japan.

It was several days before news of the *Clove*'s arrival reached William Adams and several weeks before he was able to set out on the 600-mile voyage from Edo to Hirado. But at the end of July 1613, he crossed from Kyushu to Hirado Island and caught sight of the *Clove* at anchor in the bay. At last—after more than thirteen years in Japan—he would meet fellow Englishmen again.

Saris was extremely excited when he learned of Adams's arrival. He had heard a great deal about the English pilot and knew that he held the key to trade with Japan. He also knew—for it was contained in his instructions for the voyage—that he must treat Adams with all possible respect. With this in mind, he ordered his men to prime their cannon in honor of the shogun's English adviser. "I receaved him in the best manner I could," he wrote. But as Adams approached the vessel, Saris's smile turned into a frown. He had expected to meet a down-to-earth English sea dog, much like the men he had aboard the *Clove*. Instead, he found himself gazing upon an extraordinary apparition. The man was English, of that there was no question, but one who was dressed and acted as if he had been born and brought up in Japan. He gave "so admirable and affectionated commendations of the country as it is generally thought amongest us that he is a naturalised Japanner." William Adams of Limehouse had gone native.

Captain Saris realized that this was not the moment for criticism. Adams was intelligent, spoke the unfathomable language, and was exceptionally well informed. Although it grieved Saris, he knew that he had little option but to fuss and fawn over his eccentric guest. "I entreated him to make choise of any chambers in the howse," he wrote, "and to acquaint the cooke what diet he best affected, and [ordered that] it should be provided." He wanted Adams to be as comfortable as possible and told him that whenever he felt in need of some fresh air, "Mr Cocks and who-else of the marchants should, at his pleasure, accompany him in the towne."

Adams halted Saris in mid-speech. He thanked him for his kind offer, but said that he had a Japanese friend in town—a merchant called Yasuemon—at whose house he usually stayed. Nor

did he wish "any marchant or other to accompany him," informing the captain that he was quite happy to make his own way to
Yasuemon's house. Saris, who had expected Adams to be delighted with English company, noted that "all was very strange."
He was offended by his attitude and curtly informed Adams "to
doe what he thought best." But he could not stop himself from
hinting that he thought Adams was behaving with the greatest
discourtesy. He said that the sea voyage in the *Clove* had been extremely wearisome and that he—for one—would have been "glad
to enjoye his most acceptable company."

Adams listened with a sympathetic ear, but refused to change
his mind. He told Saris that "he would be with me when I
pleased to send for him . . . ether at his own howse, or at the
Dutch." This further infuriated Saris. He was prepared to accept
that Adams wished to stay with his Japanese friends, but was most
unhappy at the thought that he was on good terms with the
Dutch. It was Captain Brouwer, after all, who had just refused to
hand over the cargo of what Saris considered to be English sappanwood.

Several of the *Clove*'s crew were keen to chat with Adams and
asked if they could accompany him back to his accommodation,
"but he entreated the contrarye." They too were offended and
told their captain that they were "not well pleased, thinking that
he thought them not good enoffe to walk with him." Saris was
completely taken aback by Adams's mannerisms and viewed what
he considered to be his affectations with scarcely concealed contempt. He confused his aloofness with arrogance and failed to understand Adams's very real anxieties about the arrival of the *Clove*,
with its crew of unkempt and unruly Englishmen. Nor was Saris
aware that Japan was unlike any other realm that he and his men
had visited during their long voyage from England. Etiquette and
politesse were of the utmost importance in the Land of the Rising
Sun—qualities that were in very short supply on board the *Clove*.

Saris was usually ready to criticize those who failed to please him, but on this occasion he held his tongue. This was not the moment to speak his mind, for these were not normal circumstances. He even tried to fathom the cause of Adams's strange behavior. He wondered if he was expecting some presents—as was the custom in Japan—and sent him a selection of cloth and trinkets "whereby he might have some feeling of his brothers." When this brought no response, Saris sent a second parcel, which contained a Turkish carpet, silk garters, leather slippers from Spain, a flamboyant white hat, and a pair of detachable cuffs. This, at last, appeared to have pleased Adams. A few hours later he sent a return present—a finely crafted salvatory, or repository, from Macao. Saris accepted it "kindly," but noted in his diary that his own gift had cost a small fortune, while Adams's was worth about six shillings.

Adams caused Saris further aggravation when the captain asked him to assess the value of the *Clove*'s cargo on the Japanese market. Adams made a careful survey of all the goods and cloths in the ship's hold and was dismayed to discover that virtually nothing would have a ready market in Japan. Assuming that Saris wished to be told the truth—rather than what he wanted to hear—Adams informed him that "such thinges as he had brought was not very vendibel." Cottons, he said, were "very cheep" while tin sold for a song. Cloves, which Saris had been careful to acquire in the Spice Islands, were not used at all in Japanese cookery. When the captain asked for an overall assessment of his likely success, Adams was noncommittal. He said "it was not allways alike, but sometimes better, sometimes worse, yet dowted not but we should doe as well as others." Such honesty did not please Captain Saris. Unused to criticism, he suspected that Adams was deliberately trying to undermine his mission.

Saris had by now been in Hirado for about seven weeks and was anxious to visit the shogun's court. This had been impossible without Adams, but now that he had arrived, Saris suggested that they make their voyage without further ado. Adams agreed and, having secured the assistance of King Foyne, who lent the men a galley and some money, they prepared to depart. Before setting off, Saris handed over authority to Richard Cocks, the most senior merchant aboard the *Clove*. Cocks was ordered to uphold the strictest discipline on board ship during Saris's absence. This was to prove easier said than done.

Adams led Saris out of Hirado in the first week of August 1613, along with ten other Englishmen, including a surgeon and a cook. He also brought an escort of seven Japanese guards who had been hired to protect the men as they traveled through the remoter stretches of countryside. The voyage to court entailed four weeks of continual travel. The city of Shizuoka, which Ieyasu had made his principal residence, lay more than 500 miles from Hirado. The quickest and safest route was to follow the Japanese coastline around the fractured northern coast of Kyushu. The men would then have to push their little galley through the treacherous Kanmon Channel, which led into the Inland Sea and on to the city of Osaka. From here, their voyage would take them across country until they joined the Tokaido, or Great Highway, which led to Shizuoka and beyond.

The men soon found that they were not everywhere treated with the same courtesy as in Hirado. When they stepped ashore at Hakata, on Kyushu's northern coast, they were surrounded by an angry mob, "hooping, hollowing and making such a noise about us, that we could scarcely hear one another speake." The town's youth hurled stones at them, which, Adams informed them, was because they had been mistaken for Koreans. In Saris's eyes, many of the women looked like the devil incarnate, for "their eyes, by continuall diving, doe grow as red as blood."

When the men reached the Kanmon Channel, they pointed their galley southeast and entered the Inland Sea, which provided them with a relatively safe passage all the way to Osaka. The sheer scale of this city left a deep impression on Saris, as it had on Adams. It was "as great as London within the walls" and its monumental castle was a work of technical genius. Saris marveled at the bulwarks and battlements; "the stones are great," he wrote, ". . . and are cut so exactly to fit the place where they are laid out [so] that no mortar is used." The castle was home to the young Hideyori—the boy for whom Ieyasu had originally been appointed regent. He was now twenty years old and had recently been married to Ieyasu's granddaughter.

The little party moored their galley at Osaka and continued to Fushimi by barque. Here, Saris caught his first glimpse of the formidable fighting force that Ieyasu could call upon in times of crisis. He watched the local garrison changing the guard "in most souldier-like manner, marching five abreast, and to every ten files an officer." There was no pomp and pageantry, as there was in England, "neither had they any drums or other musicall instruments." Nor was there any slovenly and disorderly behavior, as was usual when any English soldiers were on the march. The rigid, straight-backed foot soldiers carried their weaponry with pride and made for a menacing sight as they marched in formation through the countryside. Only their captain-general allowed himself any concessions to luxury. His horse was richly caparisoned in felts and furs and "he marched in great state," proceeded by his crimson velvet palanquin carried by six officers.

The sight of these men on the move, and the discipline with which they were governed, was something that Saris would never forget. "Such good order was taken for the passing and providing for of these three thousand soldiers," he wrote, "that no man, either travelling or inhabiting upon the way where they lodged, was any way injured by them." Indeed, the owners of roadside inns and hostels were delighted to have the business and "cheerfully entertayned them as other their guests, because they paid for what they took."

Adams led the men along the famous Tokaido, which connected Edo with Kyoto. It was thronged with merchants, ped-

William Adams and Captain Saris traveled by boat on the first leg of their voyage to court. They moored their galley at Osaka (above) and continued to Fushimi in a little barque.

dlers, and peasants whose strange hats and traditional costumes made for a colorful sight. "Ever and anon," wrote Saris, "you meet with farmes and countrey houses, with villages . . . with ferries over fresh rivers, and many *futtakeasse* . . . which are their temples." Saris was astonished when he saw the quality of the road. Its sand-and-gravel surface was "wonderfull even" and "where it meeteth with mountains, passage is cut through." The road was divided into leagues, and at the end of each league was a marker in the form of a "faire pine tree trimmed round in the fashion of an arbour." The purpose of these trees was "so that the hackney men, and those which let out horses to hire, should not make men pay more [than] their due."

The contrast with travel in England could not have been more striking. When Saris traveled from London to see his family in Yorkshire, he suffered the ordeal of broken roads and pitiful lodgings. English roads were muddy, potholed, and often impassable in the wetter months of the year. "They are often very deep and troublesome in the winter," wrote William Harrison in 1587 in his *Description of England*. He said that landowners often refused to clean roadside drains, "whereby the streets do grow to be much more gulled [rutted] than before, and thereby very noisome for such as travel by the same."

Adams had sent a letter to the court informing them that he would soon be arriving with a small band of English visitors. When Ieyasu received this message, he immediately sent a palanquin and horses to make their progress even more pleasurable. Saris was particularly pleased to have been given a slave whose sole purpose was to run in front of him carrying a pike. The men stopped each night in roadside lodgings, where the owners would

The Tokaido, or Great Highway, was thronged with merchants and travelers. It connected the vast city of Edo (above) with Kyoto and Osaka; transport was tightly regulated and highly efficient.

cook them rice and fish with "pickeld herbes, beanes, raddishes and other roots." Saris noted that there was an abundance "of cheese," unaware that he was actually eating tofu, or bean curd.

There were few dangers on the road, and Adams's presence meant that the men were rarely abused or insulted. He explained to Saris that Japan had a tightly regulated system of local government, which imposed a rigorous discipline on the population: "[There is] not a lande better governed in the worlde by civil pollecy." Each town had a governor, and every street was gated. Houses were divided into clusters—with a headman charged with maintaining order—and everyone kept a close eye on the doings of their neighbors, especially after dark when a curfew was imposed. "Each street is closed at dusk," wrote the Spaniard Rodrigo de Vivero y Velasco, "and soldiers are always on duty . . . If any crime is committed, the alarm is raised and in next to no time the gates are shut in order to catch the wrong-doer." The only sight to disturb the pleasure of the men's journey came at the approach to each town, where the road was lined with the crucified remains of thieves and murderers. As the party approached Shizuoka, the number of dead along the road began to alarm Saris. First, they passed a scaffold bedecked with several human heads. Next, they saw row upon row of crosses, "with the dead corpses of those which had been executed remaining still upon them." Worse still, there were gobbets of flesh lying on the ground, "pieces of others, which after their executions had been hewn again and again by the triall of others' *cattans* [swords]." These were scattered across the road and caused the men "a most unsavourie passage."

The party arrived in Shizuoka at dawn on September 6, exactly a month after leaving Hirado, and Adams secured lodgings for everyone. Then, while Saris and company relaxed after the long journey, he went "to the court to let the secretarie understand of my coming." He soon returned with good news. Ieyasu was delighted to learn of their arrival and promised to grant them an audience within a few days. Saris used the intervening time to select suitable presents: a gold basin and ewer, a satin quilt, a silk carpet, and three Dutch napkins.

At last the big day arrived. A splendid palanquin arrived outside their lodging and Adams and Captain Saris clambered inside. Flanked by guards, the litter was carried to the gates of Shizuoka Castle, where it was met by two "grave comely men." Chief of these was Ieyasu's secretary, Honda Masakumi, whose courtly title was *Kodzuke-no-suke*. Adams had gone to great lengths to explain to Saris the importance of conforming to the strict system of Japanese etiquette. Each rank in the court had its own title, and each courtier needed to be greeted with the greatest deference. Saris listened in silence but, unwilling to abase himself before the Japanese court, he contemptuously dismissed Adams's advice. He showed a distinct lack of graciousness when he was introduced to the courtiers and bluntly informed Ieyasu's secretary—whom he nicknamed Codskin—that he intended to deliver King James I's letter in person. Honda was horrified. Such a demand interfered with courtly protocol, for letters to Ieyasu could only be delivered by his secretary. Saris became obstinate and, according to Adams, churlishly announced "that if he might not delliver it himself, he would retourn again to his lodging." Honda was so distressed that he berated Adams for bringing such uncouth Englishmen to the court and said "that I had not instruckted him in the manners and coustoum of all strangers." Saris was determined to win the war of words and swore that he alone would hand the letter to Ieyasu.

With tensions running high, Adams and Saris were led into an antechamber, which contained Ieyasu's chair, "to which they wished me doe reverence." Then, after a long wait, they were ushered into an inner room where Ieyasu was seated. Saris still refused to follow the rules of courtly etiquette, which demanded that he should fall to the floor in obeisance. Instead, he marched straight up to Ieyasu and "delivered our king's letter unto his majestie, who took it in his hand, and put it up towards his forehead."

That, at least, is how Saris chose to record the meeting. Adams remembered it rather differently, reporting that Honda snatched the letter from Saris just as he was about to give it to Ieyasu and personally handed it over. Whatever the truth, Ieyasu seemed untroubled by Saris's unseemly behavior. He glanced at the letter and, using Adams as his interpreter, told Saris "that I was welcome from a wearisome journey, [and] that I should take my rest for a day or two." He said he would use the intervening time to compose a suitable reply to King James's petition for trade. In the meantime, the men were to enjoy themselves and take the opportunity to see something of the courtly city.

Ieyasu also suggested that Saris should visit Edo, where his son Hidetada resided. Saris was delighted. He asked Adams to accompany him on the eighty-mile trip, during which they stopped at the ancient city of Kamakura to visit some of the extraordinary shrines and temples. Kamakura lay some fifteen miles to the north of Adams's estate at Hemi. It was once "the greatest city in Japan" and had, in the distant past, been the imperial capital. It was said to be four times larger than Edo—which itself was "as bigge as London"—but large parts of the city were now in ruins. However, it was still an important pilgrimage center, whose streets were dotted with dozens of "sumptuouse" Buddhist temples and grandiose shrines, lofty pagodas and rambling monasteries. Each was surrounded by delightful pleasure gardens planted with peonies and magnolias, flowering apricot bushes and brilliantly colored hydrangeas. "There are many faire pagodas or heathen temples standing to this day in woods of pine trees," wrote Richard Cocks, when he visited on a later occasion, "with pleasant walkes about them kept in good reparation."

Neither the English nor the Jesuit fathers could understand the peculiar rituals of the monks who lived in such places. Some beat drums as they prayed to their idols, while others performed their devotions in large, two-pointed hats. The strictest followed a rule that seemed designed to cause physical suffering. "In the depths of winter they bathe in water that has been put out into the open air in order to become chilled," wrote one monk, ". . . and in the hot season they bathe in almost boiling water."

One of the city's strangest sights was a "monestary of heathen nuns, being shorne, all the haire off their heades as the papist nuns are." This was the famous Tokeji temple, which had been founded more than three centuries earlier as a refuge for battered wives. Women who stayed for more than two years were considered legally separated from their husbands, and it was said that "no man may take any woman out of that place by force." Yet men, and even lovers, were free to come and go as they pleased, for the nuns "hold venery nether sin nor shame, but live at their pleasure."

Saris was particularly struck by Kamakura's famous, and monumental, copper statue of a *daibutsu*, or Great Buddha, which stood more than forty feet tall. Completed in 1252, this immense image was constructed of thick bronze plates bolted onto a hollow frame. It stood alone in a field of willowy grasses and wildflowers. It was, wrote Saris, "in the likenesse of a man kneeling upon the ground, with his buttockes resting on his heeles, his armes of wonderfull largenesse, and the whole body proportionable." This was quite unlike the statues and gargoyles that he was familiar with in England. The Buddha had elongated ears, hair in ringlets, and a mustache that looked like two slugs pinned in the middle. It was seated cross-legged, with its arms folded in an attitude of contemplation. Captain Saris and his men were delighted to discover that they could clamber inside. "Some of our people went into the body of it," he wrote, "and hoope[d] and hallowed, which made an exceeding great noise." In a time-honored English tradition, they ended their visit by vandalizing the Buddha, etching their names in the soft copper.

Two days later, the men arrived in Edo—a city of exquisite beauty—whose gilded roof tiles and lacquered doors "made a

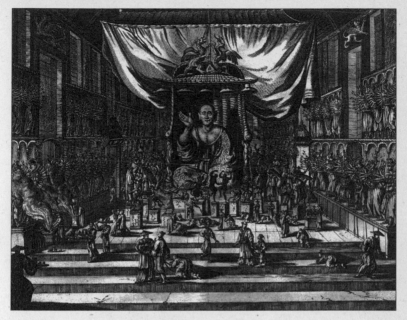

There were several Great Buddhas in Japan; this illustration shows the
Sanjusangendo temple near Kyoto. Captain Saris's men clambered inside
Kamakura's Buddha "and hoope[d] and hallowed, which made
an exceeding great noise."

very glorious appearance to us." Unfortunately, there was little
time for sightseeing, for as soon as they entered the city they received word that the young Hidetada was eager to meet them.
When Saris handed over his gifts, Hidetada responded by present-
ing him with two varnished suits of armor for King James I
(which are today housed in the Tower of London) and a *tachi*, or
long sword, "which none wear there, but souldiers of the best
ranke."

Adams suggested to Saris that, instead of returning directly to
Ieyasu, they make an excursion to the nearby port of Uraga. This
was situated at the entrance to the bay of Edo, and Adams thought
it would be a much better site than Hirado for the English factory.

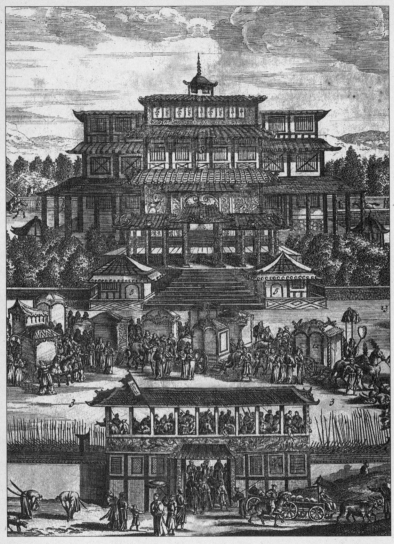

The Japanese emperor lived in splendid isolation in his magnificent Kyoto palace. Although he was accorded every possible dignity, he lacked the power and authority of the shogun and was little more than a puppet.

It was close to the shogun's court, where wealthy nobles were regular visitors, and was also far from the factories of the Portuguese, Spanish, and Dutch.

Saris was indeed impressed by Uraga. "[It] is a very good harbour for shipping," he wrote, "where ships may ride as safely as in the river of Thames before London." He also agreed that "it will be much better for our shipps to sail thither than to Hirado." One of the vessels at anchor in the bay was Spanish, and Adams had been commissioned to sell the vessel and cargo to the highest bidder. He offered it to Saris for £100—"which to our judgements was verye deare"—and refused to be drawn into bargaining. Saris rejected the offer, but did take the opportunity to acquire some of the cargo, including four writing desks and eight folding screens.

The men now returned to Shizuoka in order to collect Ieyasu's reply to King James's letter. This was written in Japanese, but Adams had it translated into the flowery language of international diplomacy. Ieyasu informed King James that he was "not a little glad to heare of your great wisdome and power" and urged "the continuance of friendshipp with your highnes," asking that more ships be sent to Japan. There was tacit praise for Adams and Saris, applauding "their worthines in the admirable knowledge of navigation" and expressing admiration that they had not been deterred by "the distance of so mightie a gulfe, nor greatnes of such infinite cloudes and stormes, from prosecuting honnorable enterprises of discoveries." Ieyasu also handed Captain Saris a copy of his trading privileges, in which he gave the East India Company "free licence" to "abide, buy, sell and barter" in Japan. He offered all Englishmen his full support and protection. Saris was delighted that his mission to the court had been such a triumph. He thanked Ieyasu, bid his farewell, and, on October 9, 1613, prepared to head back to Hirado.

Shortly before the party rode out of Shizuoka, Adams had a second, private meeting with Ieyasu in which he repeated his appeal that he be allowed to sail for England. "I mad[e] myself soumwhat bold," he wrote, "find[ing] the emperor in a good mood." Adams had tucked inside his kimono the document, signed by Ieyasu, that had granted him the estate at Hemi. Now, following Japanese custom, "I took [it] out of my bosom . . . and laid it down before him, giveing His Majesty most humbell thanks for his great favour unto me." Ieyasu was silent for a moment while he collected his thoughts. "He looked ernestly upon me," wrote Adams, "and asked me if I was dessirous to go for my country." Adams explained that he was homesick and that after fifteen years away, he was desperate to renew contact with his family and friends. Ieyasu graciously agreed to his request. He was convinced that English ships would revisit his land and "answered [that] if he should dettain me he should do me wrong, insomuch that in his service I had behaved myself well."

Adams could scarcely believe what he was hearing. For years he had begged Ieyasu to allow him to leave Japan. Now, unexpectedly, he was told that he was free to return to England in the *Clove.* "So," wrote Adams, "I thank God [that I] got my liberty out of my large and evill service." He returned to Hirado in buoyant mood, "being not a littell joyfull."

The party arrived in Hirado at the beginning of November and was welcomed with a tremendous blitz of cannonfire. Saris had received no news from the *Clove* during his time at court and feared that the crew would have used his absence as a pretext for disobedience. The men had indeed begun to misbehave just a few days after his departure, using the Japanese Bon festival as an opportunity "to flitch and steale, to go to tavernes and whorehouses." Christopher Evans had led the way, swimming ashore and testing the local brothels. When caught and upbraided, he "stood boldly in it, that he was a man, and would have a woman if he could get her." Events took a more serious turn when Francis Williams got so drunk that he lost his senses and "did strike one of the old king's men with a cudgell." He was fortunate to escape being cut to pieces by King Foyne's executioners.

Richard Cocks's leniency had only served to encourage the men; just two days after Williams's scuffle, Simon Colphax and John Lambart slipped ashore, drank themselves senseless, then fought each other with such ferocity that Lambart was seriously wounded. Evans, meanwhile, had got into a brawl with John Boules over a pretty little whore. Cocks repeatedly sent his more trusted lieutenants ashore to drag his men out of the brothels and soon earned the wrath of the pimp who controlled the whorehouse, "[who] gave it out that if I come any more into his house to seeke for our people, he would kill me and such as came with me." All pretense of discipline on the *Clove* had broken down at the beginning of October, when Cocks awoke to the news that seven men had absconded, led by the truculent Christopher Evans. King Foyne promised to help Cocks find them and said he would "fetch them alive or dead." He had added, with characteristic generosity, that he "would be loath to kill them, in respect we might want men to carry our ship back for England." In the event, Evans and company proved more accomplished runaways than mariners. They were never seen again—despite repeated searches—and were believed to have escaped to Macao aboard a Portuguese vessel.

The unpredictable weather had only added to Cocks's woes. A typhoon struck Hirado with a force "that I never saw the like in all my life." More than a hundred houses were instantly flattened, and the tumultuous seas ripped apart the town's principal wharf, sinking fifty boats. Only the *Clove*'s five anchors prevented her from being swept onto land. The newly rented English warehouse was less fortunate. A monstrous wall of water struck the town "[and] broke downe our kitchen wall at the English house, which was newly made, and flowed into our oven and broke it downe." The wind was so strong that it "blew downe the tiles . . . and the house did shake like as if there had been an earthquake." In the panic that followed, scores of terrified locals ran through the town carrying firebrands to light their way. Sparks flew into houses, the wind fanned the flames, and entire houses were "carried away." Cocks had watched in horror as "the wind whirled up the fire which was in them, and carried it into the aire in great flakes, very fearefull to behold." Only the torrential downpour had saved the wooden town from total destruction.

Saris was disappointed to learn of the crew's behavior and was less than pleased to learn that Cocks had sold almost nothing during his absence. Cocks explained that Hirado's merchants would not do business with them until Ieyasu had given his official permission and added that there was another, more important hindrance to trade. The English had hoped that Japan would be a good market for broadcloth, but the locals had good reason for refusing to buy it. " 'For,' said they, 'you commend your cloth unto us, but you yourselves wear least thereof.' " This was true: not a single man on the *Clove* was wearing broadcloth. Saris and his lieutenants were decked in silks and satins, while the common sea dogs dressed themselves in fustian. Saris realized that the Japanese were justified in their refusal and criticized his men (but not himself). "I wish that our nation would be more forward to use and spend this natural commoditie," he wrote, ". . . so shall wee better encourage and allure others."

Saris's long voyage to court had done little to alter his opinion that Adams was haughty and disdainful. He still failed to appreciate Adams's concerns about the arrival of so many Englishmen, even though the behavior of the *Clove*'s mariners had caused considerable alarm in the local community, and he was offended by Adams's detached manner. Weary of listening to Adams's advice and determined to reassert his authority, Saris launched a blistering attack on Adams's Hirado trading partner, Yasuemon, who had remained in the port during the voyage to court. Saris asserted that Yasuemon had cheated the English when accompanying them to market and berated Adams for "his man's dishonnest and villainous dealing, being put in trust and to cheate us so unreasonable." Adams was aghast and took this as a personal affront.

He said it was "very evill that his servant should be so thought of."
Saris did not care a jot and was prepared to take the matter further, when Richard Cocks intervened and defused the situation.

But Saris had already said too much. Adams took exception to
the captain's attitude and began to harbor serious doubts as to
whether he could face several years in his company on the voyage
home. He was also alarmed to discover that he had very little
money with which to return to England. His wealth was tied up
in land and property, which would all be lost if he left Japan. The
time to make a decision came soon enough. Saris was keen to set
sail as soon as possible and asked Adams if he intended to join him
on the *Clove*. Adams declined his offer: "I awnssered him I had
spent in this country many yeeres, through which I was poor . . .
[and] was dessirouss to get something before my retourn." He also
made it clear that he was disgusted by the accusations that Saris
had implicitly leveled at him. "The reason I would not go with
him was for divers injuries done against me," he wrote, "the
which were thinges to me very strange and unlooked for." Saris
did not waste his breath with apologies. He accepted Adams's refusal and offered him employment as one of the East India Company's factors in Japan.

Adams was happy with this compromise, so long as it was on
his own terms. He knew that the company required his services
far more than he needed them and held out for the highest possible wage. Saris initially offered him a salary of £80 a year and said
that the London merchants had already given Mrs. Adams £20 for
food and clothing. "I do most humbly thank the Wourshipfull
Company for this deed of Christian charity," wrote a grateful
Adams, but he scoffed at such a low figure. He demanded £144
and argued that the Dutch paid him as much as £180 a year for
his services. After much wrangling, the two men settled upon
£100. It was a more generous salary than the £40 offered to the
other factors remaining in Japan—but precious little for someone
with such influence at court. It would also take many years for the

money to reach Adams from England. The Dutch tried to woo him with a more lucrative offer and "did what they could to have gotten him from us," wrote Cocks, but Adams's loyalty to his countrymen led him to accept Saris's terms. On November 24, 1613, he signed a two-year contract and became a full-time employee of the East India Company.

One dilemma still needed to be resolved before Saris set sail: the site of the English factory. Adams's preferred choice was Uraga. Close to the courtly capital and the city where all the richest lords and merchants resided, this was by far the most sensible place for the trading post. But Saris was no longer prepared to listen to advice from Adams. He favored Hirado: swayed not by its trading prospects but by the machinations of its canny feudal lord. King Foyne was hoping to reap vast profits from foreign trade and did everything in his power to ingratiate himself with the English captain. "The old king sent me word he would come and visit me," wrote Saris, "and bring me the dancing beares [prostitutes]." King Foyne was true to his word. "Soon after, he did [bring them], being three whores of the countrey." Saris was enchanted by Hirado's hospitable lord. At the end of November, he summoned a council of his men and told them that he had decided to base the English factory in the port.

Nine days after this meeting, he named the seven men who were to remain in Japan and serve alongside Adams. On the same day, all the crew were brought on board in readiness for the *Clove*'s departure. There was no time for farewells; no time for second thoughts on the part of the factors. With the wind blowing a stiff northerly, Saris weighed anchor and set sail. On the quayside of Hirado, a little band of Englishmen watched the ship disappear over the horizon.

Chapter 8

AT HOME WITH RICHARD COCKS

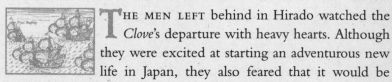

THE MEN LEFT behind in Hirado watched the *Clove*'s departure with heavy hearts. Although they were excited at starting an adventurous new life in Japan, they also feared that it would be many years until the next English vessel reached these distant shores. Loneliness was the scourge of factors in the East, and petty jealousies and rivalries quickly soured relationships. It would require great strength of character if they were to avoid clashing with each other.

Captain Saris had prepared a long list of instructions—his "remembrance"—which set out in considerable detail the day-to-day running of the factory. It also assigned specific duties to each of the men and suggested a hierarchical chain of command. The obvious choice as leader was William Adams. He had by now lived in Japan for more than thirteen years and had all the necessary contacts at court. He was also on good terms with many of the country's richest merchants and knew which commodities fetched the highest prices in Japan. But Captain Saris could not bring himself to appoint Adams to such a lofty position. Disdainful of Adams's humble origins and jealous of his knowledge of Japanese, he chose instead to give the position to the merchant Richard Cocks.

Cocks was a cheerful, happy-go-lucky fellow whose easygoing charm enabled him to make friends wherever he went. Known to his men as "honest Mr. Cocks," his passion in life was growing his own fruit and vegetables, and he was already looking forward to nurturing new and exotic plants. He described himself as "unlettered," but spent many an hour poring over his favorite book, a "Turkish History," and devoted his evenings to compiling a colorful, rambling diary. He was happiest when planting seedlings, examining his carrier pigeons, and tending to his collection of prize goldfish.

Like Captain Saris, he was a younger son with little prospect of inheriting the family fortune. This had forced him to set his gaze on horizons that lay far beyond his native Staffordshire. He had traveled to London at an early age to become an apprentice to a wealthy cloth worker, then moved on to Bayonne in southwest France. In 1605, he was recruited as a spy by his patron, Sir Thomas Wilson, and instructed to monitor the movements of English Roman Catholic exiles passing through Bayonne on their way to Spain.

Cocks was described as "one of the better sort," but he had a weakness of character that more forward-sighted merchants might have considered a major drawback for the position of chief factor. He had an endearing belief in the goodness of mankind and, although he claimed to have a sharp eye for "trix" and sleights of hand, his honesty had almost ruined him during his time in Bayonne. He had been conned by a Portuguese trickster and lost so much money that he was unable to pay his English creditors. He returned home in disgrace and found his name so blackened that he was shunned by friends and womenfolk. In a letter, he bemoaned the fact that his problems "hath been an occasion to hinder me from one or two good mariages." Sick at heart and aware that—at forty-five—his best years were almost behind him, he decided to leave England for a new life in Japan.

Cocks realized that the six men under his charge would require careful handling if he was to benefit from their skills. Richard Wickham, a Wiltshire man, was the most experienced, having led a life of rare adventure. His first voyage to the East, in 1608, had ended in disaster when he was captured and imprisoned by the Portuguese. He was then taken to Goa, where he spoke to his captors with an arrogance that astonished his fellow prisoners. He was eventually transported to Lisbon in a ship carrying an ambassador from the Persian court. Wickham befriended this ambassador, who reciprocated with "great affection" and secured him lodgings in his house. Wickham soon made his escape, boarded a ship bound for England, and arrived just in time to sign up for the voyage to Japan.

Such pluck and derring-do ought to have delighted Richard Cocks, but Wickham had a major defect in his character that would quickly sour their relationship. Greedy and unscrupulous, his sole motivation in traveling to Japan was to line his own pockets. Captain Saris described him as "capricious" and had been appalled by his behavior following the death of one of the Clove's crew: Wickham had produced a dubious copy of the dead man's will in which he was named sole benefactor.

Saris had been further angered by Wickham's demand for a wage increase shortly before the Clove's departure and refused to countenance it. But Wickham proved so persistent that he eventually caved in. "To be free of the exseeding and intollorable trouble I have dayly with him, I have offered to double his former entertainment." Even this generous salary increase did not satisfy Wickham and he vowed to make his own wages by engaging in private trade. His behavior was scandalous, yet he held a trump card. He was a friend of Sir Thomas Smythe, and knowledge of this friendship caused Saris to hesitate in disciplining him.

While Wickham succeeded in making himself enemies, William Eaton, the next in the pecking order, was busily making friends. He was a diligent and warmhearted individual whom Cocks described as a "true honest man, and a friend to his friend." Eaton was initially given the task of managing the day-to-day affairs of the English factory, but proved himself to be so hard-working that he was quickly promoted to "factor," or merchant. His previous position was filled by William Nealson, whose quarrelsome manner made him totally unsuited to life in a land far from home. Nealson was perpetually homesick and soon sought solace in the bottle, drinking copious quantities of sake and home-distilled poteen. This proved to have disastrous consequences, for alcohol had an adverse effect on his temperament and "fustian fumes." Captain Saris had viewed him as one of the *Clove*'s troublemakers and held him in low esteem. "[He is] to keepe the buttery," he told Cocks, "post your bookes, and [in] what other necessaries you see fitting may be employed." Even these menial duties proved too much for Nealson. He frequently absconded from work and made his way to the hot springs on nearby Iki Island, where alcohol was plentiful and the whores were attractive.

The other three members of the English community were to be directly involved in trade. The most experienced was the splendidly named Tempest Peacock, an adventurous individual who was "well experiensed in marchandising." He had a quick, mathematical mind and soon realized that he and his colleagues would need higher salaries if they were to make ends meet in this ruinously expensive country. "To live in this place is very charge-able," he wrote to the merchants in London, "and to receive no more . . . will make us returne home with empty purses." To his disgust, his pleas fell on deaf ears.

Peacock's deputy was Walter Carwarden, who had probably

trained as a gold or silversmith, while the young Edmund Sayers—who was possibly a kinsman of Saris—was still learning his trade.

Captain Saris had not been impressed by the men that the East India Company had selected to stay in Japan and was particularly critical of Nealson and Wickham. But he reserved his greatest contempt for William Adams, the eighth and most important member of the English factory. His jealousy of Adams had festered during his time in Japan and, by the time he came to prepare his "remembrance," it had turned into a passionate hatred. He denied Adams any role in the running of the factory and informed Cocks that he was "only fitting to be master of the junk, and to be used as a linguist at court when you have no employment for him at sea." He claimed that Adams was lazy and selfish—a grotesque travesty of the truth—and said that "it is necessary that you stirr him . . . otherwise you shall have little service of him." He further warned Cocks to be on his guard against duplicitous behavior, suggesting that Adams was likely to spend much of his time fraternizing with the Dutch, since he was "more affected to them than his own nation."

Saris's criticisms were so vehement that it is surprising that he offered Adams employment at all, but he was enough of a realist to know that Adams's expertise was essential if the English factory was to be a success. For this reason, Cocks was warned to treat him with respect, "[or] he shall leave you and betake him[self] to the Spaniards or Dutch." If that happened, the English would find themselves in deep trouble.

As soon as the *Clove* had left Hirado, Adams introduced Cocks to the local merchants. He also helped him to prepare the factory's warehouse and create living quarters for the men. A contemporary picture of the building shows a small, pitch-roofed dwelling with a huge flag of St. George fluttering in the sea breeze. The reality must have been somewhat different, for Cocks spent a great deal of time and money enlarging the factory. He had originally rented the place for six months for the princely sum of £19. Aware that at least a year would pass before the arrival of the next ship, he decided to buy the place outright and turn it into the "good and strong howse" that the East India Company merchants had requested. As he prodded the walls and poked at the ceiling, he quickly realized that the place was in a pitiful state of disrepair and was obliged to spend more than ten times the purchase price on making it habitable. Timbers and boards were purchased to extend the building, while plasterers were employed to make the living quarters less drafty in winter. Cocks also tried to minimize the risk of fire, which had presented a constant hazard to the English in Bantam. He tiled the roof of the main building and constructed a three-foot-thick perimeter wall around the entire site.

Cocks harbored dreams of presiding over a huge, highly profitable factory in Japan. He also hoped to produce large quantities of homegrown fruit and vegetables, which would preclude spending money on expensive victuals. The accounts are filled with notices of his acquiring neighboring properties in order to flatten buildings and plant vegetable plots or erect outhouses. In January 1614, he spent £12 on "the purchase of five old houses, and their backsides . . . whereby we daily stood in fear of fire." The site was cleared and transformed into an orchard, while other land was turned into a vegetable patch. In February, Cocks bought the house of their closest neighbor outright, "which is to be converted into a yard to prevent fire." He continued to acquire nearby properties until a sizable area of land around the factory was in his possession. The shacks and houses were then put to more appropriate use. Several were converted into godowns, or storehouses, another was turned into a showroom to display the merchandise, and another became a warehouse for ships' victuals. Cocks next improved the living quarters, where the seven men would sleep, eat, and while away long hours of boredom. The floors were covered in Japanese tatami mats, and a few items of furniture were procured locally to create a less spartan atmosphere. Cocks had hoped his men would sleep on the floor, like the Japanese, but they balked at such an uncomfortable arrangement and refused to adopt local customs. After many sleepless nights on rush mats, Cocks sent out an order for bedsteads. Henceforth the men would get some rest.

Within a few months of Captain Saris's departure, they had settled into a routine that proved to be far more lax and enjoyable than it had ever been on the *Clove*. During the voyage to Japan, Saris had assembled his rebellious crew on deck every morning and evening, "so as all may jointly, with reverence and humility, pray unto Almightie God." They were given readings from Scripture and reminded that the harshest punishments would be meted out for "blasphemeinge of God, swearing, thefte, drunkennes, or other disorders." The men had also suffered from the atrocious diet that was a hallmark of all long sea voyages. Their staples were "biscuit" and "oatmeale"—both of which were crawling with weevils—while the salt beef and dumplings smelled so bad that the men had to hold their noses as they ate. Nor were they ever

Hirado was a small, picturesque port with a mountainous backdrop. Richard Cocks spent time and money enlarging the English lodgings, but the Dutch factory (above) was larger and more imposing.

given enough to fill their gnawing bellies. Saris believed that he was being more than generous with the ship's food supplies and kept a daily record of the crew's meals, but many "aspersions were cast upon the captain for scantinge of his people" and he was alone among commanders in returning to England with "good store of victualls."

Cocks called an immediate halt to the frugal diet that Saris had inflicted upon his crew. Food was abundant in Hirado, and the men soon found that rarely a day passed without gifts of fresh meat and fruit being delivered by members of King Foyne's courtly retinue. Cocks's diary is filled with references to his men being presented with platters of viands, fruits, and freshly caught fish. There were gifts of "chestnuttes and powndgranetes; peares, grapes and walnuts; marmalades and sweetmeates." The game birds were especially delicious—the men dined on "duck roasted," "wood pigions," or "hennes"—and delicately flavored "codd-fish" was plentiful in Hirado harbor. They even munched their way through "seaweede" brought to them by local townsmen.

Cocks began to pride himself on preparing sumptuous feasts, especially when dignitaries came to dine. Adams had told him of the importance of ingratiating himself with Japan's feudal lords. Cocks followed this advice to the letter and went out of his way to prove his culinary skills to King Foyne, who was a connoisseur of fine cuisine. When Cocks learned that his lordship was planning a fishing expedition in Hirado Bay, he summoned his men to the scullery and "made ready two pigs, two ducks, two hens and a loin [of] pork." The meats were roasted over an open fire and accompanied by a "banquet [of] sweetmeates." The only drawback was the fact that the king and his retinue were enjoying the fishing so much that they were reluctant to come ashore. Cocks was undeterred; he "carried it aboard the kinge's boat, where they did eat what they pleased." Such generosity and thoughtfulness made a deep impression on the Japanese; Adams's knowledge of local customs won Cocks many friends in the Hirado community.

Hirado was home to many fishermen. Richard Cocks and his men often dined on "codd-fish" caught in the harbor. They were delighted to discover that food was plentiful in Japan, and hired cooks to prepare their feasts.

The men surprised themselves in the speed with which they grew accustomed to the comforts of their new home. At first, they had been delighted with their rich and varied diet, but they soon became choosy about the quality of the food, demanding new flavorings and different spices. Cocks had hired a cook shortly after Saris's departure, but the men complained that he did not satisfy their tastes, so he was ignominiously sacked. "We put Yoske the cook away," wrote Cocks, "having over-many lazy fellows in [the] house, and he one that could do littell or nothing." Other servants proved rather more useful. In addition to the factory's interpreters, Tome and Miguel, Cocks hired a small army of Japanese helpers to run the household. A butler, called Eurque, served the men their sake, and a scullion nicknamed Hatchman performed the role of caretaker. There was a cook and several general domestics, as well as a number of low-paid laborers. The men thought nothing of treating these servants harshly, particularly if they proved disobedient, clumsy, or dishonest. One was flogged "by all the servantes in the howse . . . [each] giving him ten lashes with a double rope over the naked body and buttockes." He was whipped "till all the skin was beaten off, and after washed . . . in brine." Cocks wrote in his diary: "I wish it may be a warning to the fool, for so I esteem him."

Each of the men was also given a boy-servant to undertake menial tasks. These unfortunate children were rented for next to nothing from their parents, who surrendered all rights to their offspring for the duration of their hire. They were treated roughly by some of the men, especially Nealson when he was in one of his "fumes." His boy, Larrance, soon ran away "because he did beate him . . . overmuch." Larrance's parents might have been expected to support their son when he returned to them in tears. Instead, they sent him straight back to the English factory. Cocks noted that Larrance was "the best boy in the howse"—small consolation to the bruised and battered lad.

The men's greatest gratification was the fact that they soon found themselves sharing their beds with the local women. When they first landed in Hirado, they had been reluctantly celibate for more than two years. The few that had risked the fleshpots of Bantam had been disgusted by the grubby and pox-ridden whores. Hirado's strumpets offered a rather more pleasurable route to sexual satisfaction and the men quickly formed dalliances with the town's womenfolk—something the London merchants had been keen to prevent. The puritanical Sir Thomas Smythe had been horrified by sordid stories filtering back from the East Indies and urged captains to stop their crews from visiting brothels. He vainly hoped that his men in Japan would live in a "frugall and sparing" manner, leading chaste and spotless lives to "their best endevours." But this was asking too much from men who were desperate for the company of women. Cocks frequently hired "dancing bears" to enliven their evening drinking sessions, while his men spent their paltry salaries on whores and long-term concubines. They were quite open about this in their diaries and letters, although they sometimes concealed their boasts of sexual conquest by writing in code.

The ease with which Japanese women could be hired for sex had already drawn critical comment from the Jesuits, the Franciscans, and even some merchants. "It often happens that a girl's own father, mother or brothers . . . will, without hesitation, sell her as a prostitute before she is married, for a few pence, under the pressure of poverty." So wrote the Florentine adventurer Francesco Carletti, who had arrived in Japan just three years before Adams. He had landed at nearby Nagasaki and had been shocked at the extent of prostitution. Girls were available for either long-term or short-term hire and were often extremely cheap. "It often happens that they [the foreign traders] will get hold of a pretty girl of fourteen or fifteen years of age, for three or four *scudi* . . . with no other responsibility beyond that of sending her back home when done." Carletti was scandalized and concluded his account by claiming that Japan offered the "means of gratifying the passion for sexual indulgence, just as it abounds in every other sort of vice."

Adams makes no mention of visiting Hirado's fleshpots. Indeed, the disdain he showed toward the *Clove*'s crew was almost certainly in response to their licentious and rowdy behavior. Cocks and his men were less choosy than Adams in their quest for physical pleasure and were delighted to enter into liaisons with the local wenches. They soon made arrangements with Hirado's "brokers" and looked forward to nights of passion with their new and exotic concubines.

Cocks, whose history of success with English women had been woeful, took a shine to a girl called Matinga, who became his mistress. He quickly realized that she was no submissive house drudge. She came from good stock and expected constant gifts of clothes and trinkets. Cocks found to his dismay that a large percentage of his salary was disappearing on the maintenance of Matinga, who demanded her own lodgings and a retinue of servants and slaves. He bought her five gold rings and spent substantial sums on silk kimonos, finely stitched girdles, and costly jewelry boxes, yet Matinga was rarely happy with her presents and was even less impressed with Cocks's sexual prowess. She had a hankering for more virile men and it was not long before she was looking for those who could provide more physical stimulation. Rumors of her infidelity rapidly spread through Hirado, and "there were rhymes cast abrode and sung up and downe towne against Matinga." Cocks was upset by the lewd songs and ordered that "handes should be laid upon such as were heard to sing it hereafter, and punishment inflicted upon the offenders." Only later would he discover that she was being unfaithful and that her dalliances were taking place very close to home.

Cocks was not alone in finding himself a female consort. Wickham was consumed with passion for a local girl called Femage, while Eaton hitched himself to a young lady called O-man (who was given the nickname Woman). Both men showered their concubines with gifts of silks and satins but, for Eaton at least, the spark of passion was quickly extinguished. He tired of O-man and sold her to Wickham, a transaction that infuriated the girl's mother, who complained that Eaton "[had] sold away her daughter to one that will carry her out of the land of Japan."

Although Adams helped Cocks and his men to establish themselves in Hirado, he had little time to join them in their merrymaking. He was preoccupied with an exhilarating project that Ieyasu had personally assigned to him. The shogun had long been fascinated by Adams's knowledge of geography and astronomy and was surprised to discover that even the Jesuits were impressed by his knowledge of the science of navigation. Padre Carvalho went so far as to describe him as "a great engineer and mathematician." Ieyasu decided to put Adams's talents to good use, giving him informal employment as cartographer to the court. Adams responded by making a terrestrial globe, in order that the shogun might better understand the relative positions of realms and kingdoms. He also wished to demonstrate to Ieyasu his belief in the existence of a sea passage to England along Russia's northern coastline—the route that Captains Pet and Jackman had attempted more than thirty years earlier. All subsequent attempts had also met with failure, and no vessel had successfully penetrated the icy Kara Sea.

Adams's idea was to tackle the voyage from the other end—from the east. The enthusiastic shogun quizzed him at great length about the reputed route "[and] asked me if our countrimen could not find the norwest passadg." Adams told him: "We doubted not but there is a way [across the top of Russia] . . . and called for a map of the wholle world, and so [he] sawe that it was very neer."

Ieyasu was fascinated and gave Adams the task of planning and leading a voyage of discovery. "He told me [that] if I would go, he would give me his letter of friendship to the land of Yedzoo [Hokkaido], where his subjects have frindship." Adams warned that it would require a great deal of expertise and wrote to the East India Company directors in order to inform them of the project and ask them to send "good marriners to saill with." He told them to dispatch only experienced explorers, since "the peopell of this land are verry stoutt seamen." He also informed them that he had a desperate need for "compasses, rounningglasses, a pair of globes . . . and some cardes or maps, one containing the wholl world." Such equipment would enable him to explain the hazards and logistics of the voyage to Ieyasu, as well as the route he intended to follow.

Adams was realist enough to know that any expedition was likely to be several years in the planning. He also knew that any such discovery would be "one of the most famous that ever hath been," and this thought spurred him on in his endeavors. He spent much of his time studying in his lodgings at the house of his merchant friend, Yasuemon, while his compatriots indulged in a raucous cycle of drinking and partying.

Cocks and his men knew that they would soon have to call a halt to their pleasure pursuits and start trading with the Japanese, but claimed there was little they could do until the factory and its warehouses were repaired and made waterproof. Adams was content to let them behave as they pleased. It was Cocks, not he, who was head of the English factory, and Cocks who would have to answer for any failings. Yet Cocks himself seemed remarkably untroubled by the burden of responsibility and spent long hours indulging his passion for gardening, tending his vegetable patch and newly planted orchard. The Japanese were bemused by his hobby and sought to humor him by bringing gifts of trees. On one occasion, a friendly Buddhist priest arrived at the factory with fifteen orange, lemon, and chestnut trees. Four days later, another three were unexpectedly delivered. Cocks himself traveled to Nagasaki to buy "two fig trees, an orenge tree and a peach tree." When he arrived back at the factory, he discovered that an anonymous donor had left him a quince tree and a pear tree. It was not long before Cocks's orchard was in blossom and promising a heavy crop of figs, grapes, oranges, and lemons.

There was the occasional setback. On one wet June afternoon the upper slopes of the orchard "did shrink with the extreme rain, and three panels of our orchard wall fell downe and spoiled divers fruit trees." Cocks rushed out to save what he could but noted that "all the rest of the wall [was] much shaken and like to fall, the ground giving way."

Cocks also developed a passion for goldfish, which he collected with an avidity that surprised even the Japanese. His enthusiasm had been sparked by Li Tan's brother, who presented him with "a littell fishpond (or jarr) with live fish in it." Cocks soon started a collection, buying so many prize fish that they became the talk of Hirado. His aquarium attracted the envy of the local nobility, who tried to get their hands on some of the finer specimens. Often, they were extremely blunt in expressing their desire for one or other of Cocks's golden friends. On one occasion, King Foyne's brother learned that Cocks had a particularly fine fish "and sent desire to have it." Cocks was reluctant to part with it, but knew that he would cause great offense by refusing, "so I gave it him." Nobutoki was delighted and showed his gratitude by sending back "a great black dogg."

Cocks soon grew annoyed at the constant plunder of his goldfish and did his best to ignore the requests from Hirado's fish-obsessed nobles. But all too often he was forced to relent: "The King of Hirado sent to beg my two golden fishes," he wrote on one occasion, ". . . which, much against my will, I gave him."

The English quickly learned to adopt the best of the local customs. They had washed neither themselves nor their clothes during their long months on the *Clove*, and their fetid skin was rank and offensive when they first arrived. The Japanese were appalled by such disregard for personal cleanliness and could not understand why foreigners had no desire to bathe. They had observed the same unpleasant trait in the Portuguese, who shunned Japanese steam baths and ate their food with unwashed hands. Padre João Rodrigues noted their disdain in his book *Historia da Igreja do Japão,* in which he wrote with passion about Japanese cleanliness and bathing habits. "They are greatly astonished by eating with the hands," he wrote, and said that the sight of filthy clothes and food-stained table coverings "causes both nausea and disgust." Even in a provincial backwater like Hirado, the nobility were scrupulously clean and prided themselves on their scrubbed and scented skin. "All the houses of the nobles and gentry have bathrooms for guests," noted Rodrigues. "These places are very clean and are provided with hot and cold water, because it is a general custom in Japan to wash the body at least once or twice a day." The Japanese were uninhibited by nudity; they stripped naked in their public baths "and do not worry at all if their privy parts are seen." First they washed themselves in running water. Then they slipped into huge baths and languished in the naturally heated pool.

When Cocks and his team tried this strange custom, they were surprised to find it much to their liking. Indeed, they enjoyed it so much that they decided to construct their very own *o-furo*, or bathhouse, in which they could relax and entertain their Japanese guests. The principal chamber was the steam bath; this was constructed of scented wood, which absorbed the moisture and turned it into perfumed droplets. Before entering, the men changed into baggy loincloths. Once inside, they lounged around in the steam, which "gently softens the body . . . [and] brings out and loosens all the adhering dirt and sweat." It also worked wonders in curing their hangovers. When their skin was pink and their aching joints relaxed, they entered a cooler room and refreshed themselves by splashing each other with chilled water.

Cocks's building works had been extensive, and the factory soon enclosed a significant area of land in Hirado. Yet there was one important outhouse that receives no mention in the accounts. The Japanese were in the habit of performing their bodily functions in special privies, which were set apart along a paved path. Unlike the English, whose drains were nonexistent and whose streets often overflowed with excrement, the Japanese prided themselves on their pristine sewers and latrines. "The interior," wrote Padre Rodrigues, ". . . is kept extremely clean . . . [with] a perfume-pan and new paper cut for use." He added that these privies were "without any bad smell, for when the guests depart, the man in charge cleans it out if necessary." Every morning, a team of cleaners would visit each privy and pay good money to remove the waste matter, which was then used on their fields and vegetable plots. Cocks and his men must have been utterly bewildered by such strange habits, and it is not clear whether they adopted this particular custom.

The English factory soon began to resemble a Japanese household. It was built in the local style and kept extremely clean by its army of Japanese servants. Although the cooks did not always prepare food to the men's liking, they knew how to keep the kitchen in order. Their attention to hygiene came naturally, for even in the meanest of Japanese households pots and pans were scrubbed with the greatest diligence before use, while any uncooked food that was touched during preparation was washed and sterilized. "[The Japanese] have special people who cut up fish, and the flesh of birds and animals of the chase," wrote Rodrigues. "All the food is cut up on spotless thick tables with iron forks, knives and cleavers and nothing is touched with the hands."

The Japanese paid great attention to hygiene and cleanliness, especially when preparing food. "[They] have special people who cut up fish, and the flesh of birds," wrote the Jesuit João Rodrigues circa 1620. This had been standard practice since the Middle Ages, as this late-fourteenth-century manuscript illustration shows.

This attention to cleanliness, coupled with the healthy Japanese diet, ensured that the men were blessed with good health. This was in dramatic contrast to their time in Bantam, where so many of the *Clove*'s crew had succumbed to mysterious tropical fevers. Cocks was surprised that his men stayed in such rude health, especially as they had arrived in such a weakened condition, and he wrote to one of the factors in Bantam to express their good fortune. "All the Englishmen which came in the *Clove*, except myselfe, have [he means "had"] been very sick, so that I expected no life of any one of them." Yet ever since they landed in Hirado, "they [are] recovered and in good health."

There were a few occasions when the men fell ill, especially in the early months when their stomachs had not yet adjusted to the strange Japanese diet. Terrified that they had contracted some unknown disease and anxious to find a cure, they turned to Adams for advice. "I have been much tormented with an ague," wrote Cocks on one occasion. "[It] turned into an extreme ache in my bones in all partes of my body, so that I had thought I should have lost the use of my limbs and was become a very crippell." A diet of fresh fruit and seafood quickly helped him to recover his strength, and after a few days at the hot springs he made a full recovery.

Richard Wickham was unfortunate enough to fall sick while undertaking a voyage to Kyoto. "[I am] troubled with a burning ague," he wrote to his friends in Hirado, and added that "this fever does so vex me that I cannot get no rest night nor day, want of sleep much offending me." As he grew weaker and paler, he urged Cocks to send some alcohol, which he thought would do him good. He also took the drastic decision to resort to surgery, informing his friends that he intended to "play the surgen myselfe, for I have a very good lancet." Cocks was alarmed when he read this and wrote an urgent reply, begging Wickham not to perform surgery on himself. "My councell," he wrote, "is that yow give not yourself too much to physick, except upon greate extremity."

The Japanese would have agreed wholeheartedly, for they were horrified by the barbaric medical practices of Europeans, especially the obsession with letting blood. "The Japanese would rather die than use our painful surgical remedies," wrote the Jesuit padre Luis Frois. They preferred natural medicines made of boiled roots and herbs, sea snails and seaweed, and took candied pills that were believed to purge the body. Their widespread use of acupuncture also astonished foreign observers. "In nearly all their sicknesses they are accustomed to having their stomach, arms and back etc. pierced with silver needles," wrote one incredulous monk, "and at the same time they cauterize with herbs." The needles were inserted into the most sensitive points in the body and were remarkably effective in relieving pain.

Japanese physicians paid a high price for failure, since poor diagnosis and treatment was punishable by death. "During the emperor's sickness," wrote Wickham, "he caused his chiefe physition to be cut in pieces for telling him . . . that in regard he was an old man, his medicine could not worke so effectually."

Such wanton brutality was a way of life in Japan, and the English never ceased to be amazed by the terrifying rule of law. Adams had written at length to his compatriots in Bantam to warn them that unruly behavior was punished with the utmost harshness in Japan. "In justice [they are] very severe," he wrote, "having no respect of persoons." He warned that thieves were rarely imprisoned, "but pressently executed," while cities and towns were governed with the greatest rigorousness. Adams must have been aware that many newly arrived mariners were likely to be drunkards whose uncontrollable rabble-rousing often ended in violence. In order to preempt any trouble, he had warned his colleagues that "no murther[er] for the most part can escape," because the Japanese judicial system relied upon informants and rewards. A price was placed on the head of any escaped criminal—up to £300—which was paid out to whoever provided incriminating information.

Adams, who had grown up in the violent back streets of Lime-house, quickly became a keen advocate of strict Japanese justice. He said that the shogun's policy of "eye for eye, touth for touth" meant that "in their citties, you may go all over in the night with-out anny trobell or perill."

King Foyne was as inexorable as any other Japanese lord. He governed his fiefdom with a razor-sharp sword, crushing disobe-dience and refusing mercy. Cocks's men were no strangers to the spectacle of public beheadings and grisly disembowelments—for they were a common occurrence in London—yet they were sur-prised to discover that Adams was not exaggerating the inflexi-bility of Japanese justice: even minor transgressions were capital offenses. Worse still, the sentence was inviolable, and King Foyne

Like all Japanese lords, Foyne maintained a troop of well-armed retainers who could be called upon in times of crisis. They were well equipped (above) and liked to test their swords on the corpses of criminals.

would not "revoke or mittigate the severitie of it." Once judgment was passed, the punishment was immediate. The victim was instructed to kneel and the executioner cut off his head. Then the head and body were chopped into tiny pieces.

Cocks and his men were horrified by such violence and watched in dismay as young children were executed for minor crimes. In their first months, they had been too nervous to intervene. But when they were more familiar with their new home, they began to lodge complaints with King Foyne. On a December afternoon in 1615, Cocks learned that "a boy of sixteen yeares old was [to be] cut in peeces for stealing a littell boat and carrying it to another island." Cocks felt that the death sentence was unduly harsh and "sent [an appeal] to the king to beg his life." He also dispatched a message to the executioner, asking him to refrain from killing the boy until he had learned of King Foyne's reaction. The executioner, infuriated by the English petition, was further angered when he learned that Foyne intended to pardon the lad. Without further ado, he unsheathed his sword and "put him to death before the [official] pardon came, cutting him in many mammocks."

Life was cheap in Hirado, and death was so commonplace that the local populace was untroubled by the sight of corpses lying in gutters or fields. Cocks was rather more sensitive, and such horrific spectacles would remain forever etched on his mind. One day, he was enjoying a walk on the edge of the town when he "fownd a young girl of some eleven or twelve years of age, dead on the backside under the walle [of a little lodge]." He was disgusted to see "doggs feeding on her, having eaten both her legges and her lower parts." He was unable to discover her identity or the cause of death, but noted that "it is thought some villen had ravished her and after killed her, or else, being a slave, her master had killed her upon some displeasure and cast her out to be eaten of dogges, an ordenary matter in these partes." He added that the lives of slaves were in the hands of their masters "to kill them when he will, without controle of any justice." Even the corpses of the *Clove*'s mariners who had died in Hirado were not allowed to rest in peace. On one occasion, Cocks was passing the little graveyard where a crew member had been buried when he noticed that "some villanouse people had digged up the coffin and stolen the winding sheete and his shert, and left the karkasse naked upon the ground."

King Foyne was bemused but untroubled by Cocks's criticism of his draconian rule. The English became regular visitors to his palace, climbing the long stone staircase accompanied by their "boys"—for it was the custom of the country for "any person of quality, from the highest ranking to the lowest, to be accompanied by a lad who takes his [the man's] sandals at the entrance."

The palace itself was a fine wooden structure atop the Tomigake, a rocky hill set back from the town. A decorative map of Hirado, drawn some seven years after the *Clove*'s arrival, depicts it as a large, walled complex of buildings with a roofed gatehouse and a huge inner courtyard. In common with all noble buildings, its lacquered interior was sparsely furnished. Sliding doors led onto cedarwood verandas, which had a panoramic view of the deepwater bay and surrounding pine-clad mountains.

On each visit, Cocks and his men were expected to arrive bearing choice and costly gifts. When Saris first met King Foyne, he had given him rich cloths and trinkets. Cocks took rather more unusual items. He discovered that his lordship had developed a taste for traditional English cooking, especially hearty stews in a thick gravy. His favorite was made with salted meats—"a piece of English beefe, and another of porke, sod with onions and turnips." Thus began a bizarre exchange: Foyne would present Cocks with local fish—yellowtail, red snapper, shellfish, and crabs—and Cocks would hand over chunks of two-year-old meat, some of which had traveled all the way from England.

King Foyne was a devotee of the tea ceremony, a ritual so bizarre—and of such complexity—that it was quite beyond the comprehension of Cocks and his men. Inspired by the hermit philosophers of Zen Buddhism, it was intended as a means of. contemplating the mysteries of the soul. Padre João Rodrigues described it as "a kind of solitary religion," which necessitated much physical and mental preparation. King Foyne and his guests would change into pristine robes and shave their heads before starting to sip their soupy green tea, which was believed to have powerful medicinal properties. The leaves were ground to powder and a few spoonfuls placed in a porcelain vessel. Hot water was then added and any lumps broken up with a bamboo whisk. The tea was served in special bowls, but before it could be drunk the guests were obliged to rinse their mouths and hands. Cocks and his men tried this unusual drink, and a couple of them found it to their liking. William Eaton grew quite fond of it, while Richard Wickham sent "jarrs of chawe [tea]" to Hirado on several occasions. But they much preferred more intoxicating beverages and spent many of their evenings glugging wine, eau-de-vie, and locally brewed sake.

The men found themselves socializing more and more with their Dutch counterparts, and there were numerous Anglo-Dutch drinking sessions to keep them merry. Captain Specx returned to Hirado shortly after the departure of the *Clove* and quickly formed a deep and lasting friendship with Richard Cocks. The English soon discovered, as William Adams had done many years earlier, that it paid to remain on good terms with these fellow Europeans. Although there was stiff trading competition between the two nations, they were frequent guests at each other's factories. Their evening drinking sessions were invariably raucous, with numerous toasts and noisy singing that filled the night air. The evening was usually brought to a close with a tremendous burst of cannonfire, which woke the town's nervous inhabitants with a series of echoing explosions. "Much ordinance was shot off," wrote Cocks after one particularly drunken evening, "both at the howse and aboard the shipps." The next morning, with bleary eyes and throbbing heads, Cocks and Specx would exchange thank-you letters. These grew increasingly effusive in their compliments and were probably written while the men were still intoxicated. On one occasion, a jovial Specx told Cocks that he was "ready to doe ether me or any other of our English nation any service or pleasure he could." He was genuinely fond of Cocks and added "that the loving kindness he had received from me in espetiall could never be forgotten whiles he lived, knowing well it came from a good hart."

Although Adams spent much of his time in his lodgings at Yasuemon's house, he did accompany the men to parties and festivities at the homes of Hirado's merchants. Some of these were extremely colorful. The annual Bon festival—the feast of the dead—saw the town bedecked with pennants and candles. "All the streets were hanged with lanterns," wrote Cocks, "and the pagans vizited their *hotoke* [temples] and places of buriall with lanterns and lamps, inviting their dead frendes to come and eat with them." The townsfolk spilled into the streets, hoping to meet the souls of their departed loved ones. It made for an extraordinary spectacle: they chatted with imaginary specters and placed food offerings on their graves to help the occupants through the following year. "Then, each one retorned to their howses, having left rice, wine and other viandes at the graves, for dead men to banquet off in their absence." When they reached their homes, some hurled stones onto their roofs, explaining that this was done to drive away any spirits that were still lingering.

Huge quantities of food and wine were consumed on such occasions, and the inhabitants "did eate and drink . . . with much mirth and jesting, drinking themselves drunken all or the most parte." Drunkenness—the men discovered—was a way of life in Japan. Many Japanese saw nothing wrong in drinking themselves into oblivion and would continue with their revelries until there was no one left standing. It was one of the few Japanese customs that was eagerly adopted by the English and the only one at which they truly excelled.

After the first few months in Hirado, Cocks and his men had every reason to feel pleased with themselves. Adams had given them invaluable advice about their new home and had introduced them to many of the local merchants. He had also been instrumental in helping them create handsome living quarters and buy timber and tiling for necessary repairs. The men had acquired mistresses and servants and were enjoying a far more luxurious life than they could possibly have achieved in England. As they prepared to start trading in earnest, their thoughts turned to whether or not Saris had survived the long journey back to England. It was essential that he had, for they were dependent on him for their first shipload of supplies.

Chapter 9

CLASH OF THE SAMURAI

WHILE RICHARD COCKS and his men were settling into their agreeable new life in Japan, the *Clove* was making speedy progress back to England. She had left Hirado in December 1613 and reached Bantam after just four weeks at sea. Captain Saris had no intention of risking his men's lives by stopping there for long. After being loaded with pepper and spices, the *Clove* left Java almost immediately, heading for southern Africa's Table Bay, where victuals and water could be easily acquired. Then, with the wind in his favor, Saris headed north into the Atlantic and arrived in Plymouth at the end of September 1614.

It was customary for vessels returning to England after such a long voyage to make a brief pit stop at one of the ports on the south coast. They would take on board fresh water before heading to London, where the cargo would be unloaded. The merchants of the capital soon learned of the *Clove*'s safe arrival in Plymouth and expected her in London within a few days. But their wait

proved in vain. For more than six weeks the ship remained at anchor, delayed—according to Saris—by tremendous storms, "more
tempestuous . . . and our lives more endangered, than upon the
whole voyage." The East India Company directors were suspicious
and believed that Saris had put into port only so that he could
unload cargo that he intended to sell for private profit. Their
suspicions were increased when they intercepted two secret
letters, written by Saris to his brother and cousin, in which he
asked them to send "two trustie watermen." These men, it was
supposed, would land Saris's illicit cargo and sell it on the black
market.

The company directors were by now convinced that Saris
"had used very greate private trade for himself, and purposed to
convey away his goods out of the shipp." Furious with their captain and anxious to prevent any loss of cargo, they sent two of
their agents to Plymouth with orders to board the vessel and prevent any unauthorized deals. They sent a third official to the
"postmaster's house" with orders to intercept Saris's letters, while
a fourth was told to take lodgings in the Starre Inn in Bread
Street, a favorite watering hole of many mariners, and pick up
hearsay.

Not all of the London merchants approved of these steps. Saris
had friends as well as enemies in the East India Company, and
they argued that it would be fairer to presume him innocent until
more evidence had been gathered. They managed to reverse an
order to call Saris immediately to London—an action that would
have been tantamount to disgrace—and convinced the directors
that it was "fitting to have him kindly used untill some ill carriage
of his be certainly knowne."

But the four officials sent to Plymouth were not recalled, and
they soon had information to divulge to the London directors—
not about Saris, but about events that had taken place in Japan.
Among a parcel of letters deposited at the postmaster's house was
one written by William Adams, which revealed that seven men

had been settled in Hirado and that the "emperour," Ieyasu, had offered generous trading privileges. The letter also said that Japan was every bit as rich as the old fables had suggested, as well as being a perfect place for repairing ships battered by the long sea voyage. "Here is no want of nothing," wrote Adams, "for carpenters, timber, planking and iron . . . [are] so good and as good cheep as is in England."

Captain Saris did not arrive in London until mid-November, "havinge made his jorney overland from Plymouth." He was given a mixed reception, for there were many who remained suspicious of his six-week sojourn in Plymouth. But they quickly forgave him when he presented his report on Japan. At a great meeting of the assembled merchants, he gave a detailed account of everything that had occurred during the voyage and led a lively discussion on the goods most valued by the Japanese. He painted a wildly optimistic picture of trade with Japan, feeding his audience with information that they wanted to hear. He told them that broadcloth was particularly in demand—especially in bright colors—and added that the Japanese would pay large sums for baize, linen, and Indian cloth.

This was both misleading and wrong. Cocks had found it almost impossible to sell his cargo of colorful broadcloth and had learned to his cost that Japanese noblemen favored "sad colors"—blacks and browns—for the costumes of their retainers. Saris was also mistaken in informing the London merchants that coarse cloth would sell for more than £6 per yard, a wildly optimistic price, while his list of other highly valued commodities—sugar-candy, soap, and lascivious pictures—was as eccentric as it was incorrect.

Saris had good reason to present the London merchants with such an upbeat assessment of trade with Japan. He was in danger of disgrace and hoped that his report would offer a quick route to rehabilitating his reputation. It also vindicated his decision to found a factory in the country. Satisfied that he had won over his detractors, he now urged the London merchants to "build upone this slender advise . . . for it is trewe."

This is exactly what they intended to do. They were overjoyed to learn of the alleged profitability of the Japanese market and listened with interest to news that the Dutch had recently spent £1,500 on repairs to their Hirado factory. The Dutch were known to be cautious in matters of trade; if they were investing large sums in Japan, it could only mean there was a spectacular harvest to be reaped.

The company debated Saris's report in mid-November 1614, and excitement mounted as the meeting drew to a close. "Whereuppon they, havinge weighed all reasouns . . . were absolutely of opinion that the place is very hopefull." They acquired two vessels, the *Advice* and the *Attendant*, and began to procure a cargo.

Saris was delighted by the turn of events. Just a few weeks earlier, he had been under a cloud of suspicion and in danger of being censured. Now, he found himself being feted as a hero. His voyage yielded a 200 percent profit—derived almost entirely from his cargo of spices—and his decision to open a factory in Japan was hailed as forward thinking. All criticism of his conduct as a commander was brushed aside, and the merchants showed little interest in the letters written by the men who had remained in Japan. Cocks, Peacock, and Wickham all offered excellent advice, much of which was in direct contradiction to that brought home by Saris. Cocks's letter was particularly prescient: it warned that the Japanese were "so addicted to silks that they do not enter into consideration of the benefit of wearing cloth." He added ominously that "time may alter their minds . . . [but] in the meantime we must seek out other matters."

Saris's honeymoon with the company did not last long. Sir Thomas Smythe had lent the captain a room in his house for the storage of his goods and belongings. Shortly before Christmas, he learned that a large part of these consisted of pornographic books and pictures that Saris had acquired during his travels. When

Smythe informed his fellow merchants of this discovery, they were equally horrified and decreed that these "lascivious bookes and pictures . . . [were] held to be a greate scandall unto this company, and unbeseeminge their gravity to permitte."

Smythe was prepared to let the matter rest, although he assured the merchants "of his dislike thereof, the rather for that it was in his howse." But when he discovered that the erotica had become a source of mirth and that prattlers and gossips were making "derogatory speeches" about it in the London Exchange, he decided on more extreme measures. Angry and upset, he vowed to hold a public burning ceremony—with Saris present—which was intended to show Londoners "that such wicked spectacles are not fostered and mayntayned by any of this company." On January 10, 1615, Saris's great collection of pornography was set alight. "And thereupon, in open presense, [Smythe] putt them into the fire, where they continued till they were burnt and turned into smoke."

While Saris was making his way back to London, William Adams was growing increasingly impatient with life in Hirado. His lodgings were comfortable enough, and the company of his Japanese friends was agreeable, but he was anxious to return to his estate at Hemi and be reunited with his wife and family. He had already lost one family—his wife and daughter in England. Now, stuck in distant Hirado, he was in danger of losing another. He also needed to tend to the management of his estate. There was the rice harvest to be supervised, and constant, if minor, disputes over land and property had to be resolved. It was almost impossible to be a country landlord when living some 600 miles away.

There was another reason why Adams was anxious to return to Hemi. For more than thirteen years he had awaited with great anticipation the arrival of fellow Englishmen in Japan. Now that they had at long last pitched up in Hirado, he was disappointed to discover that he had very little in common with them. In one respect, Captain Saris had been absolutely right: Adams felt more at home with his local friends.

As soon as the building works were complete, Adams suggested that Cocks and his men turn their thoughts to trade. The repairs had consumed much of the factory's cash, while the giving of presents had been a further drain on precious resources. Adams knew that if the men did not start trading immediately, there was a very real chance that the factory would become insolvent.

But trade was not as easy or as straightforward as Cocks had hoped. Each time he entered the warehouse, he was reminded of the fact that his goods were "not very vendibel." There were fifty pieces of broadcloth, some 6,000 Indian cottons, and 124 elephant tusks. He also had large quantities of pepper, tin, and lead, as well as forty-six barrels of gunpowder and six cannon. He had hoped to dispose of these items with ease, but found that the market was flooded with ivory, there was no demand for broadcloth, and tin was as cheap in Japan as in England. Worse still, the Japanese produced their own cotton cloth and showed no interest in buying Indian imports.

Cocks hoped that the problem was unique to Hirado and that the merchants elsewhere in Japan would be keen to acquire his wares. He had been instructed by Captain Saris to spread his trading tentacles far and wide, founding subfactories and depots right across Japan. This was not going to be easy with only seven men at his disposal, but Adams made suggestions as to how Cocks could capitalize on his limited resources and manpower. It was agreed that he should send William Eaton to Osaka, Richard Wickham to Edo, and the youthful Edmund Sayers to the mountainous island of Tsushima in the Korean Straits. Peacock and Carwarden volunteered to strike even further afield—to Cochinchina or south Vietnam—while Adams himself offered to sail to distant Siam. Nealson was to remain in Hirado with Cocks to hold the fort.

Wickham and Eaton were the first to leave Hirado, bidding farewell to their friends in January 1614. Adams accompanied them on their journey, for his presence was necessary to help them find suitable houses in Edo and Osaka. Cocks, who was increasingly worried at the vast sums of money he had spent on dancing girls, servants, and building works, urged them to sell their cargo as quickly as possible. "Turn all into ready money before any other shipping come out of England," he wrote with a tone of desperation, "[so] that it cannot be said that we lie still and do nothing but eat and drink."

The three men paused briefly in Osaka to find lodgings for Eaton, before continuing to Edo, a city of such grandeur that all who came here were impressed. Saris had been astonished by the magnificence of its noble mansions. "[They] made a very glorious appearance to us," he wrote, "the ridge-tiles and corner-tiles richly gilded, the posts of their doors gilded and varnished." The wide, neatly swept boulevards were "as broad as any of our streets in England" and also a great deal cleaner. One Spanish visitor remarked wryly that they were "kept so clean that you might well think that nobody ever walks along them."

The city was divided into different quarters, with areas reserved for cobblers, tinkers, blacksmiths, and tailors. There was a special district for shops selling game birds—partridges, geese, wild duck, cranes, and hens—and another that specialized in rabbits, hares, and wild boar. The fish market was so exotic that foreigners were brought on guided tours. "They sell every kind of salt and freshwater fish you could desire," wrote the Spaniard Rodrigo de Vivero y Velasco. "Many live fish are kept in tubs full of water so you can buy just what you want." The fruit market was no less colorful: "it is just as interesting . . . because in addition to the abundance and variety of fruit, the cleanliness with which the goods are displayed gives the customers an appetite."

Edo was a wealthy city whose streets were thronged with courtiers and noblemen dressed in fine silken kimonos. The richest and most ostentatious of these feudal lords wore flamboyant robes decorated with exquisite patterns of blossoms and leaves. "They intermingle gold among the flowers," wrote Padre João Rodrigues, ". . . and they are especially clever in their use of crimsons and, even more, of violets." In summer, the men wrapped their bellies in sashes of hemp or linen, while "all the noble and aristocratic ladies . . . wear silk gloves which cover the back of the hand." Their most extraordinary item of clothing was their footwear. The Japanese were accustomed to wear goatskin slippers, which were held onto the feet by a twisted straw rope. In the rain, they changed into chunky wooden clogs that were strapped to their big toes with a thong.

Cocks had told Wickham that money was no object when he came to renting accommodation. "Take up your lodging in the best merchante's howse in the towne," he said, adding that "to live under the roofe of a naturall Japon[ner] is better than to be in the howse of any stranger." Adams was fortunate to have family contacts in Edo and he introduced Wickham to his father-in-law, Magome Kageyu, who was still superintendent of the packhorse exchange. Magome was offered employment as Wickham's sub-agent, with responsibility for safeguarding the English wares, and he was also charged with introducing the English to his business contacts. It quickly became apparent that he was a "crafty fellow" who was so adept at filching money that the English gave him the nickname Niccolo Machiavelli.

Wickham's *jurabassos*, or interpreters, were equally dishonest. They were hired for their knowledge of Portuguese, which had become the lingua franca for trade in Japan, but spent much of their time stealing supplies from the little English storehouse. Only Adams was able to keep them under control. Once he had left, they ran circles around Wickham, prompting him to write to Eaton informing him that they were "villains and deceavers every way, and not any to be trusted."

Although Wickham faced formidable difficulties, he had high

hopes of turning Edo into a successful base. He had arrived at a propitious moment, for hundreds of wealthy Japanese noblemen had flocked to the city to celebrate the rebuilding of the castle. Many of them now pitched up at his little warehouse and asked to view his selection of broadcloth.

Unfortunately, this was not possible. The goods had not yet arrived from Hirado, and Wickham found himself in the infuriating position of having potential buyers but no goods. He was so distraught that he caught "an ague" and wrote a letter to William Nealson informing him that he was "so wearied . . . that I have had no time to gather matter to write unto you." When Cocks learned of Wickham's misfortune, he was angry rather than upset: "For if we stay seven years more in Japan, we shall never have the like time to have vented our cloth as at this general assembly of the nobility."

The Dutch in Hirado soon heard rumors of the disaster and took advantage of the situation by sending their own cloth to Edo. Their timing was perfect, and they returned from their mission with large quantities of silver. This proved too much for Wickham to bear. When events conspired against him, his first reaction was to look for someone to blame. On this occasion, he did not have to look far. "I cannot tell what to thinke or speake of Captain Adams," he wrote in a private letter to Cocks, "but I much suspect playing of both sides."

Wickham's suspicions had been aroused by Adams's insistence that the goods be delivered by sea. The Dutch usually transported theirs by land, and Wickham began to wonder if Adams was deliberately sabotaging English trade. He stopped short of accusing Adams to his face "because I knew not how to remedy it." But he warned Cocks of his suspicions and told him that it would "serve for a caveat against the next occasion."

Cocks, deeply shocked by Wickham's accusations, conducted a full and thorough investigation. He quickly discovered that the fault lay with the porter charged with transporting the goods and that Adams was in no way to blame. Yet Wickham had sowed the seeds of doubt in his mind, so he took the bizarre precautionary measure of giving employment to one of the *Liefde*'s Dutch survivors, the treacherous Gisbert de Coning, who had been shunned by Adams ever since the ship's arrival in Japan. Gisbert soon proved to be as ineffectual as he was unpopular and became yet another drain on Cocks's dwindling resources.

Wickham's new home in Edo was more than 500 miles from Hirado, but he received frequent letters from his colleagues. On one occasion, Cocks wrote him a gossipy note to inform him that their former landlord, Li Tan, had serious marital troubles. He had had frequent explosive rows with Mrs. Tan and on one occasion had handed her his sword and told her to "cut off her littell finger"—a command that she would meekly have obeyed had she not been stopped by her maidservant, Maria. It was now Maria who became the object of Li Tan's wrath. "[She] paid deare for it, having her left thum almost cut off."

A few days later, Wickham received a cryptic letter from William Nealson in which his friend confessed to some extremely exciting news. The letter was written in riddles, puns, and code in order to conceal the sensitive information it contained. "For the exposition of this riddle," wrote Nealson, "construe thus: all that is not cuckolds that wear hornes." It continued in a similar fashion for almost half a page, giving tantalizing clues as to its meaning. "Read this reversed," it instructed, "*ad dextro ad sinistro*: OIGNI-TAM." Then, assuming that Wickham had solved the riddle, it ended: "What, man! What is the matter? Methinkes you make crosses, for never muse at the matter, it is true." The news was indeed exciting: Nealson had slept with Cocks's mistress, Matinga. The exuberant tone of the letter reveals his delight, but he also knew that Cocks would be distraught if he discovered Matinga's infidelity. "Be not a blabb of your toung," he wrote to Wickham. "Whatsoever I write you of hence-forward, condemne ether to flux [sea] or the fire." Happily, Wickham did not follow his friend's advice; Nealson's confession can still be read in the British Library.

Cocks, too, had been sowing his oats. Disappointed by Matinga's alleged frigidity, he took steps to find himself a more active bed companion. "I bought a wench yesterday," he wrote to Wickham. "She is but twelve yeares old, oversmall yet for trade, but yow would littell thinke that I have another forthcominge that is more lapedable [fuckable]." In an unconscious echo of Nealson, he added, "you must be no blab of your tongue," although he was sure that Wickham would convey his secret to the others and probably found the idea rather pleasing. Wickham was indeed impressed that the aging Cocks was still interested in sex and warned that he should take care not to impregnate the young girl: "You old chipps are most dangerous fuell [when] standing near such tinder boxes."

The other men would have done well to heed this advice, for it was not long before they discovered that their concubines had fallen pregnant. Eaton's woman bore him two children in succession—named William and Helena—while Sayers's mistress, Maria, gave birth to a daughter. Nealson also had a "girle," and Adams, too, found himself with an ever-growing family. He had already sired two children, Joseph and Susanna, who were living with their mother in Hemi. Now he learned that he was to be the father of another child—the product of his long and lonely months in Hirado. Unlike the other men, he was embarrassed by the birth and never mentioned it in his letters.

Cocks grew increasingly optimistic about trade as spring gave way to summer. Wickham had managed to sell his stockpile of lead, and prospects were looking good for Eaton's factory in Osaka. Tempest Peacock and Walter Carwarden had set sail for Cochinchina and had high hopes of success, while young Edmund Sayers was attempting trade in Tsushima. Cocks harbored grandiose dreams of expanding his trade empire into inland Korea, even though initial reports were not encouraging. He was told

Richard Cocks and his men enjoyed the company of Japanese prostitutes (above, note the décolleté kimono). They also had long-term mistresses, and swapped partners on several occasions.

that Korea's biggest cities were surrounded by "mighty boggs, so that no man can travel on horseback." The only way to reach them was to use amphibious "waggons or carts," which used sails to cross the waterlogged land.

Throughout the spring of 1614, William Adams had been helping the men embark on their adventures. Now that they had all left Hirado, he was keen to set off on his own intended voyage to Siam. When news of this reached Edo, Wickham begged to be allowed to join the expedition. This was not because of any desire to spend more time in Adams's company, but because he saw the voyage as an excellent opportunity to dabble in private trade. "Honest" Mr. Cocks failed to grasp Wickham's ulterior motive and willingly gave his consent. The factory in Edo was temporarily closed, and Wickham made his way back to Hirado.

It took many weeks for Adams to repair his junk, the *Sea Adventure*, and many months to hire the 120-strong Japanese crew. He also engaged two European traders—an Italian and a Castilian—who had been employed as commercial agents for the English in Nagasaki. It was November 1614 by the time the vessel finally put to sea, and the weather was on the turn. The *Sea Adventure* had scarcely left the Japanese coastline when she was battered by a ferocious electric storm. The wild seas lashed at the recent repairs, loosening timbers and pouring water into the hold. For a day and a night, the Japanese crew labored "to heave out and pumpe the water continually," but the water continued to rise. To their horror, they realized that the vessel was filling faster than they could empty her.

The attitude of their reckless English captain only increased their sense of terror. Adams appeared to be enjoying their predicament, urging them on in their endeavors and putting "the merchantes and other idle passengers unto such a feare that they began to murmure and mutiny." As the winds howled and the waves crashed over the deck, the crew rebelled and told Adams that they would refuse to pump unless he headed immediately for the Ryukyu Islands in the East China Sea. Adams had little option but to agree. With heavy heart, he steered the vessel toward the subtropical island of Great Ryukyu—today's Okinawa—which lay some 500 miles to the south of Hirado.

This palm-fringed island was one of the few places where Japanese and Chinese merchants could engage in direct trade. Until 1609, Ryukyu had been an independent kingdom and its prosperous rulers had lived in considerable splendor in the lacquered glory of Shuri Castle. Now, their hereditary lands had fallen under the control of the Japanese lord of Satsuma, who hoped that this remote outpost of his fiefdom would continue to be an entrepôt for foreign trade.

Adams and his storm-battered men staggered ashore after a harrowing voyage and "found marvelous great friendship." They were handed rice, hams, and turnips, and Adams was permitted to land his goods while the punctured ship was repaired. A more grateful crew might have considered themselves fortunate to have been washed up in this lush paradise with its pristine beaches and year-round tropical climate. But these unruly men complained about the stifling humidity and were irritated by the hungry mosquitoes. They demanded half their wages, spent it on liquor, then vented their anger on each other. "This day, all our officers, mariners and passengers rose up in armes to fight one with another," wrote an appalled Adams. He tried to stop the "bludshed," but Ryukyu's ruthless headman had already received news of the brawl. He plucked out the ringleader, unsheathed his sword, and hacked the unfortunate man into pieces.

The local officials now decided that they had shown enough tolerance toward these riotous men. They ordered the *Sea Adventure* to leave, ignoring Adams's pleas that he had not yet acquired "those necessaries that our junk wanteth." They also refused to engage in trade, leaving him to count his losses. The voyage had cost more than £140, money that the factory could ill afford, and had engendered much bad feeling in Ryukyu. Only one man aboard Adams's junk had managed to make money out of the disaster. Richard Wickham had discovered that ambergris—a perfumed resin—was far cheaper in Ryukyu than elsewhere in the East. He also knew that this rare commodity was highly prized in Japan, where it was used as a flavoring. Wickham seized his chance, buying a modest two pounds in weight for the Hirado factory and a staggering 260 pounds for himself. He later sold some of this to the factory at a 50 percent markup, yielding himself a massive profit. He sold another batch in secret through an agent in Nagasaki and sent a third supply to Bantam. It was almost two years before Cocks learned the extent of Wickham's double-dealings, by which time it was too late to take action.

The *Sea Adventure's* voyage had failed in almost every respect, and the fallout was to continue long after Adams's return. The

English factory's two Nagasaki agents, who had accompanied Adams to Ryukyu, found themselves in deep trouble with the town's Portuguese authorities. Accused of treachery for serving the English and of betraying their Catholic faith, they were thrown in prison, pending their execution.

Cocks wrote urgent letters to the governor of Nagasaki, demanding their freedom, but his pleas fell on deaf ears. "[He] used all meanes possible to get them releaste," wrote William Eaton, "and cannot." Humiliated by his lack of influence, Cocks begged Adams to argue his case with the shogun. Adams was happy to oblige. He informed Ieyasu of what had happened, and the shogun ordered the Portuguese to free the men immediately. "[Ieyasu] gave his command forthwith that the two men should be set at liberty," wrote a grateful Cocks, "and all their goodes restored to them." The Portuguese were furious, but there was nothing they could do. Once again, Adams had managed to humiliate them, and at the same time he had demonstrated his continuing influence over Ieyasu.

Adams scored a further triumph when he interceded with the shogun on behalf of Specx and his men. The Dutch had captured a Portuguese ship, the *San Antonio*, which was richly laden with ebony wood, gold, and conserves. She was heading for Nagasaki but, because she did not have the necessary Japanese trading license, they claimed her as a lawful prize.

Ieyasu was unsure how to respond and allowed both sides to come to court to plead their case. When he discovered that the Dutch were represented by Adams, he resolved the matter in their favor. They were allowed to keep the ship, her cargo, and her captured crew. "William Adams was a cheefe occation to move the emperour thereunto," wrote a gleeful Cocks, who was delighted to learn that Adams had taken the opportunity to remind Ieyasu of the Spanish and Portuguese kings' desire to dominate the easternmost parts of the world.

Cocks was also pleased with the sweet-potato tubers that Adams had brought back as a present from Ryukyu. These would become the first recorded potatoes ever grown in Japan and, tended by the green-thumbed Cocks, they produced a heavy crop. It was not long before he was writing in his diary about how he had taken a "dish of pottatos" to the food-loving King Foyne.

They proved to be the factory's only material benefit from the 1614 voyage to Ryukyu. Although Wickham had made a fortune from private trade, Cocks himself was left with empty pockets. But before he was able to take stock of the situation—and count his losses—the men found themselves facing a far more serious challenge. Japan was threatened by civil war, and Ieyasu was mobilizing his troops.

Ieyasu's anger was directed toward the Christians in his realm. He had hitherto shown remarkable tolerance toward both Jesuits and Franciscans, allowing them to construct churches and preach in public throughout the land. They had established religious colleges to instruct Japanese novices and had founded their own printing press to produce catechisms for recent converts. The Jesuits had benefited most from Ieyasu's benign rule: they had achieved a far greater success in Japan than in any other Eastern realm—the number of their converts was probably approaching 300,000—and their 116 missionaries served scores of churches spread right across the country. Ieyasu had even turned a blind eye to the conversion of several feudal lords and had appointed a number of Japanese Christians to senior positions in his court. Now, a series of unfortunate incidents caused him to rethink his entire strategy toward the foreign padres.

The visit of Sebastian Vizciano had sounded the first alarm bell. The Spaniard's haughty arrogance had infuriated Ieyasu, and his anger had increased when he learned that this disagreeable individual had many contacts with the Franciscans. Ieyasu punished these monks by closing some of their churches.

Shortly after, he faced a challenge from one of his own feudal lords. The lord of Arima, a Christian, bribed one of his coreligionists at court to forge a document that extended the boundaries of his fiefdom. Ieyasu was horrified that a courtier could place religious loyalty above loyalty to his own person. As a warning to other Christian officials, he had the man roasted alive. He also took action against Arima, stripping him of his fiefdom and sending him into exile.

Ieyasu soon received word of a far more serious incident, which finally persuaded him that Christianity was having a pernicious and divisive influence on Japanese society. A common criminal called Jirobioye was caught counterfeiting money and was brought before the authorities. He was condemned for his crime and, as a Christian, sentenced to be crucified. The crucifixion was attended by hundreds of fellow Christians and, when Jirobioye finally expired, the assembled crowd "kneeled downe upon their knees to commend his soule unto God." The priests then began preaching to the masses, telling them of their love for all Christians—even sinners like Jirobioye.

Ieyasu was disgusted by such behavior and was even more shocked to discover that these priests were openly teaching their flocks to obey the padres over and above their feudal lords. Such a doctrine was a threat to the orderly society of Japan, and Ieyasu decided he could no longer allow it to continue. In January 1614, he issued his famous edict against Christianity. It charged Christians with having come to his land "to disseminate an evil law [and] to overthrow true doctrine, so that they may change the government of the country." It added that "this is the germ of great disaster, and must be crushed." All foreign Christians were to leave forthwith, or face one of five punishments: branding, nose-slitting, amputation of the feet, castration, or death. The edict was also aimed at Japanese converts. They were allowed to remain in Japan, but only on the condition that they become members of one of the principal Buddhist sects. The head of each family was made personally responsible for the apostasy of his children.

The Jesuits were appalled by this dramatic downturn in their fortunes. After more than half a century in Japan, they found themselves summarily expelled by the very man who had shown the greatest tolerance toward them. Although some hoped to stay behind, "to remaine hid and disguised in Japan," they knew that this would be almost impossible because of "the extreme difficulty in finding means to keep them secret." With great reluctance, the fathers made their way to Nagasaki, their designated port of leave, hoping and praying that Ieyasu would rescind his edict.

Ieyasu's new law theoretically applied to all Christians in Japan, yet it was specifically targeted at Catholics. Adams had spent a great deal of effort explaining to the shogun the differences between the Catholic and Protestant faiths and informing him of the theological rift that had plunged Europe into turmoil and war for decades. His clarity and patience now paid handsome dividends. The English remained totally untouched by Ieyasu's wrath. The only consequence to them came when they were ordered to remove the flag of St. George from their factory because the cross was a cause of offense. They greeted the news of Ieyasu's selective tolerance with undisguised glee, yet they were not unduly surprised. Adams had long believed that Catholicism in Japan was ultimately doomed and had bragged to one Spaniard, "Your Honour will see that within three years there won't be a single padre in Japan." Wickham went so far as to claim that Ieyasu's edict was partly a result of English chicanery, boasting that "upon demand, as occasion offered, we have done the Jesuits little credit here." The Jesuit provincial Valentim Carvalho certainly believed as much. He wrote to the Pope to inform him that Adams and the others "by false accusation . . . have rendered our preachers such objects of suspicion that he [Ieyasu] fears and readily believes that they are rather spies than sowers of the Holy Faith in his kingdom."

The effect of Ieyasu's edict was dramatic and immediate. "All the houses and churches that did belong to the friars and Jesuits are pulled down and burnt," wrote William Eaton from Osaka. He added that all the Japanese converts had abjured their faith "so as now there is no more Christian Japanners in these parts." This was only partly true. Osaka's churches had indeed been demolished, but many of their worshipers were still at large. Nor had all the foreign priests made their way to Nagasaki. A number of friars, Jesuits, and Christian samurai had, in great secrecy, begun to seek refuge within the impregnable ramparts of Osaka Castle. A conflict was brewing, and Ieyasu was about to face the greatest—and most desperate—challenge to his authority.

The trouble had been long in the making. Ieyasu's triumphant victory at Sekigahara in 1600 had made him temporarily the undisputed master of Japan. His enemies had been utterly crushed, and all criticism appeared to have been silenced. But Ieyasu's victory had provided only breathing space. The young Hideyori, for whom Ieyasu had originally been appointed regent, was still ensconced in Osaka Castle, and there were many who saw him as Japan's legitimate ruler-in-waiting. As Hideyori approached adulthood, scores of disaffected nobles and dispossessed princelets began to rally to his standard.

Ieyasu's anti-Christian edict had strengthened Hideyori's hand, encouraging Christian samurai and soldier-priests to join his ranks. By the winter of 1614, it was clear to Ieyasu that he was facing a crisis that needed to be confronted head-on. He had long planned for his own son to succeed him and did not intend to let Hideyori's increasingly belligerent forces stand in the way. But the challenge posed by these malcontents was far more serious than that which Ieyasu had faced in 1600. Although he could count on the loyalty of a vast number of troops—including battle-toughened veterans of the Sekigahara campaign—his enemies had one significant advantage. They controlled the mighty Osaka Castle, which occupied a strategic position in the heart of Japan.

Osaka Castle was immense. It was built on such a monumental scale that all newly arrived foreigners were stunned by what they saw. Its outer defenses stretched for more than nine miles and were widely held to be impregnable, while the central keep was protected by two deep moats, both of which were surrounded by 120-foot walls. These, in turn, were protected by "very deep trenches . . . and many drawbridges, with gates plated with iron." Each gate was bristling with weaponry, and the ramparts were defended by fire-hurling mangonels. When Saris had examined the castle, he was astonished to discover that "the walls are at the least six or seven yards thick."

Ieyasu and Hideyori both knew that a military showdown was inevitable. They also knew that this battle would determine the future of Japan. There was so much at stake that their already massive armies were augmented by thousands of eager volunteers, who sought to improve their lots by backing the winning side. Ieyasu had some 180,000 troops at his disposal, all of whom were mustered outside the walls of Osaka. Their martial encampment made an impressive sight—an array of tents and pavilions that stretched for many miles. These hardy warriors faced a hidden enemy that was believed to number about 100,000 troops and included many of Japan's most ruthless samurai. Ieyasu's first challenge was to dislodge from Osaka Castle this formidable force— many of whom were fanatical Christians fighting for their faith. Once they had been flushed from their stronghold, he would have to defeat them in hand-to-hand combat. It was a dangerous and risk-filled strategy.

Ieyasu had acquired a great deal of weaponry and gunpowder from Adams and Eaton, and he decided to use these to announce the start of hostilities. At the end of December 1614, he ordered his most experienced gunners to train their thirteen-pound guns—the *Clove's* culverins—on one of the castle towers, in the hope that they would dislodge the masonry. They continued their bombardment for three days, as shot after shot pounded the fortifications, but they made little impact on the stonework. It quickly became apparent that the castle was indeed impregnable to weaponry and that Ieyasu's only hope of capturing the place was by siege or trickery.

He had long proved a master of cunning and now—in his hour of greatest need—he acted with consummate skill. He caused confusion inside the castle by sending conflicting signals to the defenders. One day, he played the peacemaker. The next, he renewed his warmongering. He dispatched negotiators to Hideyori's mother, who was known to favor peace, yet shortly afterward he bombarded the castle with cannonfire. He wooed

Ieyasu's troops were battle-hardened and well equipped. But they soon discovered that arquebuses (above) and even cannon were of little use against the massive battlements of Osaka Castle.

factional groups with bribery, but at the same time mined the moat. And then, to the bewilderment of the defenders, he suddenly capitulated. He sent a document to Hideyori in which he confessed to his folly at having hoped to capture Osaka Castle. Contrite, and with customary grace, he offered to pardon all the malcontents inside the castle and allow the young pretender to live wherever he wished. He assured Hideyori "that his person should be held inviolable" and sealed his document with a *kappan*, or blood-stamp—blood from his own finger—which rendered it sacred and binding.

Hideyori and his forces were utterly perplexed by the turn of events, but the elderly ruler appeared to be true to his word. Ieyasu's massive army struck camp and headed in the direction of Kyoto. Apparently, they were in headlong retreat.

There was much rejoicing inside Osaka Castle, for Hideyori's forces believed that they had won a significant victory without firing a shot. Only later did it become apparent that their celebrations had been premature. Ieyasu's retreat was a ruse—a brilliant piece of strategic deception. He had left behind a small band of troops whose orders were to fatally weaken the castle by demolishing the outer walls and filling the moat with rubble. Hideyori's forces were perplexed when they saw these men set to work, for no such measure had been stipulated in the peace agreement. Their concern turned to alarm when they saw the zeal with which the men were pulling down the defenses. Ieyasu's men tore a tremendous hole in the castle's outer fortifications and used the masonry to fill the moat. The castle was suddenly dangerously exposed.

Hideyori's lieutenants protested, but to no avail. They were curtly informed that, in the light of the treaty, there was no longer any need for the defenses to remain intact. Only now did they realize that they had fallen headlong into their adversary's trap. Alarmed, they ordered their men to repair the walls and re-excavate the moat. This was exactly what Ieyasu had hoped. He now played his trump card, declaring that Hideyori had broken an inviolable treaty. The only answer was war.

He moved against the much-weakened Osaka Castle with a troop of some 180,000 men. Hideyori was gravely concerned that the castle's broken defenses would crumble under cannonfire and had little alternative but to fight a pitched battle on open ground. His strategy was to pit a small number of crack troops against the cream of Ieyasu's army, while a much larger force attempted to smash through the rear of the shogun's ranks. Then, when the confusion was at its height, Hideyori himself would ride into battle, accompanied by his most loyal—and ruthless—household troops.

Many of the Christians in Hideyori's army knew that this was a fight to the death. If they lost the battle, they would be shown neither forgiveness nor mercy by Ieyasu. Confident of victory and throwing caution to the wind, they raised flags and banners that left Ieyasu in no doubt as to their faith. "Six great banners bore as devices, together with the Holy Cross, the images of the Saviour and of St James—the patron saint of Spain—while some of them even had as a legend, 'The Great Protector of Spain.' " These flags and standards were unfurled outside the castle walls, providing a colorful and defiant backdrop to the gray stone of Osaka's ramparts. More and more banners appeared, until the ranks of the defenders were awash with Christian symbols. One observer wrote that "there were so many crosses, *Jesus* and *Santiagos* on the flags, tents and other martial insignia . . . that this must needs have made Ieyasu sick to his stomach."

The two mighty armies squared up for battle on the plains outside Osaka. The hostilities began on June 3, 1615, and Hideyori's forces scored an early success. Ieyasu's right flank was rapidly dismembered by rebel gunners, while a series of daring strikes at the center brought Hideyori's troops within striking distance of Ieyasu's bodyguards. By noon, it seemed as if Hideyori had a very real chance of victory. But the slow war of attrition was to prove his undoing. By early afternoon, Ieyasu's most highly trained troops had launched a blistering counterattack and had driven the rebel army back into the castle. Hideyori feared that the battle was now lost; his only wish was to be cut down in action. In a moving address to his most loyal lieutenants, he said, "Death is what I have been ready to meet for long." But his captains urged him to defend the castle, and their fighting spirit gave Hideyori renewed confidence. A fierce sword battle ensued, in which thousands of samurai clashed in and around the castle ramparts. As Ieyasu's warriors slowly edged their way toward the inner citadel, a traitor in Hideyori's ranks set fire to the castle kitchen. The strong wind fanned the flames, and within minutes much of the castle was ablaze. Ieyasu's foot soldiers fought on through the conflagration, capturing walls and gates and forcing their way into the innermost enceinte. Hideyori and his officers now realized that this really was the end. Reaching for their *wakizashi*—their razor-sharp daggers—they plunged them into their stomachs and ritually disemboweled themselves. Osaka had fallen and Ieyasu was triumphant.

It was his most stunning victory. Hideyori's forces were annihilated and all opposition to Ieyasu was wiped out. More than 100,000 corpses lay on the field of battle and were so heaped up in the river that they formed a dike that could be crossed dry-shod. Ieyasu's triumph was to change the course of Japanese history. He was now the undisputed master of Japan, and members of his family would fill the office of shogun until 1868.

The fall of Osaka dealt a particularly crushing blow to the Jesuits, who had so closely allied themselves with the vanquished Hideyori. They and their Japanese converts had been quite unequivocal about their support for the rebel forces and had fought—banners flying—until the bloody end. In doing so, they had infuriated the attacking army and earned themselves the enduring wrath of both Ieyasu and his successors.

Cocks heard rumors of Ieyasu's victory on the day after the battle, but no one in Hirado could furnish him with any details.

Ieyasu's crack troops fought their way into the heart of Osaka Castle. At the climax of the battle, a traitor set fire to the kitchens (above). To avoid capture, the vanquished defenders ritually disemboweled themselves.

He asked newly arrived travelers for information, hoping that "amongst many lies, something may proceed from truth." He did not have to wait long to learn of Ieyasu's triumph. Shortly after dinner on June 7, 1615, a weary and disheveled "Franciskan friar" turned up at the English factory and begged for mercy. His name was Father Appolonario, and he told the men "that he was in the fortres of Osaka when it was taken, and yet had the good hap to escape." He had lost everything in the battle and claimed to have "brought nothing away with him but the clothes on his back." He also brought a gripping account of Hideyori's defeat, informing the English that "the action was so sudden; and that he marvelled that a force of above 120,000 men . . . should be so soon overthrowne." He begged Cocks for food, telling him that he had endured "much misery" over the previous weeks. Cocks—

notwithstanding his dislike of Catholics—took pity on the man and gave him some silver plate to help him reach Nagasaki.

Ieyasu's victory was conclusive, but Cocks was concerned by reports of continuing unrest. Trade had proved hard enough in times of peace—a civil war would make it almost impossible. Cocks was also troubled by a souring of relations between himself and Adams. Their dispute began when Adams's Japanese friend Yasuemon was abused by one of the English factory's interpreters, the quarrelsome John Gorezano. The ensuing argument quickly developed into a crisis. Yasuemon was incensed by the interpreter's impertinent behavior and ordered him to leave Hirado. He also told Cocks that "if I sent him [Gorezano] not away . . . [he] would kill [Gorezano] as he went in the street."

Cocks was extremely annoyed, curtly informing Yasuemon that all the factory's employees were under the protection of the shogun and that no one had the right to "meddel with me, nor no servant in my howse." He hoped that this would be the end of the matter and was extremely surprised to learn that Adams had leaped to the defense of his old friend. Not only was Adams in full agreement with Yasuemon, but he also declared that Gorezano's continual presence was causing immense damage to the reputation of the English.

Cocks exploded with rage, for he felt that his authority was being deliberately undermined. He recorded in his diary that Adams "esteemeth him [Yasuemon] more than all our English nation . . . [and] would pawn his life and soule for his honesty." When he learned that the Dutch had also sided with Adams, Cocks began muttering about treachery. "I cannot chuse but note it downe," he wrote, "that both I myselfe, and all the rest of our nation, do see that he (I meane Mr William Adams) is much more frend to the Dutch than to the Englishmen, which are his owne countrymen."

It was to be another fourteen months before Cocks finally conceded that he had been wrong about Adams and that Gorezano was indeed a liability. He admitted that "it is this fellow's foolish tricks which hath gotten him many enemies, and put me to much trouble to save his life."

Cocks was still smarting when, at the end of August 1615, he was brought the welcome news that "[a] ship was at an ancor three or four leagues from Hirado, and that the ship's name was called the *Hosiander*." Almost twenty-one months after Saris's departure, an English vessel had arrived in Japan. At long last, the factory would receive the supplies that it so desperately needed.

The Englishmen in Hirado greeted the *Hosiander* with a blitz of cannonfire. Assuming that she had sailed from England and would bring news from their loved ones, they gave her captain, Ralph Coppindale, a triumphant welcome. However, they soon discovered that their celebrations had been premature. The *Hosiander* had actually come from Bantam and was laden with a mishmash of junk that included wax, pepper, and scissors. Cocks's heart sank as he watched the goods being transferred to the warehouse. The calicoes were stained and rotten, and the wax was "so bad that no man will look at it." Richard Wickham took one glance at the cargo and recommended sending it straight back to Bantam with the caustic message that the traders there "hath bin mistaken in sending chaulke for cheese."

The ship's cargo was not the only cause for grievance. The men had been eagerly awaiting an influx of new company, but quickly found that the *Hosiander*'s crew were disagreeable troublemakers. "For truly," wrote Cocks, "I never saw a more forward and bad lewd company than most of them." Their ringleader was Henry Dorrington, a "drunken, unruly, mutenouse fellow" who accepted no authority but his own. He proudly declared that he intended to go drinking and a-whoring whenever he chose. "This Dorrington," wrote an exasperated Cocks, "hath said in open company . . . that neither captain, master, nor no other had authority to punish men with ducking or whipping." Such a statement was tantamount to mutiny and was punishable by death, and Ieyasu himself had given Cocks the right to execute any Englishman in Japan. Yet Cocks hesitated to exert his authority, fearing that it would provoke a full-scale riot. Captain Coppindale was even less capable of disciplining his men. A "peacable and quiet, honest man," he was so depressed by the unruly antics of his crew that he shut himself away inside the English factory.

Dorrington's lead soon caused a complete breakdown of discipline, and the sea dogs began fighting each other in the streets. John Shepherd, one of the common mariners, attacked the factory's cook, while John Japan, the interpreter, took advantage of the chaos "to steale and filch." Tensions heightened when William Nealson and Morris Jones, the ship's surgeon, fell to blows and "Mr Nealson drew his dagger on the surgion." He stabbed Jones in the hand and tried for his heart, but was pulled away just in time.

Captain Coppindale fell into even deeper despair when he discovered that the careening of his ship was taking much longer than expected. Two of the *Hosiander's* carpenters had died, and unusually high tides had caused complications. The weather, too, was hindering the work. There was an icy blast blowing from the north, which had frozen the ropes and sails. It numbed the men's hands and they shivered as they attempted to carry out the delicate work. "This morning [was] very cold weather," recorded Cocks on January 3, 1616, "being a greate snowe; the greatest I saw since our arivall in Japan." Rowland Thomas, the *Hosiander's* purser, was also alarmed at the plummeting temperature. Snow fell continuously for four days, blocking Hirado's streets with huge drifts and filtering into the drafty belowdecks of the *Hosiander*. Thomas wrote that it was so cold that neither a glowing fire nor a "waistcoat and a jerkin under a cloth gowne" could stop him from shivering. As he watched the relentless fall of snowflakes, he dreamed of being tucked up in two pairs of stockings, "a cloth paire upon an worsted."

A brief thaw allowed the crew to finish their work on the ship, replacing planking in readiness for her departure. Cocks was so desperate to be rid of these troublesome men that he helped them prepare their cargo and supplies. The *Hosiander* had arrived with goods valued at £2,150—much of it unsalable—and was returning with a paltry collection of Japanese swords and bowls. She was also taking some £550 of silver, which had been generated by the sale of broadcloth and weaponry. Cocks was reluctant to part with this money, for it represented the greater part of the factory's assets, but he realized the necessity of proving to the London merchants that he and his band had begun to generate an income.

Before the ship's departure, a general council was called to review trade with Japan. The men in Hirado were cautiously optimistic, even though the factory's account books made for gloomy reading. Adams had convinced them that luxury goods from Indo-China could reap rich dividends in Japan, and Cocks and his team were expecting the imminent return of Tempest Peacock and Walter Carwarden. They also had high hopes of forging trade links with the mandarins of Ming dynasty China. Such an ambitious project would be impossible without increased manpower, and Captain Coppindale was asked to loan three of his crew to serve the factory. This was a high-risk strategy, for Cocks would have more mouths to feed. But they decided to take the gamble. Their only fear was that they had been abandoned to their fate by Sir Thomas Smythe and his fellow merchants, whose only interest—and motivation—was in returning a healthy profit on their investments.

Chapter 10

A QUESTION OF LANGUAGE

SIR THOMAS SMYTHE had long been accustomed to receiving uninvited guests at his
London home. Philpot Lane was frequented by
merchants, weather-beaten mariners, and experts
in exploration—all of whom sought the good offices and influence of the governor of the East India Company. Such guests
were usually received with warmth and affection, but on the
morning of April 13, 1615, Smythe had found himself greeting
a less than welcome visitor. Mary Adams, estranged wife of
William, was so critically short of money that she had tramped all
the way from Limehouse with her begging bowl.

Mary's expenses had increased dramatically in recent years.
Her paltry savings had long ago dried up, and she no longer had
enough money to support her daughter, Deliverance, who was by
now at least seventeen years of age. Mrs. Adams was in desperate
need of cash for food and clothing, and pleaded with Sir Thomas
to be "relieved with £30 of her said husband's wages." She was

perfectly entitled to such a sum; indeed, Adams himself had asked that Mary be remunerated with money that was owed to him by the company and had "promised satisfaction . . . at Japan, or elsewhere, or to be defaulted out of his salary." But Smythe, always reluctant to part with his precious stockpile of silver, chose to prevaricate.

His cold-hearted action was endorsed by the merchants of the company, who advised him to delay and dissemble, "and see if £20 would give her content for the present, and £10 this time 12 monneth." However, Mrs. Adams refused to be browbeaten, and her persistence won the day. Whether or not she received the entire sum in one payment is not altogether clear, but she was certainly given part of the money. The uncharitable attitude of the directors did little to dampen her feisty spirit—indeed, it encouraged her to press her claims. She returned to the company headquarters on several future occasions to collect additional sums that she considered her due.

Mary Adams's unwelcome visit was soon followed by rather more alarming news that had filtered back from the East. Smythe's fearless captains had braved monsoons and typhoons in their quest for riches, and the company's trading tentacles now stretched into distant and little-known seas, with remote outposts on swampy tropical islands and coral atolls in the fragrant "spiceries." In these backwaters of the East, small bands of Englishmen found themselves rubbing shoulders with swaggering chieftains, tribal headhunters, and oriental princelets.

Many of these adventurers were living in such isolation that their behavior could not be checked by the merchants of the East India Company. The sober-minded directors assembled regularly at Smythe's house and listened with dismay to rumors of brawls, bawdiness, and rambunctious whoring. Some of the most shocking stories came from Hirado, where tales of Cocks's bacchanalian parties, enlivened by dancing damsels, chilled the blood of these puritanical merchants. But there was little they could do to rectify

*Sir Thomas Smythe and his fellow merchants were horrified
by rumors of Richard Cocks's drunken parties, enlivened by
"players" (above) and dancing damsels. "It is a misery to know that
men of such antique years should be so miserably given over to
voluptuousness," wrote one.*

this parlous state of affairs. Their few attempts to impose discipline from afar were greeted with derision and scorn by their servants in the East.

Smythe and his men were also concerned by the lack of account books from the remoter factories. Ships returned to England with pepper and spices, but it was anyone's guess as to how much of the merchants' silver had been siphoned off into the pockets of their corrupt and disreputable factors.

Sir Thomas undertook a thorough review of the Eastern trade and quickly realized that many of the problems stemmed from a lack of regulation. He proposed a complete overhaul of company management, which included the establishment of regional depots, the restoration of discipline, and the prompt dispatch of a governor-general to the East Indies. This latter idea was copied from the Dutch, whose combative approach to trade had enabled them to seize control of numerous islands and atolls in the Spice Islands.

The London merchants' most urgent task was to decide whom to appoint as their man in the East. The veteran sea captain Thomas Best proposed himself for the job, arguing that he was the only person in London who had the necessary "countenance and sufficiency." But Best infuriated the merchants by demanding a large gratuity for his past services to the company, and Smythe wisely declined his offer. Instead, he plumped for William Keeling, an altogether more flamboyant commander who had successfully undertaken two previous voyages to the Indies.

Keeling was quite unlike any of his fellow sea captains. Cultivated and refined, he enjoyed his creature comforts and saw no reason why a lengthy voyage to the East should require hunger or hardship. He had a passion for amateur theatricals—he was particularly fond of Shakespearean tragedy—and found them a useful way of relieving the tedium of the long passage. On his 1607 expedition, he had encouraged his men to perform *Hamlet* on the tropical shores of West Africa. "We gave," he recorded proudly, "the tragedie of Hamlett." It had proved a triumphant success, and soon afterward his crew was busily rehearsing *Richard II*.

When Keeling came to write his ship's log, he eschewed the custom of recording depth soundings and wind directions in favor of a more entertaining style. "Let no man expect an exact reckoning of the shipp's traverse," he wrote, ". . . nor let any think to find herein situations of countries." Instead, he had decided to relate "only . . . the accidents hapning among his fleete." When Keeling reached for his quill, it was to regale his readers with tales of furious storms, merry banquets, and carousing with native chieftains.

With his proven track record in the Indies, Keeling was offered the position of "commander of the English throughout all India." Yet there was some disquiet about his mercurial character and it was not long before the directors found themselves in dispute over a most unusual and unexpected affair. Keeling, it transpired, was so deeply in love with his wife that he announced his intention of taking her with him to the East. The directors were taken aback by such an unorthodox proposition, for it was an unwritten rule that women never sailed with their husbands. Indeed, they had already discussed "how inconvenient and unfitting it is for such women to go among so many unrulie sailors in a shipp." Keeling disagreed and petitioned the court for permission to travel with his beloved Anna.

His request threw the straitlaced directors into a quandary. A few approved wholeheartedly, arguing that it would be "very fitting in regarde of the quiet of his minde and good of his soule." They warned that it was unnatural to separate a married couple for so long and added that "a curse befalleth those that keepe a man and wife asunder." Others disagreed and attacked the proposal with vehemence. They said that Anna, who was pregnant, was "a weake woman and unfitte for travaile." They also claimed that she would stop Keeling from visiting the farthest-flung factories and that her presence would distract him from his business in the East.

Keeling was most unhappy when he was told this and informed the directors that having his wife on board would give "better blessinge in his labors." He also appealed to their puritanical natures, suggesting that sharing his cabin with Anna would free his mind "from sundry corrupt thoughts." It was a clever argument. The directors had been horrified by Saris's collection of pornography and were no less happy to learn that their factors in

Japan were dallying with local women. Some of them now championed Keeling's cause, asserting that factors were less likely to sleep with prostitutes if they traveled with their spouses. But when the issue was put to the vote, their petition was rejected.

Keeling neither appealed nor complained. Indeed, he dropped his request so promptly that it was rumored he intended to smuggle Mrs. Keeling aboard ship shortly before his departure. The directors' suspicions were confirmed when, in February 1615, a disguised Mrs. Keeling joined her husband aboard the *Red Dragon*. They were even more alarmed when they learned that she had been in secret negotiations to take a midwife with her. Loath to remove her forcibly from the ship, the directors instead threatened to discharge Keeling unless he capitulated. Keeling had no option but to accede to their demand, but he was extremely unhappy and wrote a stern letter to the directors reminding them that "there are very fewe [men] . . . who are able, notwithstandinge their best endevors, to live without the companie of women."

Keeling's four-strong flotilla set sail in the spring of 1615 and was given a more extravagant farewell than usual. This was partly because the fleet was carrying Sir Thomas Roe, England's first ambassador to India, who was being sent to the subcontinent to negotiate trading rights with the Mogul emperor. But it was also because Keeling's mission was one of critical importance. At stake was the future of England's trade with the East.

The outward voyage proved most agreeable, and the crews were given plenty of diversions to keep them merry. Keeling used rowing boats to keep in touch with his other captains and was forever sending them gifts of food and trinkets. He paid particular attention to Sir Thomas, lavishing presents and victuals on him. On one occasion, he sent Roe a sheep (which had been kept alive on the *Red Dragon*) along with one hundred "fresh" Weymouth oysters and some silk strings for his viol. A few days later, Keeling himself received a present—a set of six Italian madrigals—which he enjoyed enormously.

The fleet sailed first to India, in order to land Sir Thomas Roe, then headed for Bantam. Despite the men's healthy diet, they began to die as the fleet approached the coastline of Java. Some were ill with dysentery; others had scurvy; while a few were stricken with the calenture—a strange, mind-altering sickness in which the victim imagined the sea to be a lush green field into which he was impelled to leap.

Keeling announced his imminent arrival in Bantam with a blast of cannonfire, which quickly attracted the attention of John Jourdain, the factory president. Jourdain poured out a woeful tale of disease and bankruptcy. The corrupted air and malarial marshes had claimed the lives of many of his men, while trade had almost ground to a halt. The factory was no longer solvent, and those factors still alive had formed themselves into factions that were constantly at each other's throats. But there was another, far more alarming crisis in the making—one that threatened every English outpost in the East, including Japan. The Dutch, who had hitherto limited their attacks to the Portuguese and Spanish, had now started to assault their erstwhile colleagues. This unwelcome development was as extraordinary as it was unexpected. The English and Dutch were old allies, and the two nations regularly manned each other's ships. They shared the same religion and were united in their hatred of their Catholic rivals. Although there had always been tensions between rival traders in the East, these had escalated dramatically in recent months, and it now seemed as if the Dutch were bent on pursuing a far more hawkish policy.

They had already ejected English factors from the clove-covered island of Amboyna. Now they seemed intent on wresting control of the remote Banda Islands in order to deprive England of access to the fabulously valuable nutmeg. It was only a question of time before they would apply their aggressive policy to Japan, where Cocks and his men were already battling against insolvency.

Jourdain was particularly alarmed by the fact that violence had spilled over into the streets of Bantam. Several of his men had been set upon by Dutch mariners, while fights and brutal attacks were becoming commonplace. One factor, Richard Hunt, was strolling along one of Bantam's narrow alleys when he found his path blocked by two Dutchmen. They punched him to the ground and then called to twenty of their friends to assist in beating him black and blue. "[They] beate him very sore, and hailed him through the dirt by the haire of the head to their own howse, and set him in the bolts at their gate in the hott sunne, without hat." They said that the purpose of their attack was to demonstrate to the native Javanese that the Dutch were stronger than the English.

A band of headstrong Englishmen vowed to have their revenge, but Jourdain chose a wiser course of action, appealing to the local *pangeran*, or governor. The Dutch had no wish to anger the governor and promptly released Hunt, but they saw fit to write an insulting letter to Jourdain. The English chief factor was so incensed that he vowed to inflict reprisals on them, but was thwarted by Keeling's unexpected arrival.

Keeling soon proved himself to be altogether more accommodating than Jourdain. When he heard about the behavior of the Dutch, he brushed it aside and said he was "willing to wincke at it." This was probably because he had learned of the imminent arrival of the intrepid Dutch adventurer Joris van Spilbergen, who was midway through his circumnavigation of the globe. Keeling was anxious to chat with Spilbergen about his adventures and had no wish to antagonize the Dutch. Far from criticizing their unruly men, he welcomed Spilbergen to Bantam with a blast of cannonfire.

Spilbergen was enchanted at being received with such honor and dressed in his finery to meet the English captain. "He came like a generall," wrote Keeling, "in a Japan[ese] boate, finely built, all her ports full of silke streamers." How this boat came to be in Bantam is unclear, but it made for an impressive sight. It was rowed by no fewer than forty Japanese oarsmen, "all well clad and duly armed," and as Spilbergen approached the *Red Dragon*, the thick tropical air was filled with the "noise of trumpetts and other musique."

The Dutch captain proved a most agreeable guest. He told Keeling that he had a deep affection for the English, and Keeling responded by showering Spilbergen with flattery. He listened attentively to the Dutch captain's account of his adventures off the coast of Chile, where he had managed to sink three Spanish galleons, and was so entranced with Spilbergen's tales that he invited him on board on several other occasions, preparing lavish dinners in his honor.

Jourdain was utterly perplexed by Keeling's behavior, particularly since the attacks on his men had intensified. Several English sailors were set upon by sword-wielding Dutchmen in a Bantam hostelry, while three other Englishmen were slashed and stabbed "in such a manner as that all men had thought they had beene slaine." Their wounds were washed and dressed, but they were "so sore wounded that they will never be their owne men againe." The Dutch had also been doing everything in their power to turn the local chieftains against the English, informing them that Jourdain's men came from "a poore and base nation, [and were] deflowrers of women [and] great theeves and drunckards."

Keeling was still prepared to "wincke" at this, but realized that his dinner invitations to the Dutch were drawing considerable criticism. When he was invited to a banquet at the Dutch factory, the English commander had no option but to decline. He expressed his regret that circumstances prevented his acceptance, informing Spilbergen that he was "kept from their howse by the extreame wronges done our nation."

With his socializing at an end, Keeling now turned his attentions to finding a solution to the crisis in which the English factory found itself. He managed to procure a lading of pepper for the aptly named *Peppercorn* and secured a license from the local governor to fortify the English factory against further Dutch attacks. But he was unsure how to save the place from financial ruin. In a damning report that he prepared for the London directors, he placed the blame squarely on their own shoulders. "God send some supplies speedie," he wrote, "or else your business lies a-bleeding in all these parts for want of your foresight." He added that "all your servants [are] utterlie disheartened for lacke of foundation to endeavour the building your proffitt."

Keeling's original instructions had been to explore the extent of the crisis throughout the East. He was to "pass from port to port" in order to meet the factors and hear their grievances. He had already read letters from factors serving elsewhere in the Indies and had listened to tales of woe from men recently returned from some of the remoter outposts. The factory at Hirado was the farthest from Bantam and seemed to be in a similarly parlous state. Indeed, Keeling had already concluded that there was "no likelihood of money from Japan," at least in the short term. Yet there was a glimmer of hope. Although Cocks and his men minced no words when they wrote about their increasingly desperate situation, they continued to stress the potential riches of their new home. Wickham was most ebullient, claiming that Hirado would one day be able to export "so greate quantities of silver" that it could "stuffe all the factories betweane this and Bantam." He added that every factory in the East could "wholly depend upon this factory" and that "there never should be any more need to send any more money out of England."

Keeling fully intended to see for himself. He planned to visit each of the farthest-flung factories and offer advice on how best to proceed. But no sooner had he decided on this course of action than he received a most unexpected, although wholly welcome, piece of news. The captain of the newly arrived *Swan* handed him a letter from the London directors in which he was given "licence for my retourne for England." For reasons that remain obscure— and which Keeling himself never quite understood—they had decided to call off his mission to the East. Keeling could scarcely believe his good fortune and sank to his knees in prayer: "Thy mercy therein, O Lord, let me never forgett."

His little fleet weighed anchor in October 1616, and Keeling set sail for England in the hope of being reunited with his dear wife. It was an atrocious voyage, for the ships were leaking and supplies running low. The *Expedition* was overrun by rats, which multiplied at an alarming rate in the dingy hold of the ship. "It is almost incredible," wrote one, "the noisomness of that vermin, who have been ready to eate us living." They nibbled at the mariners in their sleep, and men who died in the night "had their toes eate quite off, and other parts of their bodies gnawen."

As the ships neared London, Keeling's thoughts turned to his wife. As he dropped anchor close to the South Downs, he saw the sight that he had dreamed of for so long. There was a small figure waving at his vessel—it was his beloved Anna. Whether or not she was holding a baby is not, alas, recorded.

William Keeling's hasty departure from Bantam was a bitter blow for England's trading prospects with the East. It also meant that the condition of the poorest and most desperate trading posts went unreported. Keeling had offered the best chance of replenishing the empty coffers of the Hirado factory. Now Cocks and his men were once again left to fend for themselves.

The autumn and winter of 1615 had proved a particularly testing time, for William Adams had been absent on a voyage to court for many months. He claimed to have received a personal summons from Ieyasu, but Cocks had his doubts. Cocks's judgment was clouded by the fear of being left alone in Hirado and— once again—he accused Adams of double-dealing and treachery. "I suspect it was a plot laid . . . by Captain Adams himselfe and the Dutch," he confessed to his diary, ". . . and, truly, I esteem he loveth them much more than us that are his owne nation." But

Adams's "plot" was no such thing. He had indeed been called to court by the shogun, who had turned to his English adviser when he learned that a Spanish ship had arrived in Japan. She was carrying three ambassadors—Franciscan monks—whose visit contravened his anti-Christian edict. Ieyasu refused to see them and gave Adams the pleasure of expelling them from his realm. "The emperour would neither receive the presents nor yet speake with them," wrote a contrite Cocks, "but sent captain Adams to tell them they should avoid out of his dominions."

Adams returned to Hirado at the end of November 1615, but his visit was extremely brief. Less than ten days after being welcomed back, he set sail on an eight-month voyage to Siam to procure a cargo of sappanwood. Cocks reluctantly let him go. He knew that Adams was the only member of the factory with the skill to pilot a ship across the East China Sea, but his absence meant that the English factory was once again left without its most important member. It also meant that Cocks would have no one to turn to for help in moments of crisis.

The freezing weather only added to the men's woes. Snow had fallen with wearisome monotony, and the temperature remained far below zero for many weeks. Icicles hung from the eaves of the factory buildings, and deep drifts blocked the paved streets of Hirado. All of the men complained of the chill, for the factory's wood-fired stove gave out very little heat. They hoped that the new year would bring ships, supplies, and prosperity.

On New Year's Eve 1615, Cocks's barber had turned up at the factory with a basketful of oranges. He had brought them so that the men could adorn the entrance to their living quarters, for it was an ancient custom "to decorate the front door with certain kinds of tree, which signify good fortune and longevity, . . . and also with bitter oranges." As dusk fell over Hirado, the townsfolk thronged the streets and prepared to celebrate long into the night. Cocks and his men were invited to raucous parties and religious feasts and they spent many hours enjoying the good-humored festivities. "All make merry," wrote Padre João Rodrigues, "and hold certain ceremonies with lighted lamps in honour of the god or spirit of the hearth, and other spirits and lares." Hirado's inhabitants also exchanged gifts—a custom to which Cocks and company found themselves unwilling participants. Their womenfolk expected costly presents, and the men had little option but to oblige. Cocks bought Matinga bundles of satin and taffeta and provided her servants with a few reels of Indian cloth.

The chill came to an end in January and the snow and ice rapidly melted. Cocks hoped that spring would bring the arrival of a vessel from England and, aware of the damage that a long sea voyage could cause, he began to buy timber planking for repairs. When he learned that there was a large supply of wood for sale in Akuno-ura, a small coastal village to the south of Hirado, he dispatched William Eaton with orders to buy up as much as possible.

Eaton set off immediately, but when he arrived at the timber yard he found himself hampered by local merchants. He quickly lost his temper and so infuriated one of the timber workers that he hit Eaton with his staff. Eaton responded vigorously, smashing the man over the head with his wooden stick. "[I] broake a little parte of his head," he admitted, "which fett[ched] blood."

The man staggered for a moment as he reeled from the blow, then recovered his balance. Stunned by the attack and intent on revenge, he lifted his club and prepared to strike, at which point Eaton unsheathed his sword and dagger. The two men now began to tussle with their weapons, each intent on incapacitating the other. "With the force of the blowes," wrote Eaton, "both he and myselfe fell into the water." This did nothing to dampen their enthusiasm for the fight, and the two men thrashed and flailed in the surf. When Eaton's interpreter realized that his master was in peril, he rushed to his aid, plunging into the water and joining the attack. He grabbed the Japanese assailant and "strooke him upon the head with a staff he had in his hand." Eaton now had the advantage, and it was only a matter of time before he delivered the fatal blow. He seized his chance when his opponent slipped in the soft sand and fell backward into the water. Eaton reached for his dagger and plunged it into the man's body. It pierced his vital organs and within seconds the man was dead.

Eaton suddenly found himself under arrest. The fight had been witnessed by dozens of villagers, who seized him and held him prisoner while the matter was referred to the local lord. When news of the affray reached Hirado, Nealson rushed to Akuno-ura in order to help his friend, but the villagers refused to listen to his appeals. Eaton's problems were compounded by the fact that William Adams was not available to help him gain his freedom. He was en route to Siam, and Eaton grew so terrified about his fate that he quite lost his appetite. "I have scarse eaten a bit of meate for very grief," he wrote. Imprisoned and in danger, he fell into deep despair.

But there was a ray of hope. The villagers had killed Eaton's interpreter, which had helped to assuage their fury, while Cocks had written to the local lord demanding clemency. He informed his lordship that under the terms of the English privileges granted by Ieyasu, he alone had jurisdiction over the English in Japan. He added that the lord would be breaking the shogun's command if he put Eaton to death. Cocks's letter secured Eaton's release. The lord declared that he was untroubled by the death of one of his subjects and had no wish to contradict Ieyasu's orders. Eaton was freed after a frightening fortnight in prison.

Cocks soon found himself in receipt of further good news. Two ships had been sighted off the Hirado coastline, and they proved to be the *Thomas* from Bantam and the *Advice* from London. The second vessel had been sent on the advice of Captain Saris—along with the *Attendant*, which had remained in the East Indies—and the men had high hopes that the cargo would be perfect for the Japanese market.

But they were quickly disappointed when they broke open the

crates. There were no silks, the broadcloth was the wrong color, and the rest of the cargo was little more than bric-a-brac. As Cocks rummaged through the rubbish, he was most surprised to discover a "lascivious" print of Venus and Adonis, and another of "Venus sleeping with two satyrs." The merchants, it seemed, had forgotten their earlier outrage at Saris's pornographic collection.

Cocks despaired as he unpacked crate after crate of jetsam. Stunned at the choice of cargo, he wrote a letter to London in which he informed the merchants that they needed to send "better commodities than yet we have had out of England." Wickham was rather less diplomatic. He was disgusted by the cargo and wrote that "[even] if we were learned alchimists, we could not so soone turne mettals into silver." The men were still wondering how to dispose of yet another supply of unwanted goods when they were interrupted by unexpected and unwelcome news from the court in Shizuoka. Ieyasu was ill, and no one knew if he would recover.

His sickness had begun after one of his customary hawking tours. He had celebrated his return with a lavish banquet, dining on freshly caught sea bream cooked in sesame oil. But the meal had disagreed with him and he found himself seized with violent cramps. The pain was temporarily allayed by medicine, but it was not long before the cramps returned and he grew weak from the pain. His friends were extremely concerned and—fearing the worst—decided to honor him with the title of *dajo-daijan*, or Minister-President, "which," wrote Cocks, "is as the names of Caesar or Augustus amongst the emperors of Rome."

Ieyasu was by now desperately ill, suffering from what was probably stomach cancer, but he struggled from his sickbed in order to accept the congratulations of his fawning retainers. It was clear to all that the end was near. In the middle of July, Ieyasu handed his sword to a friend, asking him to test it on a convicted criminal and report back on the quality of the blade. The friend performed this grisly task with relish and informed Ieyasu that it was as sharp as it had ever been. "With this sword," said Ieyasu, "I will guard and protect my descendants for many ages."

He could no longer eat solid food and managed only a few sips of hot water. On July 17, 1616, he pulled himself upright, wrote two short verses, then breathed his last. He had, in the words of the official chronicle, "passed to another world." Cocks and his men had lost their most powerful ally.

So, too, had William Adams. For more than sixteen years he had been totally dependent upon Ieyasu, who had granted him his title, his estate, and his unrivaled position at court. The shogun had also saved Adams from almost certain death back in 1600, by refusing to allow the Jesuits to crucify him. He had even come to treat him as an oracle—a window on the outside world—and had frequently sought his advice on how to deal with the Catholic proselytizers. Adams was only too aware that he owed everything to Ieyasu and must have been deeply concerned when—on his return from Siam—he learned of his death. His letters written in the immediate aftermath have been lost, but other surviving accounts reveal the deep sense of anxiety that followed the death of any great lord in Japan. It often prompted the most faithful followers to commit suicide, in order to accompany him on his journey to the land of the dead. It had long been the practice for loyal relatives to offer themselves for *junshin*—the barbaric and excruciatingly painful practice of being buried alive. But in recent years ritual disembowelment had become more commonplace. The Dutch adventurer François Caron was witness to both kinds of suicide and was so bewildered that he wrote about it at some length. "When one of the lords die," he wrote, ". . . they celebrate the parting feast upon mats and carpets . . . [and] having well eat and drank, they cut up their bellies, so that the guts and entrails burst out." Caron noted that "he that cuts himself the highest, as some do, even to the throat, is counted the bravest fellow and most esteemed."

Those who chose to be buried alive went to their deaths with steely determination. "They go with joy unto the designed place and, lying down there, suffer the foundation stones to be laid upon them which, with their weight, immediately bruise and shiver them to pieces."

There were many who expected a mass suicidal display after Ieyasu's death, but a peculiar calm fell over the city of Shizuoka. Cocks noted in his diary that just two noblemen elected to die: "they killed themselves to accompany Ieyasu in another world," he wrote. Their loyalty did not pass unrewarded, for their corpses were buried near Ieyasu's and a splendid monument was erected in their honor.

The English had not been altogether surprised to learn of Ieyasu's demise. Rumors of his sickness had been circulating for many months, and Cocks and his men had first been told of his death more than seven months before it actually occurred. They had been skeptical on that occasion, and Cocks had recorded in his diary: "I beleeve rather [it] is a fable, and given out on purpose to see how the people would take the matter." In March he had received two more warnings of Ieyasu's death, and in April he had been told that Ieyasu had fallen from his horse and been knocked unconscious "so that no man might speak with him." When he received confirmation that, on this occasion, the news was indeed true, Cocks knew that a visit to the new court was imperative. The English needed to pay their respects to Ieyasu's son, Shogun Hidetada, and—more important—they required confirmation of their trading rights.

It was fortunate that Adams returned from his voyage to Siam less than a week after Ieyasu's death. He immediately offered to escort Cocks and Eaton to court—accompanied by a small band of mariners—in order to take presents and good wishes to Hidetada. As they sailed through the Inland Sea toward Fushimi, they saw evidence of civil unrest. "We saw a dead man cast upon the shore," wrote Cocks, "whom had been murthered by some villains, yet the cuntry people let him lie, and not giveing him buriall." The men turned their heads to avoid this unpleasant sight, only to be met with one that was even more gruesome: "on the other side was a man crusefied upon a crosse for murthering a merchant's servaunt." Close by, there was a row of poles adorned with decomposing human heads. "I saw some eight or ten malefactors' heades set upon timbers by the highway," wrote Cocks.

The party rested for a few days at Osaka, before setting out on the last leg of their journey to Edo, where they intended to lodge in Adams's town house. They were given a friendly welcome by courtiers and retainers, and received gifts of sake and pigs, grapes, and bread. But scarcely had they settled into their accommodation than they found themselves in real danger. "About three a-clock in the afternowne, there happened an exceeding earthquake in this city." So wrote Cocks, who was stunned by the severity of the quake. "It was so extreame that I thought the howse would have fallen downe on our heads." His men were terrified that they would be crushed and ran out into the street "without hat or shoes, the timbers of the howse making such a noise and cracking that it was fearefull to heare."

When the earthquake subsided, a careful check of the gifts for the shogun revealed that some of them had been irreparably damaged on the journey, while others had disappeared completely. To the superstitious English, these two disasters presaged ill for their visit and they began to wonder whether their privileges would be confirmed after all.

The big day came on the first of September, when Adams and the others were asked to present themselves at the shogun's palace. Work had begun on this vast labyrinth some ten years earlier, when Ieyasu had made the city his official courtly capital. He had hired more than 600,000 laborers to help build the chambers and fortified walls, which stretched more than ten miles in circumference. It made for a most impressive spectacle. When the Spanish governor of the Philippines had visited a few years earlier, he had been stunned by the scale of the defenses. There were three tiers of walls, a fast-flowing moat, and "more than 20,000 persons between the first gate and the prince's chamber." The chambers were of exquisite beauty and were decked with painted hunting scenes chased with gold. "Although the first compartment left nothing to be desired," he wrote, "the second chamber was finer, while the third was even more splendid."

The bodyguards at the entrance to each section of the palace wore golden cuirasses that sparkled in the sun and were armed with pikes, lances, and razor-sharp scimitars. Cocks was amazed by the size and luxury of the place, for it was built on a scale that far surpassed anything he had seen in England. There was room enough within its walls to house more than 150 Towers of London. Cocks described it as "a huge thing" that appeared, at first sight, to be "far bigger than the cittie of York." But unlike York, Hidetada's castle was surrounded by "three greate and deepe ditches full of water, with strong walls about each of them . . . being all of free stone of an exceding height with faire building upon it and towers." Cocks was astonished to discover that even the roof tiles glittered with gold leaf.

The interior of the palace was no less splendid, "being gilded with gould, both overhead and upon the walls." The rooms were also richly adorned with paintings and murals—depictions of "lions, tigers, onces [lynx], panthers, eagles and other beastes and fowles, very lively drawne and more esteemed [than] their gilding." The largest chambers could be divided into smaller rooms by means of folding screens, "which go up and downe, or rather to and fro . . . [like] the shutting of our windows in England."

No less impressive were the furnishings, and Cocks was particularly taken with the exotic floor rugs. "All the roomes in his palace under foote are covered with mattes edged with damask or cloth of gold, and lie so close joined on[e] to another that you cannot put the point of a knife betwixt them."

The men were escorted into the inner chambers by two of Hidetada's chief counselors, who carried away the English gifts of broadcloth, coral, animal skins, and pots before leading them to the presence chamber. Here they stopped, for even the senior-

Protocol was all-important at the Japanese court. Courtly servants entered on hands and knees, while lords repeatedly prostrated themselves. When Richard Cocks visited the court, he found the shogun seated "cross-leged like a tailor" and flanked by shaven-headed monks.

ranking Honda Masanobu did not dare to enter the room without prior permission from the shogun.

Adams had stressed to Cocks the overriding importance of abiding by the complex rules of Japanese etiquette. He told him that he would earn great respect by following the correct protocol and that this would be of great assistance in forging good relations with Hidetada. He had offered similar advice to Saris, but the captain had ignored it, creating much bad feeling at court. Cocks was more willing to listen to advice and impressed the shogun with his deferential humility. "He [Hidetada] called me once or twice to have com in, which I refused; which, as I understood afterward, was well esteemed of." After being summoned for a third time, Cocks entered the chamber and found himself face to face with the shogun. Hidetada was seated on the floor, "cross-leged like a tailor" and flanked by four shaven-headed monks. The shogun was swarthy and well built, but cut a somewhat comical figure on account of the colorful ribbons that he was accustomed to wear in his hair. On this particular occasion, he looked quite splendid in his light summer robe made from bright blue silk.

Cocks was fortunate to be granted a private audience. Hidetada had a fondness for pomp and ceremony and liked to be surrounded by the lords of his realm, all decked in their traditional costumes and hats. When the Spaniard Sebastian Vizciano visited Hidetada a few years earlier, he had been bemused by the extraordinary headgear of their lordships. "Some had mitres on, others wore three-cornered hats like *birettas*, others had hats like clogs, others wore coloured turbans, and so on." Hidetada himself was no less flamboyant, but his colorful exterior concealed a wily and crafty nature: he was said to have inherited many traits from his father. As history would show, Cocks was absolutely correct to describe him as "the politikest prince that ever reigned in Japan."

There was no mention of trade or privileges at this first meeting. Instead, the men stuck to pleasantries and the audience passed "with many favourable words." Two days later, Adams returned to the castle "to procure . . . the renewall of the old emperor's privileges, with a *gowshin* [shogunal pass] for his junk." Hidetada listened politely to Adams's request—made on Cocks's behalf—but declined to give an immediate answer. Obliged to leave the court empty-handed, Adams returned to Cocks with the grim news that their privileges might not be renewed after all.

The next few days were spent in a hectic round of lobbying and meetings, as Adams attempted to persuade the shogun's most senior courtiers that they had nothing to fear from the presence of Cocks and his men on Japanese soil. But he quickly discovered that this was no easy matter. Hidetada, who had inherited from his father a deep mistrust of Christians, was even more determined than Ieyasu to enforce the anti-Christian edict. While he was perfectly content to allow Adams to remain in Japan, he was rather less convinced about giving his blessing to the small community of Englishmen in Hirado. Adams warned Cocks that Hidetada was naturally suspicious and far stricter "against the Romish relligion than his father was, for he hath forbidden thorough all his dominions, under pain of death, non of his subjectes to be Romish Christians."

Hidetada was also less astute than Ieyasu and he found it almost impossible to distinguish between Protestant and Catholic. It soon became apparent that his courtiers—who were well versed in Adams's views of Catholicism—were particularly interested in discovering Cocks's opinions of the Jesuits and friars. They quizzed him about Protestantism in England and the tenets of the faith so as to compare his answers with those of the trusted Adams. "The Councill," wrote Cocks, "sent unto me I think above twenty times to know whether the English nation were [Protestant] Christians or no." One of his principal difficulties had been caused by a letter, written by King James I, in which he had styled himself as "Defender of the Christian Faith." The court said that this was exactly the same title used by the Jesuits and that they must therefore share the same beliefs. Exasperated, Cocks informed them—not for the first time—"that all Jesuites and friers were banished out of England before I was borne, the English nation not holding with the pope nor his doctrine."

The courtiers listened politely, yet they remained suspicious and warned the English not to have any contact with papists. Cocks responded with his own warning—that Hidetada should watch that the Catholics in Japan did not behave "as they had done [toward] the kinges of England, in going about to kill and poison them, or to blow them up with gunpowder, and stirring up the subjects, to rebell against their naturall prince, for which they were all banished out of England." Cocks was so desperate to prove his anti-Catholic credentials that he suggested an Anglo-Japanese attack on the Spanish Philippines. It would, he said, be a great opportunity to kill Catholics and added that Hidetada "needed not to dowbte the assistance both of the English and Dutch."

This, at last, had some effect. Stiffening his resolve to eradicate the Jesuits and friars, Hidetada, at the beginning of September 1616, issued new edicts to the effect that anyone suspected of sheltering Christians would be put to death, along with all their relatives. Two days later Cocks received a visit from a courtier who brought the news that the delay in the renewal of their trade privileges was caused by a rumor that William Adams's wife was harboring Christians on their country estate at Hemi. Adams was alarmed and "wrot . . . to his folkes, to look out that no such matter were proved against them, as they tendered their lives."

Adams visited the court every morning, hoping to receive good news, but each time there was some new obstacle that prevented the privileges from being signed. One day, he was told that "foule weather" had prevented the usual business at court; another, the courtiers were too busy torturing a man suspected of helping in the defense of Osaka Castle. He was "racked and tormented very much," but refused to confess, claiming it would be dishonorable to break under pressure. This only encouraged his tormentors, who "applied exquisite tortures of fire and pressed

Torture was commonplace and gruesome in Japan. Many of the most terrible punishments, such as suspension with weights (above), were used on captured Christians.

him between boards studded with the points of spikes, and trans-
fixed him, but despite his certain knowledge, he did not confess a
single thing before he died."

Although Hidetada had yet to make up his mind about the
English trade privileges, he had a great respect for Adams and was
keen to recruit him as a master-pilot. He had learned from his father of Adams's skills as a navigator and had been aware of Ieyasu's
proposal to place Adams in command of an expedition in search
of the fabled Northwest Passage. To Adams's dismay, those plans
had come to nothing, for Ieyasu had been too preoccupied with
civil unrest to finance such an expedition.

Hidetada had his own, rather different mission for Adams and
summoned him to the court to discuss details. "He understood
there were certen islands to the northwards, very rich in mines of
gold and silver, which the emperour ment to conquer, and asked
him whether—upon good terms—he would be pilot." Adams
pointed out that he had agreed to undertake a number of projects
on behalf of the East India Company and, always a man of princi-
ple, he "could not serve two masters." But he promised to do
everything he could to discover more about these islands, and his
willingness to help evidently impressed Hidetada, for his mood
toward the English began to lighten.

By the third week in September, the English were convinced
that the deadlock was about to end. The shogun sent Cocks a
present of ten kimonos and a suit of armor, as well as two kimonos each for Eaton and Wickham. More gifts soon followed
from other courtiers and retainers, and three days later came the
greatest present of all. Adams was handed the renewed trading
privileges, which granted the English permission to stay in Japan.
The only condition was that they should not "comunecate, con-
fesse nor baptise" with Catholics, something that neither Cocks
nor his men had any intention of doing. Hidetada also gave
Adams a *shuinjo*—a document sealed with vermilion-colored
wax—that renewed his permission to sail overseas. It also provided

protection against piratical attack, for an assault on a *shuinjo*-carrying vessel was considered an assault on the shogun himself. Malefactors would be hunted down and executed.

Just hours after receiving these all-important documents, Cocks, Eaton, and Wickham set off with Adams to pay a visit to his estate at Hemi. Adams's return was a cause of great joy to his vassals and "husbandmen," who lined the roads to cheer him on his way. Cocks, as Adams's guest, was also given a hero's welcome, and "divers of his tenantes brought me presents of fruite, [such] as oringes, figgs, peares, chestnuttes and grapes." Cocks responded by handing out small gifts of cloth and money. The size of Adams's estate and the authority that he wielded over his retainers left a lasting impression on Cocks. Unlike English lords, whose power over their tenants was limited by the law of the land, Adams was truly the master of all he owned. "There is above 100 farmes or howsehold upon it [the estate]," wrote Cocks, "besides others under them, all of which are his vassals, and he hath power of life and death over them." He added that these peasants and agricultural laborers were "his slaves, and he has absolute authority over them, as hath any *tono* or king in Japan over his vassales."

After a few days of merrymaking at Adams's house, the men decided to pay a visit to the respected Japanese admiral Mukai Shogen Tadakatsu, who lived nearby. They set off on horseback. Cocks was most impressed that they were accompanied by a group of Adams's Japanese tenants, who ran alongside on foot "as homegers [vassals]." When the men arrived at the admiral's house, they were given a lavish dinner and bundles of gifts. Cocks was delighted to be presented with a dagger and wrote that Mukai "is one of the best friends we have in Japan."

The idyllic few days in Hemi came to an abrupt end on the last day of September, when the men received an express letter from Richard Wickham in Edo. This brought disastrous news. Hidetada had issued a decree to the effect that it was unlawful for Japanese merchants to buy merchandise from any foreigner residing in Osaka, Kyoto, or Sakai. If true, this would strike a death knell to England's fledgling trade with Japan, for it would mean the abandonment of all the subfactories that had so far been established. Cocks was perplexed that Hidetada should issue such a decree so soon after reconfirming English privileges and recorded that the news "seemed very strange unto me." It was only when he studied Hidetada's grant in detail—this time with the help of an erudite Buddhist priest—that he realized that the English privileges had been severely curtailed. "We were," wrote Cocks, "restrained to have our shipping to go to no other place in Japan but Hirado." He knew that unless this order could be overturned, it would necessitate the closure of the factory and would also spell the end of their charmed lives in Japan.

Adams dashed straight to Edo, accompanied by Cocks and Eaton, in order to beg the court to change its mind. Cocks was extremely upset and when he met one of the most senior courtiers, he told him that "the emperour might as well banish us right out of Japan as bind us to such an order, for that we could make no sales at that place." Cocks tried everything in his power to persuade Hidetada to revoke his decree. He even said that his life would be in danger if their privileges were not restored, for "King James would think it to be our misbehaviours that caused our privilegese to be taken from us." Cocks added, "It stood me upon as much as my life was worth to get it amended, otherwise I knew not how to show my face in England."

But Hidetada was immovable. He had not been impressed by Cocks and was determined to confine the English to their remote factory in Hirado. Only after intense lobbying did he agree to a compromise. He told Cocks that the goods already stored in the subfactories could be sold off under the terms of the original charter, but all future trade must be confined to Hirado. William Adams alone was exempt from this order: he had impressed Hidetada with the breadth of his knowledge, and the shogun renewed his position as *hatamoto*, which gave him equal status to other

Japanese samurai. Cocks held out the hope that Hidetada would change his mind about the trading privileges, recording that otherwise, "I feare me our Japan trade will not be worth the looking after." But the shogun refused, and the disappointed English decided to leave Edo.

As they set off for Hirado, they suffered a further, and almost fatal, setback. Adams was galloping along a country lane when a bird flew unexpectedly from the hedgerow. "It caused Captain Adams's horse to start, so that he fell backward and put his right shoulder-bone out of the joint and, 100-to-one, that he had broake his neck."

The men found roadside lodgings so that Adams could rest his damaged shoulder, and on the following day he felt a little better. But there was no question of him continuing on toward Hirado for the time being. "In respect [that] Captain Adams feared his arme would go out of joint againe, he thought it best to stay four or five days at Suruga."

He eventually caught up with Cocks and Eaton in Kyoto, even though his shoulder was still causing him extreme pain, and remained in their company for the rest of the journey. On December 4, 1616, the three disappointed men arrived back in Hirado, where the future looked bleaker than ever. But not everyone was quite so downhearted. Richard Wickham, in particular, had cause to be very happy indeed.

Chapter 11

KILLED LIKE FISHES

RICHARD WICKHAM had every reason to be pleased with himself. While the factory trade had faltered and Cocks moaned about decline, he had been managing his own affairs with spectacular success. He was thriving in Japan, having devoted all his energies to amassing a private fortune.

Those invited into his living quarters were left in no doubt that he was doing extremely well for himself. His room was crammed from floor to ceiling with treasures and curiosities, while his trunks were overflowing with Chinese silks. An inventory of his belongings reveals a man who enjoyed all the trappings of wealth and did not hesitate to spend his money. He ate off fine china, made his tea in a silver teapot, and drank beer out of polished "tackerdes." His dining table was draped in the choicest cloth, and there was an ointment box in the washroom for those who wished to perfume themselves. His chamber was a picture of oriental splendor, adorned with an extraordinary collection of curiosities and souvenirs from right across the East—Japanese chests, Javanese spears, and rubies from Siam. His larder was no less exotic and contained supplies of "sugar-candy" for his sweet-toothed friends, as well as "jarres [of] conserves" and a large supply of liquor.

But the possessions on display were as nothing in comparison to his extraordinary collection of clothes. Wickham had been quick to note the Japanese custom of dressing smartly and he started to emulate the local courtiers, equipping himself with a wardrobe that contained dozens of finely tailored shirts and garters. His doublets were his most extravagant gesture to foppishness. One was made from thick purple satin and trimmed with gold lace. Another had a brilliant orange collar. Wickham also had a collection of flamboyant hatbands—some embossed with gold—to add a touch of exoticism to the dandyish ensemble.

Wickham's possessions were worth more than £1,400—a significant sum for someone who was earning just £40 a year. When news of his wealth reached London, the company directors were aghast and expressed surprise that Wickham was making so much money "in a place where the company lost all theirs." In truth, they knew only too well how Wickham had amassed his fortune. Instead of working for the profit of the Hirado factory—for which he was paid and employed—he had devoted all his energy to enriching himself.

Wickham was hungry for money. He had been planning his path to riches long before he set foot in Japan and had proceeded to amass silver with a single-minded determination that had shocked his shipmates on the *Clove*. As soon as he arrived in Bantam, he began buying up goods with his own savings, hoping to sell them for a profit in Japan. When this first attempt failed, Wickham dispatched the goods back to Bantam and asked his friends to send instead a consignment of pepper or silk, "or any knowne comodity that will make me my principal againe." In the intervening months, he had been busy speculating with the cash that he had brought from England.

Private trade was the curse of the East India Company and was roundly condemned by the London merchants. They did everything in their power to limit the buying and selling of goods for personal profit, and each ship's captain was instructed to forbid his mariners from indulging in financial speculation. When Saris set sail in 1611, he was explicitly commanded to prevent Cocks's men from buying and selling on their own account, and the London merchants set down "an absolute order that no man, neither captains, marchaunts, masters or marriners, or any other person or persons whatsoever . . . do trade or deale for any [private] marchandize."

Yet it was inevitable that some men would break this command, and few mariners would ever have left England if they had not had the hope of doing deals on the side. Captains, too, were in the habit of speculating with their own money. William Keeling had been so bold as to request that in his case—as commander of an important expedition—he should be granted a special dispensation that would allow him to engage in private trade. The merchants "utterlie distasted" of the proposal and offered instead to double his wages. Keeling accepted the pay raise with alacrity, but continued to press for permission to trade on his own account. When the merchants realized that he was in danger of resigning his post, they had little option but to agree. But they made him swear to secrecy and ordered him to prevent his men from following suit. Keeling was true to his word; indeed, he surpassed himself by disciplining several factors in Bantam and warning them that they broke company rules "at your perill."

Wickham was not the only Englishman in Hirado to indulge in private trade. Nealson, Sayers, and the young Richard Hudson—one of the three men left behind by the *Hosiander*—all struck secret deals with the Japanese. Eaton established his own lacquerware syndicate, and even "honest" Mr. Cocks speculated with his own money. On one occasion, he asked Wickham to invest some of his silver, but Wickham was not interested in making other men rich. "He retorned me my money as I delivered it," wrote an angry Cocks, "and employed all his own." Such a mean-spirited attitude was a continual source of grievance, as was Wickham's habit of escaping censure by reminding Cocks of his friendship with Sir Thomas Smythe.

Unlike Adams, the men had made only a few friends among the local Japanese population of Hirado and preferred to rely upon each other for amusement and entertainment. Cocks and Wickham had appreciated each other's company on first arriving in Japan, but their relationship soon deteriorated. This was particularly galling to Cocks, who had more in common with Wickham than any of the other men. Both he and Wickham saw themselves as cultured—sophisticated, even—and enjoyed writing about their experiences in Japan. They also liked reading and spent time and money acquiring new books. Wickham amassed a considerable library of fifty-eight volumes "great and small," while Cocks had histories sent to him from Bantam. The two men occasionally indulged in intellectual banter, and Wickham delighted in dropping references to Suetonius and Cicero into his letters. Like Cocks, he also enjoyed scandal, especially when it involved women. He referred to one Japanese girl as his "little vixen."

There was much to bring these two men together, yet Cocks quickly tired of Wickham's boorish behavior. Wickham was proud, capricious, and hotheaded, spending much of his time in the society of drunkards—perhaps because they were best able to bear his company. Cocks noted with some satisfaction that Wickham was unpopular, adding that those who socialized with him were hoping to profit in the event of his succumbing to an early death. "I think all the rest of the English in these parts desire rather his rowme [chamber] than company," he wrote. As the factory's finances grew more and more desperate, Cocks became more and more impatient with Wickham. But he also realized that a complete breakdown of relations would make life impossible; after one particularly ferocious row, he wrote Wickham a letter in which he claimed to have "quite put out of my memory any wordes which have passed betwixt us." He would soon discover that Wickham was not so magnanimous.

The other factory members had also begun to wear on one another's nerves. Although there was much to celebrate in Japan, they soon tired of life in such a strange and uncompromising land and grew bored with each other's company. William Nealson was the most obviously troublesome. He had been employed as the factory's assistant bookkeeper, but he showed little enthusiasm for work and preferred to indulge his passion for alcohol. Soon after arriving in Japan, he began to display the tendencies of an alcoholic and became subject to wild and irrational mood swings. Cocks increasingly found himself cautioning Nealson for his unruly behavior, but his admonishments had little effect. Indeed, they seemed only to fuel Nealson's fury. On one occasion he rounded on Cocks and launched a scathing attack. "He fell out with me," wrote Cocks, "and called me old drunken asse, giving me many thretning speeches not sufferable." Cocks quickly grew weary of Nealson's drunkenness and his "fustian fumes." He eventually tired of admonishing Nealson and left him to his own devices. "When god is my judg," he sighed, "I have been taxed with all the English in the cuntry for suffering Mr Nealson to abuze all men as he daily does."

No less irksome was John Osterwick, who had joined the factory from the *Hosiander* in 1615. Cocks had taken an instant dislike to Osterwick, describing him as "a proud, surly young man and one that scorns all men in respect of himself." The feeling was mutual, and it was not long before Osterwick was actively stoking warfare between Cocks and his men. He formed a friendship with Nealson, then tried to poison his mind by suggesting that Cocks was hoarding company money for his own private use. Cocks was furious, but managed to keep a cool head. He informed Oster-wick that "it had been better he had told me thereof, than to speake such matters to others."

It was inevitable that such a small group of men would form themselves into factions and equally inevitable that Cocks—as leader—would find himself the object of their criticism. Yet he did have one ally, William Eaton, who was loyal, competent, and hardworking. He and Cocks quickly discovered that they had much in common. Both may even have come from Staffordshire, since Cocks refers to him as "my cuntryman." He certainly recognized Eaton as a man of uncommon ability and sent him on frequent trading missions to Osaka, Sakai, and Kyoto. Even in the darkest times, when money was scarce, Eaton remained loyal, and Cocks repaid him with frequent warm tributes in his letters and diary. He described him as "a true honest man and a friend to his friend." Eaton's loyalty may well have stemmed from the fact that he was happy in Japan. After a brief but disastrous relationship with O-man, he fell in love with a local girl called Kamezo. He showered her with gifts of silks and cloths, and Kamezo repaid his affection by bearing him a son and a daughter.

The men's most complex relationship was with William Adams. They knew that Adams's friendship with Ieyasu had proved of the greatest assistance to the factory and were forever turning to him for help and advice. Cocks freely admitted to being deeply impressed by Adams's knowledge of the language and customs of Japan. He was only too aware that without Adams to argue their case at court, they would never have been allowed to establish themselves in the country. Yet he retained a sneaking mistrust of his most valued servant and harbored suspicions that Adams was secretly working for the Dutch and the Spanish. These were never substantiated, yet it took Cocks more than three years to concede that he had misjudged Adams. Like Captain Saris, Cocks had confused Adams's aloofness with arrogance and failed to realize that Adams had good reason to be troubled by the men's drunkenness and whoring. It was Adams, after all, who had to answer for their behavior at the shogun's court—a position that won him praise neither from Hidetada nor from Cocks.

It was only after Cocks had seen Adams pleading the English cause with the shogun that he realized his previous comments had been unfair. In a letter to the East India Company directors in London, he informed them that "I find the man tractable and willing to doe your worships the best service he may." He later commented that Adams's calm demeanor was in stark contrast to that of the unruly men in his charge. "I am perswaded I could live with him seven years before any extraordinary speeches should happen betwixt us."

Adams had rescued the English factory from financial ruin in 1616. Cocks had spent a small fortune on building works and had further depleted his supplies of silver by establishing trading posts in Edo and Osaka. His parties and feasts had also eaten into precious resources, while the civil strife that followed the Osaka battle had damaged much of the stock in William Eaton's outpost. Cocks had also found himself spending more than £300 on unexpected repairs to the *Hosiander*. With such huge outgoings, it was only a matter of time before the factory lurched into insolvency.

When Adams's contract with the East India Company had officially come to an end in November 1615, his initial reaction was that he had no intention of renewing it. He had no need of the paltry salary he was paid; he was more than capable of making money from private trading voyages, as well as from rice harvested on his country estate. But he knew that Cocks was facing severe financial difficulties and, although he had little in common with the staff of the English factory, he had no wish for them to come to harm. That same month, he offered his services to Cocks for much of the next year, helping him out of a succession of crises.

His voyage to Siam, which lasted from the winter of 1615 until the summer of 1616, had thrown a lifeline to the factory. Adams sailed his junk, the *Sea Adventure*, to Ayutthaya—the site of the lit-

tle English trading post founded by Lucas Antheunis—and be-
stowed numerous presents on local Siamese officials. In return, he
was allowed to acquire vast quantities of sappanwood—a commodity that continued to fetch spectacular prices in Japan. Adams
managed to buy so much cargo that his junk was soon fully laden.
He found it necessary to charter two additional vessels to transport
the rest of the goods back to Hirado.

Although Adams was doing Cocks a huge favor, the English
factors in Siam were suspicious of his motives and were particularly wary of his close relationship with his Japanese mariners.
Benjamin Farie went so far as to condemn him for allowing his
crew to transport their own private cargo on board the vessel. He
said that the East India Company was "exseedingly abused herein
by his [Adams's] lardge priviledges [to the crew]." But Farie was
unaware that this was standard practice among Japanese mariners
and was specifically designed to discourage them from deserting
ship.

Adams had arrived back in Hirado in July 1616 to be greeted
by the news of Ieyasu's death. He had traveled straight to Edo,
along with Cocks, and it was not until the two men's return to
Hirado that they could dispose of the sappanwood. The sale in-
jected a huge sum of much-needed money into the near-
bankrupt factory. The wood sold for more than three times its
cost price—providing Cocks with a windfall of silver—while the
hides reaped a 100 percent profit. The men were delighted
and, feeling a sense of renewed optimism, decided to celebrate
Christmas in lavish fashion. The *Thomas* and the *Advice* were still
at anchor, and they blasted their cannon at dawn "in honor of
Christmas day." Now that the factory was once again solvent,
everyone was determined to have a good time, and Cocks hired
Japanese dancing girls to enliven their banquets and parties. The
Advice's master, John Totten, had noted Cocks's love of bathing
and presented him with eighteen bars of soap, while Li Tan gave
him two bundles of black taffeta and "ten great China cakes of

sweete bread." Cocks had bought presents for the children of his Japanese friends; one little girl received a fan, a perfumed pomander, and "a bundell of paper."

Once Christmas was over, the men turned their attention to a matter of pressing concern. For almost two years there had been no news from Tempest Peacock and Walter Carwarden, who had sailed to Cochinchina in the spring of 1614. They had been expected to return after four or five months—perhaps a little longer—and it was hoped that they would bring back a shipload of silks and hides. Instead, Cocks had heard numerous rumors that the men had been either killed or captured. One of the more colorful tales suggested that Peacock had drowned, dragged underwater by the weight of gold in his pockets. Another claimed that Carwarden had escaped danger and would soon be back in Japan. Such stories had continued for almost two years, yet Cocks had made no efforts to find the men. Now, in the spring of 1617, he at last had the opportunity to act when Adams offered to lead a search party to Cochinchina.

His new junk, the *Gift of God*, lacked supplies and cables, so he made a visit to Nagasaki, where such equipment could be bought for a song. When he returned to Hirado, he found that his money-saving measure had not pleased young King Figen, the fiefdom's new ruler, who would have preferred Adams to have spent his money in Hirado. Nor had it been well received by the port's principal merchants, who were still in dispute over Cocks's sale of the Siamese sappanwood. Some of the more hotheaded among them—who had long been jealous of Adams's access to the court—sent three henchmen down to the harbor with orders to punish and humiliate him. These men did rather more than was asked of them. They clambered aboard the *Gift of God*, "laid hold on Captain Adams' armes and, before he was aware, wrung him in such extreme sort that they put him to much paine." Adams was still recovering from the fall off his horse, and their arm-twisting and punches were excruciatingly painful. Indeed, his joints were wrenched with such force that the thugs almost dislocated one of his arms. As Adams cried in agony, the henchmen set upon the other members of the crew. They grabbed the boatswain, John Phebie, and threatened to slice him to pieces with their swords, while Sayers found himself seized by "the hinder part of the haire" and caught in a suffocating headlock.

The situation looked grim, for the attackers were "passing in as violent sort as might be" and eager to put the men to the slaughter. They were under the illusion that Adams was no longer under the shogun's protection and could therefore be treated in whatever way they chose. But as soon as Adams had escaped from their grip, he reached into his kimono and pulled out a document, signed and sealed by Hidetada. He waved it in the air, "kissing it and holding it up over his head, meaning to protest and take witnesse of the violence they offered him." This theatrical gesture had an instant and dramatic effect. The document did indeed provide Adams with the protection of the shogun and it was inviolable upon pain of death. The attackers blanched when they saw it. Fearful of the repercussions, they resheathed their weapons and hurried back ashore.

Adams wisely turned a blind eye to this unpleasant episode. Toward the end of March 1617 he set sail for Cochinchina. After just three weeks at sea, he observed an earthy murkiness in the water, a clear sign that he was nearing the outfall of the mighty Quang Nam River. The following morning, Adams sighted the mouth of the estuary and carefully guided his vessel upstream.

The local official in charge of this stretch of river was intrigued by his arrival and quizzed him about the purpose of his visit. Adams explained that he had been dispatched by the English chief factor in Japan in order to discover the fate of Peacock and Carwarden. He added menacingly that if they had been killed "without offence," then he intended to "seek justis." The official mumbled some excuses and left, promising to investigate the men's disappearance. Soon after this meeting, Adams found himself greeted by the local king's secretary, who also asked why he had come. This time, Adams was more forthright. "We told him . . . [we were] sent by the command of the King of England, to knowe what was become of the two Englishmen sent hither." He added that "we heard they were kild here . . . but how, as yet, we did not knowe." The secretary listened politely, feigned indignation, and washed his hands of the affair. He told Adams that Peacock and Carwarden "ware drowned by misechance in a small boat."

Adams was convinced that the secretary knew more, but was silenced by the man and warned not to delve into such delicate matters. "That is gone and past," said the secretary, "[and] is not needfoull fore to speake of this now." Adams was infuriated by the man's dismissive manner and persisted in his questioning. This provoked an unexpected response. The secretary suddenly snapped and, in a frenzy of anger, said that "the chiefeste of the two had given many skornfoull speeches, and proud not makinge any reckning of the kinge nor his countrey." Then, aware that he had already said too much, he checked himself and refused to provide any more information. He left Adams and Sayers with the growing suspicion that there had indeed been foul play.

Over the coming days, Adams quizzed a number of other local traders about the fate of Peacock and Carwarden. After receiving numerous testimonies, he managed to compile a plausible reconstruction of what had happened. Peacock, it seemed, had been lured upstream by the promise of trade and had secured lodgings with a Japanese merchant called Mangosa. This merchant was outwardly friendly, but was actually a hit man who had been paid by local officials to murder Peacock. Their motive was straightforward: they were shocked by Peacock's drunkenness and took offense at his boast that the English could cripple Cochinchina by blockading all the coastal ports. The exact manner of his death was unknown, although Cocks later recorded a rumor—probably brought back by Adams—that he was "trecharousely set upon . . . [and] kild in the water with harping irons, like fishes."

Walter Carwarden's end was less mysterious. He had remained in the river estuary while Peacock headed upstream and probably learned of his friend's murder from local merchants. Terrified that he would meet with a similar fate, he fled in a little boat. This had the misfortune to get overturned in a heavy squall; Carwarden was drowned before he could swim to the shore.

Adams had threatened to have his revenge if either of the men had been killed, but he knew that he was in no position to carry out that threat. Nor was he able to recover the huge amount of silver that they were carrying, for it had disappeared without trace. There was further bad news when Sayers, who had rowed ashore to buy silks, was robbed of all his money. With heavy hearts, the two men decided that luck was against them and set sail for Hirado. Their news was greeted with grim resignation by Cocks and his dwindling band of men.

Trade had proved difficult during the period of Adams's absence, and Cocks spent more and more time pruning his fruit trees, tending his goldfish, and writing colorful letters and entries in his diary. On one occasion, he watched in amazement as Nealson turned up at the factory carrying a giant wooden penis. Cocks asked the chuckling Nealson where he had acquired such an object. Nealson explained that he had, by chance, "found an alter of the ancient god Priapus, or lecherous god, with a greate tool." This penis was an object of devotion for women wanting to fall pregnant, and they were accustomed to process around the altar "carrying wooden pricks . . . made like unto a man's member." Nealson had quickly realized that one of these wooden penises would be a splendid ornament for the Hirado factory and had acquired one from the bemused ladies.

Nealson's tale reminded Cocks of a fertility altar he had seen in France, when he was traveling to Bayonne in the service of Sir Thomas Wilson. It, too, had a "greate tool . . . to which all baron

Richard Cocks was astonished by Japan's temples and shrines (above; possibly the Honno-ji near Kyoto) and wrote colorful descriptions to friends in England. King James I did not believe them, and declared them to be "the loudest lies that ever [he] heard of."

women went on pilgrimage." They would solemnly approach the penis with sharp knives "[and] shaved, or scraped off a littell of the prick, and put it into wine and drunck it."

Although the men were increasingly harassed by financial difficulties in 1617, Cocks never abandoned hope that he would transform Hirado into a factory of fabulous wealth. He had long held the belief that this could only be achieved by opening trade with China, and in his very first letter to the London directors— written three years earlier—he had proposed making contact with the Ming emperors. "Nothing seek," he told them, "nothing gain." For too long he had relied upon William Adams to help out in times of crisis. Now, Cocks was determined to bring to a successful conclusion one of his own initiatives. It was a tall order. Trade with China was altogether more complex than with Siam or Pattani, for it was forbidden by Peking's mandarins on pain of death. Cocks's only hope of acquiring Chinese silk was by employing middlemen.

It was his good fortune that Li Tan, onetime landlord of the English factory, was more than willing to help. Rich, influential, and head of Hirado's little Chinese community, Li was on good terms with the English and was one of the principal buyers of their goods. He was a frequent guest at the English factory and often sent gifts of food and cloth to Cocks and his men. Their friendship was sealed when Li asked Cocks to be godfather to his infant daughter. Cocks accepted and gave her the name Elizabeth.

Not everyone was as persuaded as Cocks of Li Tan's honesty and probity. A Dutch account describes him as "a sly man" and adds—with a detectable note of suspicion—that he had magnificent houses in both Hirado and Nagasaki, along with "several pretty wives and children." Others accused him of being totally untrustworthy in financial matters and said that he overstated his influence over the merchants of coastal China. Cocks dismissed such criticisms and accepted Li Tan's assurances at face value. He had already written to London, telling the company directors that he had "extraordinary hope to get trade into China." Now, convinced of a breakthrough, he decided to gamble the last of the factory's resources on gaining access to the silks of Ming dynasty China. He advanced the Chinese man a staggering £1,500—money that the factory could ill afford—and also gave him costly gifts.

News of Cocks's reckless dealings was carried to Bantam by Richard Wickham, who sailed to Java in the spring of 1617 aboard the departing *Advice*. Cocks had selected Wickham to report on affairs in Hirado, believing him to be the person with the best understanding of company affairs. Wickham soon proved himself rather too qualified for the task: he used his visit to deliver a stinging attack on Cocks's leadership, criticizing everything from his management of finances to his gullibility and foolishness.

Wickham's broadside met with a receptive audience in Bantam. The new chief factor, George Ball, was a disreputable character who derived great pleasure from undermining his peers. He had already lambasted Cocks for his rambling correspondence and regarded him as an old windbag. "Your letters are copious but not compendious; large, but stuffed with idle and needless chatter ill beseeming one of your place, years and experience." His sentiments would later be echoed by King James I, who read one of Cocks's letters with interest, but "co[u]ld not be induced to beleeve that the things written are true." He declared them to be "the loudest lies that ever [he] heard of."

Ball listened to Wickham's criticisms of Cocks with a mixture of disgust and delight and compiled a blistering diatribe on his methods, character, competence, and honesty. One copy of his report was dispatched to Hirado; the other was sent to Sir Thomas Smythe in London. Cocks read the letter with horror and disbelief. It began with the usual "hartey commendations" and salutations, but quickly descended into spiteful invective. Ball told Cocks that he had long suspected him of being "extreme hot in passion, and most miserabell cold in reason." Now, having had a chance to hear from Wickham about Cocks's ineptitude, Ball declared that his worst fears were confirmed. He criticized the accounts for being filled with trivia and gossip instead of numbers, and said that Cocks's conduct as chief factor bordered on the incompetent. He accused him of being "starke blind in promoting the unworthy" and mocked him for accepting advice from those "readiest to cut your throtte." But his most vicious attack was on Cocks's handling of the China trade. Ball informed Cocks that he had been duped by Li Tan, the "father of deceit," and berated him for lining the pockets of a corrupt trickster.

Ball was even more damning in his letter to Sir Thomas Smythe, suggesting that Cocks had lost all grip on reality. "Having his imaginations levelled beyond the moone," he wrote "[he] hath the eyes of his understanding so blinded with the expectacion of incredible wanders that it is to be feared he will feele the losse before he will be made to see his error."

Ball's letter was unfair, but not altogether inaccurate. His censure of the *Clove*'s account book was spurious, for Cocks had already given good reason as to why the ship's log was incomplete. His attack on the promotion of Eaton was also unfair. Cocks had just seven men to choose from, and Eaton was without doubt one of the more competent. But Ball's most damning charge—that Cocks had been too gullible in his dealings with Li Tan—contained more than a degree of truth. Cocks was far too trusting of Li, who was rather better at making promises than producing profits. The Englishman poured money and gifts into the Chinese man's bottomless pockets, yet failed to realize that it was not at all in Li's interest for the English to gain a foothold in China, since it would break his own monopoly. Even when it became abundantly clear that Li was a trickster, Cocks remained convinced that he offered the only hope of entering the China trade—the one "which we all sweat for."

When Cocks had digested Ball's letter, he composed a long reply to Sir Thomas Smythe. He rebutted all the charges laid against him and warned Smythe not to believe everything written by Ball. "I have ill-willers," he wrote, "which go about to bring me in disgrace with your worships, as Mr Ball by name." He said that Ball's accusations were pure "spleene" and added that he was tempted to return to England to answer the charges against him. "My best way will be to come answer for myselfe if God will permit me life to see my cuntry of England." In the event, the storm temporarily blew over and Cocks remained in Hirado. But Ball's attack had a grain of truth and sowed the seeds of doubt in the minds of the London directors. It also left Cocks with the difficult problem of deciding how to deal with Wickham on his return to Japan.

Chapter 12

A RUPTURED FRIENDSHIP

 ICHARD WICKHAM arrived back in Hirado with one last surprise for Cocks. He announced that he was weary of Japan and, after spending almost five years in the country, he was ready to bid farewell to his erstwhile colleagues.

He could have left several years earlier, for Captain Saris had granted him permission to return to England whenever he chose. But Wickham had first wanted to feather his nest, and it was not until 1618 that he had amassed a sufficient fortune to make his return a comfortable one. In a letter to his mother, he claimed that he was leaving Japan because of "some wronges and crosses sustained by some enemies." He added—more out of duty than sincerity—that "my promise [was] made unto you, most kinde mother, to return . . . within three yeares." This deadline had expired long ago, yet Wickham had shown no interest in leaving on earlier vessels. It was only after his brief stay in Bantam that he had a sudden longing for home.

Wickham wrote several other letters to his family informing them of his decision. He had never been a master of tact and his correspondence was characterized by an unpleasant bitterness. He chided them for not having written a single letter during the entire time he had been away and said that he was "much marvailing that parents and allied friendes can so much forget me." He added that while he did not wish to "tax so kinde and loving a mother," he was nevertheless appalled that "not once in seven yeares" had he received a letter from her.

In a note to his aunt, he was even more forthright, castigating her family for not having written a single line in all the time that he had been in Japan, "which makes me think they all suppose me dead, or else I am hardly induced to beleeve I can be so forgotten." He asked for his best wishes to be passed to his sisters, pointedly adding, "if they be living."

Wickham's imminent return to London was a cause of deep concern to Cocks. He had already suffered once from Wickham's mean-spiritedness and feared that Wickham would now repeat his accusations to his friend Sir Thomas Smythe. This is exactly what Wickham intended to do. He promised to inform the London merchants of the "many disorders and wrongs offered by many within these few years, to the great hindrance of the East Indies trade and dishonour of our nation."

Coming from Wickham, any such criticism of Cocks was grossly hypocritical. Wickham had displayed little enthusiasm in working for the East India Company, and his own private trading had done much harm to the running of the factory. Yet his voice was certain to be heard in London, and it was quite possible that Cocks and the others would be recalled to England in disgrace. The company had poured large sums of money into the Hirado factory and was sure to want scapegoats for its failings. But for once in his life, Cocks was blessed with good fortune. As soon as Wickham arrived in Bantam—the first stage in his long voyage home—the sickly air took its toll. He weakened, trembled with tropical fever, and was forced to take to his bed. After years of healthy living in Japan, he was prey to typhoid, malaria, and the "blody flux." Wickham soon breathed his last and took his accusations against Cocks to the grave.

When his executors finally came to count his money and assess his estates, they found him to be worth a staggering £1,400. His grieving mother, the elderly Mrs. Wickham, was amazed to learn the size of her late son's fortune and quickly dried her tears when she discovered that she was the chief beneficiary. She went straight to the offices of the East India Company and petitioned the directors to relinquish the cash. But they argued that Wickham had made his money through private trade and refused to release a single penny. The elderly Mrs. Wickham fought her corner for more than six years and even took her case to Chancery. Her persistence paid off, for the company finally capitulated and handed over the money. After a long wait, Mrs. Wickham became a very wealthy woman.

Wickham's departure—first from Hirado and then from the world—enabled Cocks to pursue his hectic social life without fear of being reported. Adams had returned to his country estate in order to spend time with his family. Then, after much planning, he set off on two privately financed voyages to Cochinchina and Tonkin (modern Vietnam). Cocks, meanwhile, continued to host frequent dinner parties and invited many of Hirado's noblemen to banquets at the English factory. These had always been lively affairs, but became even more raucous when Cocks began distilling his own "very good strong annis water"—a powerful poteen that assured a speedy path to drunkenness. Dancing girls were hired in ever greater numbers, and there was usually "a blinde fiddler to singe." Cocks's aim was to ensure that his guests were "entertained to theire own content."

Although his dinner parties were an extravagance, they served a useful purpose. They enabled him to garner news and gossip and to piece together events that were happening elsewhere in the

East. At one of his soirées, Cocks learned that an English factor in Siam had been so addled by loneliness that he had quite lost his mind. He had attacked a Dutch merchant, bound him with cord, and declared him to be his very own private prisoner. In Cambodia, one of the traders had grown so sick of the tropical heat and perpetual boredom that he had suffered a complete mental collapse. "[He] fell into a mad humour," wrote Cocks, "and meant to have kild himselfe with a pistoll charged with two bullettes." He proved a poor shot, for the bullets missed his vital organs, but the excruciating pain did at least shake him from his torpor.

Information from England—which was carried to Hirado by Portuguese or Dutch merchants—was both unreliable and bizarre. Cocks was told that "in England, [there] appeared in the firmament a very greate cross, with the crowne of thorne and nailes." Such a sign had been greeted with alarm by King James and his court, who "fell downe and worshipped it." A Catholic priest who mocked them for their devotions suffered a terrible fate. "Both the priest's eyes flew out of his head, and he died imediatly in the sight of all men."

News from Java and the Spice Islands was less sensational but a great deal more worrying. The Dutch were pursuing their trading agenda with increasing aggressiveness, targeting not only native chieftains but also their trading rivals, the English. On the clove-rich island of Amboyna, they had expelled English traders and built a string of fortifications to prevent any interloper from acquiring spices. On nearby Ceram, they vowed to sink English ships if they attempted trade. Elsewhere in the Moluccas, they forbade the chieftains from selling their spices to anyone except themselves and "threatened [them] with the loss of their heads if they dealt with the English." The situation was even more alarming in the richest of all the "spiceries," the nutmeg-producing Banda archipelago. This fragrant group of islands had been first visited by English adventurers in 1603, and they had quickly forged friendship treaties with the native islanders. Now, the

Dutch were attempting to expel the English forever, building bastions and bulwarks and forcing the chieftains to sign away all rights to their nutmeg.

A small group of adventurers led by the plucky Nathaniel Courthope had vowed to make a stand on the Banda Islands, but his troop of men soon found themselves battling against a terrifying new weapon. The Dutch, who had long admired the fighting prowess of the Japanese, had started paying them to wage war on their behalf.

One Englishman, John Alexander, had the misfortune to be captured and abducted by a band of these mercenaries. He was "carried . . . into the mountaines . . . with his hands bound with four Japanese after him with their swords drawne." He quickly discovered that they were fearless and chillingly efficient. They never failed to follow orders and killed with impunity. Poor Alexander trembled in his jerkin when he saw their scimitars and prepared himself for a violent death in the sweet-scented mountains of the Banda Islands. It was his good fortune that the mercenaries were ambushed by a large group of natives, who marched them back to the shore. But the Japanese refused to surrender their English captive graciously, even though they were outnumbered and outgunned. "They threw him into their boate bound hand and foote, treading on him in their boat's hold, having taken from him his cloathes from his back." Alexander was freed only after lengthy negotiations.

English vessels had been left unmolested during this troublesome period, for the Dutch had concentrated their energies on attacking Portuguese and Spanish ships. But events in the Banda Islands had increased tensions throughout the East and in 1617 a Dutch vessel had stormed an English ship, the *Swan*, in the waters around the Bandas. A ferocious sea battle ensued, and dozens of the English crew were mutilated in the ensuing fusillade of fire. Some were peppered with shot and bled to death. Others "lost legs and arms, and [were] almost without all hope of life, if not

The Dutch admired the fighting qualities of the Japanese samurai and hired them as mercenaries to fight the English in the Spice Islands. These fearsome warriors killed with impunity and were chillingly efficient.

dead already." Once the *Swan* was captured, her surviving crewmen were manacled, taken to the Banda Islands, and incarcerated in dungeons. Cocks had been told by his Spanish interpreter, Harnando Ximenes, that "the Hollanders misuse our Englishmen in vile sort." The truth was far worse. The English prisoners were tortured, starved, and chained under Dutch sewer outlets, "where their ordures and pisse fell upon them in the night."

Cocks was indignant at these attacks, yet remained confident that they would not be replicated in Hirado. He continued to be on good terms with the Dutchman Specx and found it inconceivable that the two factories—which stood just a few hundred feet apart—would ever find themselves at war. His confidence was partly due to the fact that the shogun forbade any fighting on

Japanese soil, on pain of death. But it also had much to do with the depth of friendship between Cocks and Specx. They had always enjoyed cordial relations and continued to wine and dine each other in considerable style. Both were cheery and easygoing, and neither had any interest in conflict. Indeed, they derived great pleasure from reciprocating favors. They forwarded letters to Bantam, passed on news, and blasted their cannon in honor of each other. On one occasion, Cocks had even allowed Specx to ship a large quantity of ebony wood to Java aboard the returning *Hosiander.*

News of this spirit of cooperation soon reached Bantam, where the English had a very different experience of their Dutch neighbors. The acerbic chief factor, George Ball, condemned Cocks's collaboration as a "heinous offence" and viewed it as yet another example of his ineptitude. But Ball had never visited Japan and had no idea how important it was for the English and Dutch to maintain cordial relations. He did not realize that Hirado was a small and isolated port, quite unlike Bantam, and that the men relied upon each other for news and information. Nor did he understand another, less tangible reason why the English and Dutch in Japan needed to stay on good terms. They were living on the edge of the world—isolated, lonely, and almost totally cut off from their respective countries. Homesickness was a very real problem, and it was vital for their sanity that they forged friendships with their respective neighbors.

When Specx learned that Cocks had been reprimanded for his cooperative manner, he took the extraordinary step of writing to John Jourdain, the newly appointed "president" of the English in the East, defending his colleague. "I was sorry to understand that in your letter to Captain Richard Cocks you appeared to be dissatisfied with the friendship and assistance given to us," he wrote. He added that he was not trying to trick the English, nor spoil their trade, and assured Jourdain that he had "the honest intention of being of service in similar cases, and not troublesome to your

Honour." His letter ended with a salient and important piece of advice: "As neighbours and mutual friends, we should not refuse to help each other."

Specx's defense of his English colleague was admirable, but the depth of his friendship had yet to be tested. So long as the factories were approximately the same size, trading rivalry between the two men was muted. But in June 1618 Cocks learned some disturbing news. Hirado's King Figen, who until now had been impartial in his dealings with both the English and the Dutch, had unexpectedly given the latter a street of fifty houses. This was not all. He had also sent a team of men to help them pull down these dwellings "and build their howse larger, with two new warehouses."

This news sent Cocks into a slough of despair. He was still smarting from Hidetada's refusal to sanction trade throughout Japan and had only just finished a letter to Sir Thomas Smythe in which he bemoaned the fact that "now is worse than ever, we being debarred of our trade into all places of Japan." He was also increasingly disturbed by news from elsewhere in the East, where the Dutch had redoubled their attacks on the English. He was particularly horrified to learn that they were openly calling King James I a homosexual and that one group of traders had pulled down the English flag, or "cullers," and "tore them in pieces in disdain and wiped their backsides with the peeces."

Cocks did his utmost to hide his alarm when he heard about King Figen's gift to the Dutch. He even made a point of going to inspect and admire Specx's building works. He was quite taken aback by the size of the new factory, "which truly is greate," and was surprised to find that the Dutch were adding many other fine buildings. There was a "mantion howse" with a great hall, a series of elegant chambers for the merchants, two warehouses, a gatehouse, and a dovecote. Most impressive of all was the "stronghouse" built of stone. Cocks realized that the enlarged Dutch factory would transform their trade in Hirado and make it almost impossible for the English to compete.

He was soon to discover that trading rivalry was the least of his problems. At around midnight on August 8, 1618, Cocks was relaxing in the sultry night air when he received word that a vessel had been sighted from a headland near Hirado. She was making slow progress toward the shore, for it was "calm hott wether" and the gentle breeze had died as evening fell. It was almost impossible to determine to which nation she belonged, for the sky was already dark, but it was rumored that she was a Portuguese or Spanish prize ship that had been captured by the Dutch. She had apparently been involved in a dramatic sea battle, for "her mast [was] cut overboard . . . and the ship much broaken."

It was most unusual for the Dutch to bring their captured prizes into harbor, and Cocks was intrigued. He sent Sayers over to the Dutch house to discover the ship's identity and offered Specx the use of the English factory's pinnace "to helpe to toe her in, she being but a littell distance without and the wether calme." Cocks did not have to wait long to learn more about the captured ship. A surgeon employed by the Dutch factory knocked on his door and asked for a private meeting. "[He] came to me in secret," wrote Cocks, "and told me that this shipp without was an English shipp, and one of four which the Hollanders have lately taken at Moluccas."

Cocks was aghast; he had not even considered that she might be English. But on the following morning, he received official confirmation that the ship had been captured after a ferocious sea battle, with the "slaughter of many men, and the rest taken prisoner." At noon, his pinnace was returned by the Dutch with the curt message that the vessel had been taken "by order of war." There was a sarcastic postscript, which informed Cocks that the Dutch "had no need of our helpe to bring her [into the harbor]."

Cocks realized that he had an emergency on his hands and—

with Adams absent from Hirado—he assumed personal control of the situation. He went straight to Doi Toshikatsu, a high-ranking official, and asked him for Japanese support "to go abord this shippe betime tomorrow." He also asked for help in discovering "whether the Hollanders take themselves enemies of the English or no." Once all the necessary information had been gathered, Cocks intended to lodge a formal complaint with the shogun.

The vessel—the *Attendance*—was towed into Hirado harbor in broad daylight, to the unbridled delight of her Dutch captors. These newly arrived mariners spared no effort to humiliate the English, jeering at them and mocking them for their misfortune. "[They] brought in our shipp in a bravado," recorded a dismayed Cocks, "and shot off many guns out of her." Jacques Specx did not share the bullish good humor of his compatriots. He was as surprised as Cocks by the turn of events and quickly foresaw the problems that would follow. Embarrassed by the incident and anxious to express his regret, he sent his interpreter to the English factory "to certify me he was sorry for what had happened." He added that he was willing to hand over the craft immediately.

Cocks was so mortified by the incident that he bluntly refused the offer. Specx was upset by his reaction and "came to the English howse . . . using many complementall words, offring the shipp and what was in her at my comand." It was a generous offer, but it was also a hollow one. The ship's timbers had been smashed by cannonfire and the Dutch captors "had well emptied her before." There was not a single item of cargo left on board.

Cocks played for time, maintaining his dignity throughout the meeting. He told Specx that he "was sorry for that which was happened, and wished it had not been so." He was particularly upset that the Dutch had towed the prize into the harbor, in full view of the local Japanese. "It had been enoffe for them to have taken our shipp and goodes," he wrote, "without bringing in of the shipps in such scornfull sort." Specx could do little more than apologize. He was genuinely upset by Cocks's anger and said that the removal of the cargo had been undertaken on the orders of his superiors in Bantam. Cocks responded by arguing that there was moral and immoral behavior, even in times of war. " 'Why then,' said I, 'it seemes your masters command you to be common theeves, to robbe English, Spanish, Portuguese, Chinese . . . without respect.' "

Specx listened with patience. He was anxious to regain Cocks's confidence and told him that even if there was a full-scale conflict between England and the Netherlands, his own men would not necessarily be bound by a Dutch declaration of war, but "would doe as they thought good." Such conciliatory words did little to assuage Cocks's anger. Bitter and hurt, he told Specx that he could show friendship if he wished, "but for my parte, I did not care a halfe-peny whether they did or not."

The Japanese in Hirado were as bewildered as Cocks by the unexpected turn of events. They flocked to the Dutch factory and "asked the Hollanders wherefore they took Englishmen and their shipping in this sort." The Dutch told the Japanese that it was because the English were importing weapons and gunpowder, but this only further increased their sense of perplexity. " 'Why,' said [one], 'are the Englishmen your vassals that they are bound to observe [your command?]' ." Only one man in Hirado was not surprised by what had happened. King Figen's brother had been keeping a close eye on relations between the English and Dutch for some months. He had come to the conclusion that their friendship was a precarious one and could easily be broken. "He told me," wrote Cocks, "that he had noted a long time that the Hollanders and we were frendes but from the tooth outward, and not cordially as neighbours and frendes ought to be."

After a series of meetings with Specx, Cocks summoned an emergency council of the three factory members in Hirado—Nealson, Sayers, and Osterwick—to decide if they should make a formal protest to the shogun. He wanted to "proclaim against the insolencie of the Hollanders in presuming not only to take our

shipps, but openly to bring them in [the harbor] to our disgrace."
After a short debate, it was decided that the Dutch offense was
too heinous to be ignored. Cocks himself was selected to "take
that long and troblesome voyage in hand" and was to be accompanied by Adams and Nealson.

At every point of crisis that had been faced by the factory,
Cocks and his team had turned to Adams. He was the only one
with the contacts and the language to resolve problems and repair
relations. Now, once again, the men needed his help. They were
about to embark on a delicate mission and they knew that it
would be impossible for them to secure an audience with Hidetada without Adams. But as soon as the men had taken their decision, they realized that they faced a major problem. Adams was
not available. He was already on his way to court in the service of
the Dutch, having been employed by Specx on a mission to bol-
ster relations with the shogun. Specx had hired Adams because,
according to Cocks, he was the "only instrament that the Hollanders have to mediate for them with the emperor."

Cocks was seriously alarmed. Hidetada was most unlikely to
take his protest seriously if he had just received a Dutch deputation headed by an Englishman. Adams had to be stopped in his
tracks, and there was not a moment to be lost. He had left Hirado
eleven days earlier and would soon be nearing the court. Cocks
hired a "swift bark" and sent a messenger to Edo, hoping he
would overtake Adams before he reached the shogun. His orders
were blunt: "he should retire himselfe from them [the Dutch],
and stay my coming." Adams was explicitly commanded "not [to]
go with them before the emperour."

Cocks, meanwhile, attempted to lobby influential Japanese
courtiers. He won the backing of Matsura Nobutoki, King Figen's
brother, who had visited the English factory in order to learn
more of their grievances. Cocks told him that he intended to inform Hidetada that the Dutch "were common theeves and sea
rovers," and that he would ask the shogun to place an embargo on

their ships and goods. Nobutoki approved of his mission and wished him every success.

Cocks and Nealson set off for court within two weeks of the incident, having prepared gifts of velvets and satins for Hidetada. They paused briefly at the port of Shimonseki, where they were told that Cocks's message had reached Adams and that "Captain Adams meant to stay for me at Kyoto." But good news was almost invariably followed by bad in Japan, and this occasion was no exception. Adams had no intention of halting his Dutch-led voyage to the court. He had pledged to lead Specx's deputation to the shogun and was not prepared to break his word. Far from accepting Cocks's request, he warned him of the folly of his mission. He said it was ludicrous to ask the shogun to punish Specx for an assault that had occurred in the Malay archipelago and told Cocks that he could do irrevocable harm to the English cause if he presented his petition.

Cocks was furious when he read Adams's letter. He said that it was "such an unseazonable and unreasonable letter as I littell suspected he would have done." He was particularly annoyed by Adams's claim that "he was none of the Companie's servant" and—not for the first time—accused him of being "altogether Holandized." What Cocks failed to realize was that Adams's advice was apposite and born from experience. He had seen the Portuguese and Spanish lead similar missions to the shogun; all had been dismissed by Hidetada, who had been extremely irritated at being disturbed by an issue that had taken place outside Japanese waters.

Cocks soon found that his mission to court was impeded by more serious obstacles. Scarcely had he and Nealson left Shimonseki than there was "an exceeding great earthquake" that demolished buildings and uprooted trees. This was followed by storms and torrential bursts of rain. By the time they reached the river crossing at Ishibe, "we were constrained to stay all night, because the waters were up." They finally forged the river and continued on toward the town of Mitske, where they were seized and attacked by unruly boatmen. When they arrived at Oiso, Cocks was struck down with a terrible stomach bug. "I was taken on a sudden with such an extreme wind collick and stopping of my water that I verily thought I should have died." The owner of the hostel showed a distinct lack of sympathy and asked Cocks to leave. He and Nealson were forced to find lodgings elsewhere.

The men soon had embarrassment to add to their woes. No sooner had they resumed their journey than they encountered the Dutchmen returning from their reception with the shogun. Cocks gave them a frosty reception. "There was small greeting betwixt us," he wrote, "and so they passed." Shortly afterward, he and Nealson stumbled into Adams, who had discreetly fallen behind the main party. "[He] came to meete me ten leagues from Edo," wrote Cocks, whose anger was somewhat assuaged by the news that horses and footmen were on their way. He was also pleased to learn that Adams had unexpectedly retracted his earlier refusal to accompany Cocks to the court. Although he still believed the mission to be unwise, Adams realized that Cocks would not be deflected. To persist in criticizing him was both pointless and unproductive, so he reluctantly offered to help organize an audience with Hidetada.

The three men received a triumphant welcome as they reached the city. King Figen of Hirado was in Edo and sent a troop of pikemen to greet them, while Adams's son and daughter, who were also staying in the city, prepared a splendid banquet. Edo was celebrating a great assembly of Japanese lords, who had gathered to visit the Shinto shrine where Ieyasu had been buried in the previous year. Temples, streets, and pleasure gardens were all thronged with people, and the Englishmen joined in the festivities, banqueting with courtiers and visiting shrines. Their only sadness came when they visited King Figen and found him to be riddled with syphilis. He was "very weake," wrote Cocks, "and full of the French disease, so I think he will not live longe."

Each day brought more and more people into the city until the streets were overflowing. On one occasion, the men followed a vast throng to the great temple of Yemia Fachman, the god of war. "I doe verily thinke there were above 100,000 people," wrote Cocks, "men, women and children, which went this day upon devotion to that place." It made for a picturesque spectacle, for the route was lined with actors and comedians in the most fanciful costumes. "And before the temple the sorcerers or witches stood dancing, with knottes or bunches of hawks' belles made fast to sticks." Cocks was astonished by the generosity of the pilgrims, "[who] thronged into the pagoda in multetudes, one after another, to cast money into a littell chapell."

The men were granted the honor of being allowed to visit the sepulchre of Ieyasu, which was guarded by a phalanx of monks. "[They] used us very kindly," wrote Cocks, "and opened the doores of the monument, and let us enter in." It was one of the most splendid tombs he had ever seen—"a wonderfull peece of

Edo was a magnificent city; the largest complex of buildings was the shogun's palace (above), but there were also scores of temples and pleasure gardens. At festival times these were thronged with nobles and their retainers.

work"—and alongside there was a shrine to the two noblemen "which kild themselves to accompany Ieyasu in another world." Cocks was even allowed into the inner sanctum, "the secret place where the idol of the dececed was placed, whereat all the Japans fell prostrate and adored it."

Every morning Adams went to the court in the hope of talking with Hidetada. But every morning the shogun was busy—indulging in festivities or hawking for wild swans. Hidetada had lost his patience with Cocks, and Adams—the factory's reluctant intermediary—was refused an audience. The futility of the mission soon sapped both his and Cocks's patience. "Captain Adams went againe to court to get our despatch," wrote Cocks, "but retorned only with a nod from the counsellors."

He was concerned that Adams might never be granted an audience, and his fears seemed confirmed when, on November 7, the heavens added their own portentous sign: "There was a comett (or blazsing star) which hath appeared this five or six days some hour before day." So wrote Cocks, who observed that "it is so near the sunne that we could see nothing but the tail, it being of a hudge length."

No less spectacular, but a great deal more terrifying, was another earthquake that struck the city at midmorning on the same day. It caused widespread panic, and the inhabitants fled into the streets to escape falling timbers. Cocks had by now experienced several earthquakes and devised a theory to explain their cause. Noting that they usually occurred at high tide, he reasoned that "[there] is much wind blowen into hollow caves undergrownd at a loe water." This wind was blocked in by the sea, which "stopping the passage out, causeth these earthquakes to find passage or vent for the wind shut up."

The earthquake was followed by a devastating fire, which threatened to destroy the buildings that remained standing. Nealson, who was suffering from consumption, was nevertheless so excited at the prospect of watching the city burn to ashes that he clambered onto the roof of his lodging, "sitting in his shirt and a gowne two or three hours together." He paid a high price for his curiosity, for he "fell sick on a sudden of a fever with a bloody flux, in great extremity." The shogun's physicians were called, but there was little they could do to reduce his temperature or stop his uncontrollable shaking. Nor could they say if Nealson's alcohol-weakened body would recover from yet another "excesse of fever."

The turmoil in Edo, coupled with the temple celebrations, conspired against Cocks and Adams. They were refused an audience with Hidetada, who showed no interest in Anglo-Dutch rivalry and washed his hands of the whole affair. He said that it was up to the pox-ridden King Figen "[to] see justis performed." It was much as Adams had warned. He was vindicated in his criticism of Cocks's mission, while Cocks himself was mortified to discover that he no longer had the protection of the shogun. When the Dutch learned of Hidetada's lack of interest they were jubilant. They now knew that the English could be attacked with impunity—and with no risk to themselves.

Cocks returned to Hirado to be told that there had been a dramatic downturn in relations between the English and Dutch in the East, and that there was now a state of virtual war between the two nations. Tensions had been heightened by the dispatch of a large and heavily armed fleet from London with orders to forcibly protect English trade. It was under the command of Sir Thomas Dale, "a heroike lion," who had acquired a reputation for ruthlessness and brutality while serving in the Netherlands and Virginia. Dale, relishing the opportunity to do battle with the Dutch, sailed his armada directly to Java. The Dutch were outnumbered and outgunned, for many of their vessels were on duty in the "spiceries," and Sir Thomas decided to capitalize on their weakness. He commenced battle on January 2, 1619, with a tremendous burst of cannonfire. One Englishman on board remarked that they had given the Dutch "such a breakfast that they will not abide a second, but fly before us."

The Dutch had indeed fled the battle, but not through fear of the English guns. They headed east to make contact with the rest of their fleet, then returned to the fray with renewed confidence. This time they proved rather more effective. They picked off English stragglers, hounded the weaker ships, and dispersed the great fleet. Dale's stately armada was soon scattered far and wide, and his strategy lay in ruins. Broken and humiliated, he sailed his remaining ships to India, where, in the summer of 1619, he contracted malaria and died. A second, breakaway squadron fared no better. John Jourdain, president of the English in the East, led his vessels to Pattani, where they were attacked by waiting Dutch warships. Jourdain himself was shot dead by a sniper.

Cocks and his dwindling band first learned news of the catastrophe in August 1619 when the Dutch ship *Angell* sailed in triumph into Hirado harbor. She was carrying additional staff for the Dutch factory as well as three English prisoners. This was an extremely alarming development. The Dutch treated their English captives with appalling brutality, shackling them together and subjecting them to beatings and torture. Elsewhere in the East, they had paraded their captured seamen through streets and ports to demonstrate to native populations the extent to which they dominated the high seas. It was quite possible that they would do the same in Japan, where such a display would be guaranteed to make a deep impression on the local authorities.

Cocks and his men believed that there was little they could do to rescue the English captives aboard the *Angell*, for the vessel lay at anchor in the middle of the bay. But Adams was determined to act. Although he was suffering from a tropical disease and was "sickly" and "minded to take physic," he raised himself from his sickbed and began masterminding an audacious rescue mission. His plan was kept totally secret, and he left no clues as to how he managed to sail across the bay and clamber onto the *Angell*. Nor did he explain how he freed the prisoners from their shackles. But somehow he smuggled himself aboard the Dutch vessel, freed two of the three English captives, and brought them back in safety to the English factory.

When Cocks heard of Adams's triumph, he was embarrassed that he had made no efforts to rescue the men. In a letter to Sir Thomas Smythe, he described the incident with an uncharacteristic terseness, recording only that "William Gourden and Michael Payne escaped ashore by the assistance of Mr William Adams." He was even less forthcoming about the events of the following night, when Adams scored a second coup by managing to secure the release of the third captive—a Welshman called Hugh Williams—who had not been freed in the first attempt. It was a typically understated act of heroism on the part of Adams and even more remarkable given that he was jeopardizing any future employment from Specx and his men.

The Dutch were furious to learn of their prisoners' escape and demanded their immediate return. But the English were delighted to hold the upper hand for once and steadfastly refused to hand them over. This infuriated the Dutch still further; they vowed to recover their captives in whatever way they could. "When they saw they could not by any meanes get back the Englishmen," wrote Cocks, ". . . they laid secrett ambushes ashore to have taken them." But their strategy failed, for the men remained safely behind the locked and bolted doors of the English factory gates.

Specx's men now decided on a show of force outside the factory, hoping to intimidate Cocks and his men into submission. "They came to outbrave us in the streets before our own doors," wrote a worried Cocks, "urging us with vile speeches." Their numbers were swelled by scores of unruly mariners from the *Angell*, who tried their utmost to provoke a fight, aware that they far outnumbered the little band of Englishmen. Cocks steadfastly refused to open the factory gates, much to the chagrin of the rabble outside. They grew "so mad that they came on shore by multitudes, thinking by force to have entered into our howse and cut all our throates." Wave after wave of attackers advanced on the English factory, watched by an increasingly alarmed Cocks, whose men were soon outnumbered a hundred to one. It was fortunate that the building was surrounded by a strong perimeter fence that was relatively easy to defend and almost impossible to scale. But as ever-greater numbers of Dutchmen came ashore, their bravado fueled by alcohol, the Englishmen feared that the end was near. They were exhausted—both physically and mentally—and knew that it was only a matter of time before the sheer weight of men told against them.

But luck, for once, was on their side. The Japanese authorities were horrified to see such unruly behavior on their streets and dispatched a detachment of Japanese troops to defend the English against the Dutch mob. "[They] took our partes," wrote Cocks, who watched with relief as the Japanese dispersed the crowd and restored order. The Dutch had no option but to beat a hasty retreat.

Cocks assumed that the intervention of the Japanese would be the end of the matter and went to bed that night safe in the knowledge that Dutch violence was now at an end. But his wishful thinking had been premature. A troop of Dutch mariners crept ashore at dawn the following morning and took the English by surprise, forcing their way through the main gates and inside the factory. "A company of ten entered our howse armed with pikes, swordes and cattans [swords] . . . ," wrote a terrified Cocks, "[and] wounded John Coaker and another, thinking that they had kild one of them." The intruders soon broke into the living quarters of the factory building where Cocks and his men were still asleep. Awakened by the terrifying clatter of swords and muskets, they immediately saw the gravity of the situation.

It was now—in their moment of crisis—that Adams's good relations with the local Japanese in Hirado paid the richest dividend.

Cocks raised the alarm and, within minutes, a platoon of Japanese soldiers came rushing to his aid, storming into the factory and evicting the Dutch interlopers. "Had it not been for the assistance of the Japanese, our neighbours, which tooke our partes, they [would have] kild us all." The Dutch intruders were forced off the premises, leaving a weary and terrified band of Englishmen.

Cocks was now so fearful for his men's safety that he was "constrained to keepe in our howse a guard of Japanese night and day, armed, at meate, drink and wages, to Your Worships greate charge." He was reassured to learn that King Figen was so alarmed by the disorder that he warned the Dutch that any future disturbance would be crushed with the utmost severity. Yet Specx's mob broke King Figen's command almost immediately, and Cocks wrote a desperate letter to Sir Thomas Smythe, informing him that the Dutch had "proclaimed open warrs against our English nation, both by sea and land, with fire and sworde." They threatened "to take our shipps and goodes and destroy our persons to the uttermost of their power, as to their mortall enemies."

This volatile situation was inflamed still further by the arrival of a large Dutch fleet whose bellicose commander vowed to murder Cocks and his men. Aware that this would not be easy, for they were still protected by Japanese guards, he put a price on their heads, promising a financial reward to anyone who managed to kill them. "[He] sett my life at sale," wrote a terrified Cocks, "offering 50-reals-of-eight to anyone would kill me, and 30 reals of same for each other Englishman they could kill."

In the space of just two years, the Dutch had gone from being the closest of friends to the bitterest of foes. Cocks and his men could no longer leave their factory compound without fear of being assassinated.

Chapter 13

LAST ORDERS

RICHARD COCKS feared that London's merchants would not believe the seriousness of his predicament and decided to send news of his plight to his old friend Sir Thomas Wilson. He informed Wilson that his men were surrounded by an angry and baying mob—"an unthankfull and theevishe rabble . . . who make a daily pracktis to rob and spoile all." The behavior of these unruly Dutch mariners was so menacing that Cocks begged Hidetada to come to his aid. But the shogun dismissed his pleas for help and refused to intervene. Although he gave "good words and promise that we should have justice," he was not interested in domestic squabbles and insisted that it was for the lord of Hirado to enforce the law. Nor did he show any sympathy when a Portuguese delegation arrived at court in order to protest. Hidetada bluntly informed them that "he would not make nor meddell in other men's matters," arguing that the capturing of their ships had occurred outside Japanese waters.

The shogun was far more disturbed by news filtering out of Nagasaki. He had heard rumors that a number of expelled Jesuit priests had secretly slipped back into Japan and were being cared for by local communities of covert Christians. It was not long before the rumors were confirmed. Small groups of Jesuits had indeed returned to Japan, transported aboard the annual trading ships from Macao. They had found it relatively easy to enter the country unnoticed, for there was much chaos and confusion that followed the arrival of the great ship. Once they had landed in Japan, they vanished like phantoms, living in safe houses and only venturing out at night. They had a network of "underground" contacts throughout the land and could celebrate Mass in secret with little fear of being caught. The penalties for such a flagrant disregard of Hidetada's anti-Christian edict were torture and death, yet this did not deter the most fervent of these padres.

Hidetada had first received definite news of the Jesuits' return in the spring of 1617. He was particularly incensed by the behavior of two of the priests—a Jesuit and a Franciscan—who held his anti-Christian edict in such disdain that they began preaching in public. One of the two, Padre Jean-Baptiste Machado, claimed to have yearned for martyrdom in Japan since the age of ten—the result of some potent childhood stories—and said that the day of his death would be the happiest of his life. This claim was soon put to the test, for he was seized in the fiefdom of Omura and accused of disobeying Hidetada's edict.

He neither denied the charge nor showed any remorse. Indeed, he told the lord of Omura that he would be happy to be executed in the Japanese fashion—dismembered and chopped to morsels. In the event, he was cut into just two pieces—head and body—suffering three painful strokes of the sword before his head finally thumped to the ground. Between each stroke, he thanked Jesus for his plight. His fellow priest was also beheaded, not by the common executioner "but by one of the first officers of the lord." The corpses were placed in a common grave and guards posted beside it, but this did not prevent scenes of wild hysteria and public zeal. "The sick were carried to the sepulchre to be restored to health," wrote one eyewitness. "The Christians found new strength in this martyrdom [while] the pagans themselves were full of admiration for it." Far from deterring the local Christian community, it gave them the courage to begin worshiping in the open. "Numerous conversion and numerous returns of apostates took place everywhere."

The Omura fiefdom was home to a large Christian community, and the local lord now found that his land was in turmoil. His troubles deepened when two more foreign padres, marveling at the effect of this martyrdom, threw caution to the wind and began preaching in full priestly garb. One of the two, Padre Alphonso, brazenly decreed that he did not recognize the emperor of Japan, but only the emperor of heaven. The lord of Omura ordered both priests to be summarily executed, and this time he took an added precaution. According to Cocks, he organized a secret burial to prevent their bodies' becoming relics. "Because the people carried away the blood, in handkerchefes and clothes, of the other two," he wrote, ". . . [the lord of Omura] caused these two to be cast into the sea with stones tied about their necks." Even this grim fate served only to fuel the ardor of people's faith. Every time a new martyr was burned or beheaded, there was "so great fervour and courage in all the Christians . . . that now they did not thinke nor talke of any other thing but only how to prepare themselves to imitate and follow them."

The Jesuit authorities continued to blame William Adams for their woes. Their private writings contain many complaints against his "malicious and most vile reportes," and it was not long before they began accusing him publicly. In one book, *A Briefe Relation of the Persecution Lately Made Against the Catholike Christians in the Kingdome of Japonia*, the author singled out Adams as the cause of their misfortunes. He claimed that the Japanese nobility had turned against the Jesuits because they were "incited by the wordes of an English pilot, who spake most bitterly against religious men and Spaniardes." Adams was said to have made "their persons odious unto him [the shogun], and all that they did suspitious." Another book claimed that the entire ruling elite had been "not a little provoked by the foolish words of a certain pilot"—William Adams. It accused him of informing Hidetada that the Jesuits were actually soldiers in disguise who had come to Japan in order to "make war against them and, overcomming them, take possession of their kingdom and estates."

Although Adams had indeed made such accusations and had done much to harm those who had once tried to crucify him, the foreign priests had also been the authors of their own misfortunes. They had infuriated the shogunate by fighting with the rebels at the siege of Osaka and had persistently challenged the feudal order by demanding total obedience from their converts. Most heinous of all, they had blithely ignored Hidetada's edict. Unlike Ieyasu, who had repeatedly "closed his eyes" to their disobedience, Hidetada was determined to act. As he was less interested in foreign trade, while also anxious to tighten his control over Japan, his policy was to crush anyone who could challenge his rule. If that meant slaughtering Christians—both European and Japanese—then he was only too willing to do so.

The English realized that events were rapidly spiraling out of control and kept a close eye on developments. They had noticed that the lay Christian community in Nagasaki had so far been virtually untouched by the violence, even though the town harbored large numbers of Christians. This was all the more surprising given that the Japanese governor was fanatically anti-Christian. But Governor Hasegawa was a busy man and left the town's day-to-day affairs to his deputy, Murayama Toan, who had converted to Christianity some years earlier.

Although Toan's conversion was an open secret, the authorities had hitherto chosen not to act. But in the tense months that followed the Omura executions, Toan found himself accused by one of his bitterest foes. He and his family were charged with being Christians "and maintainers of Jesuits and friers who were enemies to the state." Toan denied that he was financing the Jesuits' covert operation in Japan, but steadfastly refused to abjure his faith. Such intransigence infuriated the authorities, who ordered him to be roasted alive, along with his entire family. The sentence was carried out with customary Japanese efficiency.

Cocks wrote that "it is thought greate persecution will ensue at Nagasaki." His prediction was correct, for the city now bore the brunt of the regime's anti-Christian wrath. Many of Nagasaki's churches had already been destroyed after the first anti-Christian edict, but a few—like the magnificent Santa Casa da Misericordia—had been spared. Now, every chapel, church, and tombstone was hacked to pieces in an attempt to eradicate all traces of Christianity. The English, who watched the destruction with considerable excitement, felt that this spelled the end for Catholicism in Japan. "All is quite pulled downe," wrote Cocks, "and all graves and sepulchres opened, and dead men's bones taken out."

Hidetada compounded Catholic woes by ordering "pagodas to be erected" on the sites of the wealthiest and most prestigious churches. He also sent "heathen priests to live in them, thinking utterly to roote out the memory of Christianity out of Japan." He insisted that even little family shrines must be destroyed and ordered the felling of flowering trees planted by Christians in memory of the deceased. "All the said trees and altars are quite cut downe," wrote Cocks, "and the grownd made even, such is his desire to root out the remembrance of all such matters." By the time Hidetada's demolition squads had finished their work, every Christian edifice in Nagasaki lay in ruins, while the churchyards were scattered with human bones and putrid, flyblown corpses.

Adams and Cocks both felt a malicious twinge of excitement at the fate of the Jesuit fathers, yet they were surprised by the extent of Hidetada's wrath and viewed the wrecking of the churches with a sense of misgiving. "I doe not rejoice herein," wrote Cocks in a letter to Sir Thomas Smythe, although he said that he was pleased that the English could now visit Nagasaki without being insulted by priests and lay people. "In the time of that bishop," he wrote, ". . . one could not passe the streetes without being by them called *Lutranos* [Lutherans] and *herejos* [heretics]." Now, he added, "none of them dare open his mouth to speake such a word." The monks who had once tried to kill William Adams had now been silenced, and the few brave Catholics remaining in Japan found themselves in the greatest danger.

It was not long before the wave of persecutions began to envelop Japanese converts. In the autumn of 1619, Cocks was spending a few days in Kyoto when he heard rumors that there was to be a spectacular public burning of local Christians. He investigated further and discovered that no fewer than fifty-two of the most devout townsfolk were to be roasted alive in the dry bed of the Kamo River. They included several entire families as well as many mothers and children who had steadfastly refused to apostatize.

Mass executions were extremely common in Japan and always drew a large crowd. There was particular excitement on the eve of a public burning, in which suffering and pain were overlaid with a barbaric theatricality. Spectators participated in the organization of the event, helping to prepare the firewood and fix stakes into the ground. "When anyone is to be burnt," wrote Dutchman Reyer Gysbertsz, "it is given out and publicly proclaimed on the evening before, that each house which lies near the place . . . must bring two, three, four or five faggots of firewood." Gysbertsz was writing of a later execution, but all were similarly brutal and horrific. Local officials dressed themselves in their finery and arrived early to supervise the event. "[They] erected as many stakes as there are persons to be burnt, and the wood is laid around at a distance of about five-and-a-half fathoms from the stakes." When the public arena had been prepared, the victims themselves were brought forth and bound to the stakes with ropes attached to their arms. As the heat of the fire increased in intensity, they would be forced to hop and skip in pain, making fools of themselves as they went to their grisly deaths.

On this occasion, the fifty-two Christians were taken to the place of execution in chariots. The women and toddlers were seated at the middle of the procession, while the men and boys were placed in the front and rear. As this solemn group made its way to the Kamo River, the crier announced their fate to the assembled masses: "The shogun, ruler of all Japan, wants and commands that all these people are burned alive for being Christians."

With such a large number of people to be burned, the executioners were obliged to tie several to each stake. The men were bound together, back to back, while the mothers were entwined with their children. It made for a desperate spectacle, and many of the onlookers were moved to tears. This execution was on an unprecedented scale, and the carnival atmosphere came to an abrupt end when people realized the full horror of what they were about to witness. One of the mothers, Tecla, was to be burned with her five children. Another, Madeleine, was roped to her two-year-old daughter Regine. Marthe was to be burned with her two-year-old son Benoit. One eight-year-old was blind.

Cocks was distraught as he watched the children tied to the stakes with their parents. "Amongst them," he wrote, "were littell children of five or six years ould." The Jesuits had helped to prepare such victims for their ordeal, publishing religious tracts on how to bear the pain of torture and fire. "While being tortured, visualise the Passion of Jesus," reads one prayer manual. "Think intently that Santa Maria, many angels and blessed ones are looking upon your fight from Heaven."

Cocks was present when the kindling wood was lit and the flames began to lick their victims. He was amazed to note that "they would not forsake their Christian faith," even when suffering the most terrible agony. They bore their pain with a stoicism that astonished those who had gathered. The mothers stroked

Executions and burnings were publicly proclaimed on the evening before they took place (above). Local inhabitants would help to prepare an arena, and often brought stakes, faggots, and firewood.

Public burnings always drew a large crowd in Japan, especially when the victims were Christians. Richard Cocks was surprised to note that "they would not forsake their faith," even when suffering intense pain.

their children's heads as the flames began to roar, and the children moaned softly as the pain grew too great to endure. "[They were] burned in their mothers' armes," wrote a despairing Cocks, "crying out, 'Jesus receive their soules.'" Tecla was clutching her four-year-old daughter Lucy so tightly that their charred corpses—when eventually removed from the stake—were fused together. The assembled crowd had never seen such a pitiful spectacle and many wept openly. All declared that they no longer had fear of anything.

The public burning in Kyoto heralded a dramatic increase in the scale and intensity of the persecution. In the immediate aftermath, the focus of the killings switched back to Nagasaki, where the martyrdoms continued apace. "There was sixteen more martyred . . . ," wrote Cocks, "whereof five were burned and the rest beheaded and cut in peeces and cast into the sea in sacks at thirty fathom deepe." One of these was Domingo Jorge, a Portuguese trader who stood accused of sheltering two Jesuits. He was sentenced to be hacked to pieces. In spite of the widespread brutality, the executions did little to dampen public enthusiasm for Christianity. Nor did they stop the desperate clamor for relics. Even the corpses dumped at sea soon found their way back to dry land, "[for] the Christians got them up againe and keepe them secretly for relickes."

The English were fortunate that Adams had persuaded Hidetada of their anti-Catholic credentials, for they remained untouched by the persecution. But they were still in grave danger of being murdered by their Dutch rivals and they also faced an increasingly acute financial crisis. Their warehouse contained small stocks of skins, hides, and hemp, but the men could find no buyers. They had plentiful sappanwood, but a glut meant that sales were sluggish, and the market in silk had slumped in the previous few months. No one at the factory spoke any longer of profits; all the talk was about how to generate enough income to keep themselves alive. Eaton said that they faced the stark prospect of not being able to feed themselves over the coming winter. In a letter to London, he bemoaned their plight and added a desperate post-script: "Here are many mouthes which eat a great deale," he wrote. "God helpe us."

Most of these additional "mouthes" had arrived in Japan over the previous few months. The Hirado factory was still sheltering the three Englishmen whom Adams had rescued from the *Angell*, while several other mariners had been left behind by the various ships that had called at the port. The additional personnel had become a real burden for a factory already in deep crisis, for the men were often sick or wounded and therefore unable to work.

Cocks was thankful that five of the original eight founders of the factory were still alive and able to help him grow food in his vegetable garden. But in March 1620, William Nealson fell extremely sick. He had never been in good health, and his prodigious consumption of alcohol had only served to weaken his already battered constitution. After each relapse, he had convalesced at the hot springs of Iki and made a partial recovery. But on this occasion he was too ill to travel to the springs, and Cocks recorded that Nealson was "so extreame sick" that he harbored serious doubts of his recovery. He was stricken with fever and soon became too weak to raise himself from his sickbed. Cocks wrote that he was "wasted away with a consumption" and knew the end was near. At some point in March—the exact date is unknown—Nealson breathed his last. The factory had lost its most truculent and unruly member.

Nealson died intestate, but the factory members all swore that in his lifetime, "being in good and perfect memory," he had named Cocks as his intended heir. Cocks was genuinely touched and was filled with remorse at his previous harsh words. He wrote in his diary that "if God had called me to His mercy before Mr Nealson, then . . . he [would have] had as much of mine."

Nealson's death was a blow to the morale of Cocks and his men. Although he was a drunkard and a wastrel, he was nonetheless one of the founders of the English factory in Japan. The men were proud of the fact that they had survived against all the odds on the far side of the globe, and their confidence had grown with every year that passed. But they rapidly lost heart as their numbers diminished, wondering who would be next to fall sick or be killed. Peacock and Carwarden were long dead, murdered and drowned in Cochinchina, while Wickham had expired in Bantam. Now Nealson's death left just four of the factory's original team—Cocks, Adams, Eaton, and Sayers. But Adams, too, was not well. Cocks could not determine the exact nature of his illness, but it may well have been a recurrence of the sickness that had struck on his return from Cochinchina. The tropical coastline was notorious for malaria, and it is quite conceivable that this debilitating illness had returned with a vengeance. Just a few weeks earlier, Adams had been strong enough to challenge Cocks to a longboat race. Now such athleticism seemed a lifetime away. Soon after the race, the fifty-five-year-old Adams went into a catastrophic decline.

This was terrible news for Cocks and his men. Unlike Nealson, who had achieved little of note during his seven years in Japan, Adams had proved critical to the survival of the factory. At every point of crisis, the men had turned to him for help. They had relied upon him for their audiences with the shogun and had utilized his contacts within the merchant community. It was Adams who had rescued them from insolvency by sailing to Siam and who had discovered the truth about the mysterious disappearance of Peacock and Carwarden. Three of the men in the factory owed their very lives to Adams—those rescued from the Dutch prison ship—while the others had survived the regime in Japan only because of his help and advice. Now he lay sickly and wan, and the men soon realized that he was not going to recover.

So, too, did Adams himself. On May 16, 1620, he called Cocks and Eaton to his bedside to dictate his last will and testament. "I, William Adams, mariner, that have been resident in Japan the space of some eighteen or twenty yeares, being sick of body but of a perfect remembrance—laude and praise be to Almighty God— make and ordeine this my present testament."

His will needed careful thought, for he was a man of means. In addition to his country estate at Hemi and his town house at Edo, Adams had accumulated the considerable sum of £500. He divided the main parcel of his estate into two parts, with half going to his estranged family in England and the other half to Joseph and Susanna, his children in Japan. His third Japanese child, born of his Hirado maid, was not even mentioned.

Adams was determined that his English daughter, Deliverance, should be the principal beneficiary in England, and ordered that the first Mrs. Adams should receive no more than half the money, with the rest going to his child. "For it was not his mind [that] his wife should have all in regard she might marry another husband and carry all from his childe."

Adams did not forget his friends in Japan. To Cocks, he bequeathed his valuable celestial globe, his sea charts, and his finest sword; Eaton was to inherit all his books and navigational equipment. His son Joseph was given his fine collection of weaponry; Osterwick and three other Englishmen were each given one of his kimonos. Although Adams had frequently been accused of being "Hollandized," he left nothing to any of his erstwhile Dutch colleagues.

Cocks and Eaton, his principal executors, watched with great sadness as he put the finishing clause to his will. "And so hereunto I have set my hand, these whose names are hereunder being wittnesses." It was the last thing Adams ever wrote. Shortly after setting his signature to paper, his breathing became shallow and his life slipped away. Samurai William—the first Englishman in Japan—was dead. It was the end of an era.

His place of burial remains unclear. It is likely that he was interred in the little English cemetery in Hirado, set in a shady grove of trees in the hills above the town. Yet it is just possible that his final resting place was in Hemi, on his country estate, where his Japanese wife would eventually be interred. It was left to Richard Cocks to write Adams's epitaph—a magnificent tribute to the man who had enabled the English to establish themselves, and survive, in the Land of the Rising Sun. "I canot but be sorrofull for the losse of such a man as Capt William Adams," he wrote, "he, having been in such favour with two emperours of Japan as never was any Christian in these parts of the worlde." He recorded that Adams had such a towering presence that "[he] might freely have entered and had speech with the emperours, when many Japan kings stood without and could not be permitted."

Adams had indeed wielded enormous influence. He had also played a significant role in the expulsion of the Jesuits from Japan and had ensured that the shogun's anti-Christian edicts did not touch Cocks and his men in Hirado. He alone had been able to guarantee their survival during their long years in Japan. Now he was dead, and he took to the grave his enormous influence at court. From this point on, Cocks's dwindling band of Englishmen would have no one to argue their case—and fight their corner—at the court of the ruling shogun.

The death of Adams broke Cocks's spirit. He had long realized that his time in Japan was nearing an end, and Adams's demise was a stark reminder that he was living on borrowed time. Cocks was now in his mid-fifties and was rapidly approaching old age.

To his surprise, he discovered that he was no longer saddened by the idea of leaving Japan. In a letter to Sir Thomas Smythe—written in the spring of 1620—he confessed that he was "all-together a-weary of Japan." His efforts to open trading links with China and Siam had singularly failed, and the factory continued to teeter on the brink of financial ruin. The constant threat of insolvency had dented Cocks's ebullience and he was now "out of hope of any good to be done in Japan."

He was far more troubled by the fact that he had failed to feather his nest during his seven years in Hirado. Unlike Wickham, who had devoted much of his energy to enriching himself, Cocks had only occasionally dabbled in private trade. Yet he had constantly lived beyond his means and had spent large sums of his own money on food, female entertainers, and prize goldfish. But the most constant drain on his resources was Matinga. Over the years, Cocks had bought her jewelry, silks, and satins. He had paid for her house in Hirado and given her several maids and servants. Now he learned that she had repaid his kindness by being unfaithful. He recorded that she had behaved with "villany" and "abused herself with six or seven persons."

Cocks had long feared that news of his lavish lifestyle would lead the London merchants to conclude that he had engaged in private trade. In a letter to Sir Thomas Smythe, he insisted that he had always behaved with probity and honesty. "I came a poor man out of England," he wrote, "[and shall] retorne a beggar home." He also attempted to justify his parties by arguing that they had been primarily business functions: "Your worships shall never find that I have been a gamester or riatouse person."

Cocks was still wondering how the factory would fare without Adams when he received news that was as astonishing as it was unexpected. On July 23, 1620, he heard rumors that a large English vessel had been sighted off the coastline of Hirado and that she was the vanguard of a huge fleet. The rumors soon turned out to be true. Captain Martin Pring of the *James Royal* confirmed that he had indeed sailed as part of a vast armada; he brought the even more startling news that the Dutch and English—who had been virtually at war for more than four years—were now allies. A peace accord had been signed by company directors in London and Amsterdam, and all hostilities had been suspended. Their accord went much further than reestablishing the status quo. The directors had established a joint squadron of ships—a "Fleet of

Defense"—whose mission was to "make spoile and havocke of all Portuguese and Spaniards, wheresoever we meet them."

Cocks could scarcely believe his luck. He had lost one protector—Adams—only to have another take his place. The *James Royal* was followed in quick succession by three more vessels: the *Moon*, the *Elizabeth*, and the Dutch ship *Trouw*. A few days later, the *Palsgrave* sailed into the bay, followed by a squadron of other ships. Their arrival changed everything. Overnight, the warring factions in Hirado made their peace and the blockade of the English factory was lifted. Cocks and Specx managed to patch up their ruptured friendship and found themselves being encouraged to work together in a way that had earned them criticism in the past.

The wretched and hungry men in the English factory—still grieving over Adams's untimely death—received the surprise news of the accord with great joy. Eaton wrote that "it was wellcome news unto us that live here . . . and to all others which are honnest men." They had lived under constant threat of death for many months and had been able to leave their factory compound only if accompanied by Japanese guards. Now they could sleep without fear of attack. The newly arrived fleet brought security, desperately needed supplies, and four large chests filled with silver coins.

But it also brought more than 1,000 unruly sea dogs, who were desperate to seek pleasure in the local whorehouses. The pimps of Hirado were delighted by the arrival of these men and saw it as a fine opportunity to make money. "As our men go along the streets," wrote Cocks, "the Japanese kindly call them in and give them wine and whores till they be drunk, and strip them of all they have (some of them stark naked)."

Adams had long ago warned of the dangers of unruly mariners being unleashed on the town of Hirado. Now, when that advice was most needed, it was brushed aside in the exuberance of the moment. Some of the men were so enchanted with the oriental pleasures ashore that they spent all their savings on prostitutes. Others preferred to riot and fight, attacking anyone who blocked their path. On one occasion, they found themselves brawling with some local Japanese. "Being drunke, [a group of men] did brabble with the Japanese, and drew out their knives." This proved a fatal mistake, for the men were seized, dragged to a field, and given a swift lesson in Japanese punishment. They were decapitated "[and] left in the fields to be eaten by crowes and dogges."

It was inevitable that news of the fighting and debauchery would soon reach Java, where the puritanical Richard Fursland had recently taken up his position as England's president of the Council of Defense. It was equally inevitable that he would react with fury and contempt. Fursland was a strict disciplinarian who had already vowed to purge the East India Company of its more disreputable characters. He had begun by putting his own house in order. Incompetent factors in Java were sent home in disgrace; others were punished for boorish behavior. One of his men, the Italian-born John Vincente, was put in the stocks after being caught flagrante delicto with a local prostitute.

As Fursland cast his eyes elsewhere in the East, he discovered a sorry picture of degeneracy and insolvency. Several outlying factories had long been abandoned, while trade in the Moluccas was in terminal decline. England's only remaining toehold in the nutmeg-producing Banda Islands had been lost in 1620, when the last pocket of heroic English resistance had been snuffed out. The little factories at Jambi in Sumatra and Pattani were insolvent and "allmost decayed." At Pattani, the factor was in debt to the tune of more than £120 and was forbidden from leaving by the local ruler. At Ayutthaya, it was a similarly depressing story. The dreams once harbored by Lucas Antheunis—of a factory thriving off trade with Japan—had proved hollow indeed.

Nor did the Fleet of Defense achieve the spectacular success that had been predicted. Its first foray into the South China Sea, in January 1621, was dogged by poor command. It missed the big Portuguese prize and captured just five poorly laden junks. The second voyage proved little better. An attack on Macao was repulsed by the Portuguese, while most of the plunder from captured ships was spent on reequipping the fleet. Fursland took the bold decision to redeploy the English ships of the Fleet of Defense and, in doing so, he effectively terminated the Anglo-Dutch alliance. The spirit of cooperation was over before it had achieved anything of note.

Fursland also vowed to bring discipline to the chaotic regime in Hirado. He was horrified by the moral depravity into which—in his eyes—the men of Hirado had fallen. He was particularly disgusted by tales of banquets, feasts, and dancing girls, and he singled out Cocks as the author of the factory's misfortunes. He informed the London merchants that Cocks's bacchanalian antics "not only consumes so much of your estate, but also utterly ruins the most part of your men by their most beastlie living." As Fursland received more and more information about partner-swapping, concubines, and illegitimate children, he was sickened to the core. He said that "it is a misery to know that men of such antique years should be so miserably given over to voluptuousness, regarding not what they consume therein."

Fursland wanted to see Cocks and his men punished for their misdemeanors and decided to recall them to Java. In the spring of 1622, he sent a message to Japan ordering that Cocks, Eaton, and Sayers, "who have been a long time at Japan, [are] to come away from there."

Cocks had no intention of obeying Fursland's command. He was terrified of being blamed for all of Hirado's woes and was equally worried by the chaotic state of his accounts. He decided to contravene the order to leave Japan, justifying his disobedience by arguing that his books were not yet up to date. Misjudging Fursland's mood as well as the seriousness of his own predicament, he wrote a letter in which he joshed that if he were to arrive in

Java with inaccurate records, "your worshipp may bid me retorne back againe, like an old fool as I am, and do it."

Many months passed before Fursland received Cocks's letter, by which time the monsoon had started. For more than four months the winds blew in Cocks's favor and Fursland was unable to dispatch a single vessel to Hirado. In the twilight of his time in Japan, Cocks returned to a quieter life, tending his beloved orchard, feeding his goldfish, and reliving his ten years in the Land of the Rising Sun. There was much to remember and celebrate: voyages to the shogun and banquets with courtiers; visits to temples and feasts with Buddhist monks. He was proud to have established a trading post on the far side of the world, separated from England by a two-year sea voyage, and kept it more or less solvent. He was also proud to have preserved his men in good health and ensured that they were amused and entertained in a way that few could ever have imagined. Yet Cocks knew that none of this would have been possible without Adams, who had been the unsung guardian of the English factory.

He kept in regular contact with the Japanese Mrs. Adams after her husband's death, sending her gifts of baubles and trinkets. In March 1622, he presented her with a large quantity of white silk, along with damasks and taffeta for Joseph and Susanna. He also gave her silver and offered to pay for Joseph's schooling. When he visited the family on the first Christmas after Adams's death, he handed Joseph his father's sword and dagger. The young lad was grateful "[and there] were tears shed at delivery."

Joseph was soon to receive a far more valuable gift. Shortly after his father's death, the shogun summoned him to his palace and conferred upon him all the privileges that had been granted to William Adams more than a dozen years earlier. "[He] hath confirmed the lordship to his son," wrote Cocks, "which the other emperour gave to the father." Joseph Adams was also granted continued rights to his father's estate at Hemi, along with all the villages and rice fields.

It was with heavy hearts that the English watched the good ship *Bull* sail into Hirado a year later with the first of the summer winds. She was carrying a letter, written by the still-furious Fursland, which could not have been more forthright in its demands. Addressed contemptuously to "Mr Cocks and the rest," it lambasted the men for their "greate disobedience" in ignoring his previous orders. "What mooved you hereunto," wrote Fursland, "we know not," but he expressed shock that someone of "so many years" had not yet learned to obey his superiors.

The first part of Fursland's letter was littered with veiled threats; the second was filled with orders. Cocks was to hand over his authority to the newly arrived Joseph Cockram—who was charged with closing the factory—and was also to surrender his account books. In addition he was told to recover all the money owed by Li Tan, who "hath too long deluded you." Fursland was so concerned that Cocks would once again refuse to set sail that he repeated his orders at the end of the letter, "lest, having read it in the former part thereof, you should forgett it before you come to the end."

Cocks read the letter with a heavy heart. He knew that it spelled the end of his time in Japan, as well as the end of his service with the East India Company. If the London merchants decided to withhold his wages, he would end his life in destitution. It was a terrifying prospect for any Jacobean gentleman—but more so for one who had few friends left alive in England.

The closure of the factory took time. Officials had to be notified and a visit had to be made to the shogun and his court. Small gifts of money were presented to the factory's servants, and the few goods in the warehouse were loaded aboard the *Bull*. Fursland would later describe it as "trash and lumber" and he was probably right. There was little of worth to be carried away from Japan. Cocks and his men stalled for time and spent their last few days engaged in tearful farewells. On December 22, 1623, "many of the townsmen came with their wives and families to take leave of the factors, some weeping at their departure." It was an especially sad day for William Eaton's mistress, Kamezo, who was saying farewell to both her partner and her son. She begged Cocks to look after the young lad and would soon write to him to beseech his help. "I am relying on you [more] than on my own father," she wrote. "Please be kind enough to take good and gentle care of him."

The English, too, were sad to be leaving the women and children they loved. Eaton embraced his daughter, Helena, while Sayers said his final farewell to his mistress and daughter. Cocks was alone in being glad to leave his mistress, the unfaithful Matinga, who had cost him a fortune. He had singularly failed to get her pregnant, despite many jokes about his virility.

On December 23, a few of the Dutch factors and many "Japanese friends" came on board the *Bull* to say their last good-byes. Captain Cockram was anxious to set sail, but he was moved by the tears and decided to postpone the departure so that there could be a final night's party. The men and women celebrated late into the evening, and the dark harbor of Hirado echoed with the sound of revelry and music.

It was late by the time the last guests had returned ashore, and there was precious little left of the night. The men snatched a few hours' sleep before the sun rose above the horizon and the crew were called on deck. The *Bull*'s anchors were raised; her great sails were unfurled. The wind was blowing from the north and there was snow in the air. It would be a cold day at sea.

The town receded into the distance, until the houses were a blur and the palace scarcely visible. Next, the land retreated to a shadow—the steep, pine-clad hillside standing darkly against the sky. Hirado was fast merging with the horizon. After ten years, six months, and thirteen days, the English were abandoning Japan.

Cocks and his men were leaving under a shadow that had been stalking them for years. They might have redeemed themselves if they had had treasure to take back to London—the sacks of silver so keenly desired by the company. But the Hirado factory was bankrupt; there was nothing to carry home. Their abandoned lodgings were the only reminder of the East India Company's dreams—the warehouse and the chambers that had consumed so much money. Even these sturdy buildings were not to last for long. Battered by hurricanes and ruined by rain, they quickly crumbled and collapsed. Within a few years, every trace of the English had disappeared. It was as if they had never come.

The company had long hoped to pin the blame for failure on their servant Richard Cocks. But Cocks was already a broken man, and his ebullient spirit had been shattered by his recall. He was weary and depressed and of a "testie and wayward disposition." He was also desperately sick, having contracted a dangerous tropical disease shortly after leaving Japan. Cocks breathed his last on the long voyage to London and was laid to rest at sea, "under a discharge of ordnance."

Edmund Sayers, too, died before he reached home, leaving William Eaton as the only original member of the factory to make it back to England. He managed to avoid censure by refusing to cooperate with company inquiries. When quizzed about his licentious behavior, he gave only "cold and uncertain answers" and the merchants dismissed him in disgust. Although he lived to a ripe old age, he never again served with the East India Company.

The English had left Japan unwillingly and in disgrace, yet their departure came at a fortuitous moment. Shortly after they set sail from Hirado, Hidetada was replaced as shogun by his sadistic son, Iemitsu. He harbored a passionate hatred of foreigners and proceeded to hound them out of the country with a barbarity that had never before been witnessed. The Jesuits were the first to feel his wrath. The few remaining priests were tortured in the most gruesome fashion, along with the converts who refused to apostatize. Next it was the turn of the Portuguese traders. They were expelled in 1637 and ordered never to return. When one of their vessels broke this command, everyone on board was trussed up and decapitated. The Dutch, too, did not escape the shogun's wrath. With Adams no longer alive to fight their corner, they found themselves evicted from Hirado and confined to the tiny island of Deshima in Nagasaki Bay. Although allowed to continue a trade of sorts, they were closely watched and denied all contact with the Japanese.

The Land of the Rising Sun had entered a period known as *sakoku*—the closed country. She had seen enough of troublesome foreigners and their bitter internecine wars. Now, after a century of contact, Japan closed her windows on the world and denied traders entry into her profitable markets and cities. The few mariners who dared to sail there—or were unlucky enough to be shipwrecked—were arrested, tortured, and killed.

It was to be more than 200 years before Englishmen—and other foreigners—would once again set foot in this Eastern realm. When they did eventually return and explored the pagodas and temples of Tokyo, they were astonished to discover that William Adams's name was still famous throughout the land. They were told the marvelous story of Adams's rise at court: how he had been spokesman and adviser, tutor and oracle. His title, estate, and extraordinary friendship with the shogun had left a deep and lasting impression on the Japanese. As a mark of their respect, they had named an area of Tokyo, Anjincho, in his honor.

They had also kept his name alive in their prayers. In the sacred gloom of the Jodoji temple, close to where William Adams once had his town house, a crowd of believers gathered once a year to honor his memory. They chose the Jodoji for their pilgrimage because this was where Adams himself was said to have made his devotions.

Two centuries earlier, Adams had stood in humility before the pantheon of deities. Now, amid a flicker of lamps and candles, the crowds came to remember Anjin Sama—the mariner from Limehouse—whose name was still famous throughout the land.

As incense thickened the air, and bells clanged in the twilight, they prayed for the soul of Samurai William.

NOTES AND SOURCES

ACKNOWLEDGMENTS

INDEX

Notes and Sources

William Adams and his men left a wealth of material about their new lives in Japan. But their handwritten letters and journals—mostly housed in the British Library—are extremely hard to decipher. Until very recently, only a few of these had been published, often in editions that were far from satisfactory. Richard Cocks's colorful diary, for example, first printed in 1883 for the Hakluyt Society, was heavily expurgated by its Victorian editor.

In researching and writing *Samurai William*, I have been fortunate to have access to new and scholarly printed editions. Anthony Farrington's two-volume *The English Factory in Japan, 1613–23*, published in 1991 by the British Library, is indispensable. It contains all Adams's letters and logbooks, along with those of his colleagues, and it also includes the factory's account books, wills, and diaries. It supplants Thomas Rundall's *Memorials of the Empire of Japan in the XVI and XVII Centuries*, published by the Hakluyt Society in 1850.

The three-volume edition of Richard Cocks's diary, published 1978–81, is also invaluable (see notes for Chapter 8); it contains all the material missing from the volumes published in 1883.

Derek Massarella's superb *A World Elsewhere: Europe's Encounter with Japan in the Sixteenth and Seventeenth Centuries*, published in 1990 by Yale University Press, provides a detailed analysis of both the English and the Dutch in Japan, and considers the reasons for the economic decline of the Hirado factory.

The history of the Catholic missions in Japan remains underresearched. C. R. Boxer's *Christian Century in Japan* was published by Cambridge University Press in 1951, yet it remains the standard text on the missions. It is best read in conjunction with Michael Cooper's *They Came to Japan: An Anthology of European Reports on Japan, 1543–1640*, published by Thames & Hudson in 1965. This contains generous extracts from Padre Alessandro Valignano's *Historia del Principio y Progresso de la Compania de Jesus en las Indias Orientales*; Padre Luis Frois's *Historia do Japão* and *Cartas*; and Padre João Rodrigues's *Historia da Igreja do Japão*.

Michael Cooper's book *João Rodrigues's Account of Sixteenth-Century Japan*, published in 2002 by the Hakluyt Society, is a welcome addition to his *This Island of Japan: João Rodrigues' Account of 16th-Century Japan*, published in Tokyo and New York by Kodansha International, 1973.

An excellent background to the period is provided by Donald Lach in his monumental *Asia in the Making of Europe*, published in nine volumes by the University of Chicago Press, 1965–93. Much of the relevant information about Japan can be found in Volume 3, Book 4, Chapter 23. Another invaluable reference book is the *Kodansha Encyclopaedia of Japan*, published by Kodansha in Tokyo.

Many of the books listed below are long out of print, and some—especially those published in the aftermath of World War II—are not available in the UK. The most comprehensive collection of material relating to the English in Japan is housed in the Japan Foundation in Tokyo.

A full reference for each book will be given when it is first mentioned in these notes.

Prologue, pages 3–8

The saltiest and most piquant Elizabethan worldview is to be found in Richard Hakluyt's twelve-volume *The Principal Navigations, Voyages, Traffiques and Discoveries of the English Nation*. Hakluyt collected his material firsthand—from newly returned captains and mariners—and his book contains a wealth of material on the Indies, Africa, and the Americas. Japan—yet to be visited by an Englishman—receives only cursory coverage. First published in its enlarged edition between 1598 and 1600, it was reprinted as a Hakluyt Society Extra Series in 1903–5.

William Adams belonged to a generation whose horizons were continually expanding. The newly awakened sense of global possibility is expressed most eloquently and enthusiastically by the Arctic adventurer George Beste. His preface to the account of Martin Frobisher's 1576 expedition can be found in the Hakluyt Society's *The Three Voyages of Martin Frobisher*, 1867.

Chapter 1, pages 9–31

An outline of the voyages and accounts of the first Europeans in Japan—including an investigation into their veracity—can be found in Chapter 1 of C. R. Boxer's *Christian Century in Japan*. Michael Cooper's illustrated *Southern Barbarians: The First Europeans in Japan*, published by Kodansha International in 1971, focuses on the Jesuits in Japan and includes generous extracts from Frois and Rodrigues. Additional material on early Portuguese adventurers can be found in the fourth volume of Georg Schurhammer's monumental *Francis Xavier, His Life, His Times*, published by the Jesuit Historical Institute in Rome in 1982; see especially p. 260 ff., notes 95–118.

The first English translation of Fernão Mendes Pinto's *Peregrinaçam*, entitled *The Voyages and Adventures*, was published in 1663.

The Otomo family fortunes are dealt with in some detail in *The Cambridge History of Japan*, published by Cambridge University Press in 1993; see Volume 4, edited by John Whitney Hall, pp. 350–5.

The brief outline of Japanese history during the *sengoku jidai* (the era of civil wars) is drawn largely from James Murdoch and Isoh Yamagata's *A History of Japan during the Century of Early Foreign Intercourse, 1512–1651*, first published by the Asiatic Society of Japan in Kobe in 1903.

Jorge Alvarez's report on the Japanese can be found, in an English translation, in the first chapter of C. R. Boxer's *Christian Century in Japan*. Francis Xavier's mission to Japan is covered in exhaustive detail in Georg Schurhammer's biography. The footnotes in Volume 4 contain lengthy quotations from original sources.

The best account of Portuguese traders in Japan is to be found in C. R. Boxer's *The Great Ship from Amacon*, published by the Centro de Estudios Historicos Ultramarinos in 1959. This includes a year-by-year account of trading voyages, as well as extracts from Japanese state papers.

Chapter 2, pages 32–55

The account of Pet and Jackman's disastrous 1580 expedition to Japan is published in Volume 3 of Richard Hakluyt's *Principal Navigations*. This includes William Borough's instructions, pp. 259–62; Dr. Dee's advice, pp. 262–3; Richard Hakluyt's notes, pp. 264–75; and the journal of the voyage, pp. 282–303.

Richard Willes's *A Historye of Travaile* was published in 1577; his reports on both China and Japan can also be found in Hakluyt's *Principal Navigations*. Willes's account of the "monstrous muchaches" of the men of Hokkaido was no flight of fancy: see the illustrations in Savage Landor's *Alone with the Hairy Ainu*, published by John Murray in 1893.

Icebergs were feared by all Arctic adventurers and presented a significant threat to Elizabethan galleons. For a graphic account of the dangers, see Thomas Ellis's "A true report," in *The Third Voyage of Martin Frobisher to Baffin Island*, edited by James McDermott, Hakluyt Society, 2001, pp. 197–200.

For references to biographies of William Adams, see the notes for Chapter 5. Adams, as apprentice to Nicholas Diggins, would have had access to William Bourne's *A Regiment for the Sea*, 1577, Martin Cortes's *Art of Navigation* (translated by Richard Eden and published in 1561), and Lucas Waghenaer's *Spieghel der Zeervaert*, 1585. Adams was an experienced pilot by 1598 and his letters reveal that he owned at least some of his own navigational equipment.

Chapter 3, pages 56–82

The most comprehensive account of William Adams's voyage to Japan is contained in the three-volume *De Ries van Mahu en de Cordes*, edited by Dr F. C. Wieder. This was published by the Lindschoten Society between 1923 and 1925 and has a wealth of information about captains, crews, equipment, weaponry, and objectives. Unfortunately, it is only available in Dutch; I am most grateful to Marjolein van der Valk for translating large sections of this book.

A shorter account of the voyage is available in English translation. Constantine de Renneville's *Recueil des Voyages*, 1702, was published in English in 1703 under the title *Collection of Voyages Undertaken by the Dutch East India Company*. Extracts from Sebald de Weert's account can be found in English in the second volume of Samuel Purchas's twenty-volume *Purchas His Pilgrims*, republished as a Hakluyt Society Extra Series between 1905 and 1907. William Adams's own accounts of the voyage, written circa 1605 and 1611, are published in Anthony Farrington's *The English Factory in Japan*.

I have drawn on other contemporary accounts for background material. For further information about scurvy, see Sir Richard Hawkins's *The Hawkins Voyages*, Hakluyt Society, 1878, p. 138 ff., and Sir James Lancaster's *Voyage to the East Indies*, Hakluyt Society, 1877. For the dangers of the doldrums, see *The Troublesome Voyage of Edward Fenton*, Hakluyt Society, 1959. For more on the Cape Verde Islands, see Sir Richard Hawkins's account in *The Hawkins Voyages* and the description of Thomas Cavendish's 1586 circumnavigation in Hakluyt's *Principal Navigations*, Volume 11, p. 291 ff. For more on West Africa's voluptuous womenfolk, see Pieter de Marees's *Description and Historical Account of the Gold Kingdom of Guinea*, 1602, published in English by the Oxford University Press in 1987.

A good general background to Dutch exploration is to be found in George Masselman's *The Cradle of Colonialism*, published by Yale University Press in 1963.

Chapter 4, pages 83–108

Alessandro Valignano's mission to Japan is covered in considerable detail in J. F. Moran's *The Japanese and the Jesuits*, published by Routledge in 1993. The book investigates Jesuit attempts to integrate themselves and includes sections on Japanese Jesuits and the Jesuit printing press in Japan. There are also lengthy quotes from Valignano's *Sumario* and *Historia del Principio*, and his *Advertimentos*, sometimes known in English as *The Customs and Ceremonies of Japan*. The Jesuit mission is also investigated by C. R. Boxer in his *Christian Century in Japan* and by Michael Cooper in *Southern Barbarians*.

There are two Portuguese accounts of the *Liefde*'s arrival in *The Travels of Pedro Teixeira*, Hakluyt Society, 1902. These include extracts from Diogo de Couto's *Decada Decima* and from Fernão Guerreiro's *Relaçam Annual*.

Adams's fear of crucifixion was real enough; Francesco Carletti's description is taken from Michael Cooper, *They Came to Japan*.

Osaka impressed all foreign visitors, as did the beautiful interiors of the city merchants' houses. Padre Luis Frois's description, and João Rodrigues's account, can be found in *They Came to Japan*.

The only English-language biography of Tokugawa Ieyasu is L. Sadler's *The Maker of Modern Japan: The Life of Tokugawa Ieyasu*, published by Allen & Unwin in 1937. His wiles and his battles are dealt with in detail in James Murdoch and Isoh Yamagata's *A History of Japan*. An entire chapter is dedicated to an analysis of the battle of Sekigahara.

The best description of an audience with Ieyasu is taken from the account of Rodrigo de Vivero y Velasco, reprinted in *They Came to Japan*. The pungent account of a Japanese prison, written by Father Diego de San Francisco, is quoted in Murdoch and Yamagata, Volume 2, p. 604.

Chapter 5, pages 109–131

William Adams has been the subject of several biographies and essays; few offer more than cursory coverage of Adams's relationships with Saris, Cocks, and the others.

P. G. Rogers's *The First Englishman in Japan*, published by the Harvill Press in 1956, provides a useful overview; Richard Tames's *Servant of the Shogun*, published by Paul Norbury Publications, 1981, is short but reasonably accurate. Other, older accounts include Arthur Diosy's "In Memory of Will Adams," in *Transactions and Proceedings of the Japan Society*, 6, London, 1906; and Ilza Vieta's "Englishman or Samurai: The Story of Will Adams," in *Far Eastern Quarterly*, 5, Wisconsin, 1945. More recently William Corr has written *Adams the Pilot*, published by the Japan Library in 1995, and the privately published *Orders for the Captain*, Wild Boar Press, Sakai, 1999. Both contain interesting material but require some background knowledge of the period.

The account of Adams's shipbuilding can be found in his own letters; the colorful story of Friar Juan de Madrid is retold by Cocks in a letter to Sir Thomas Wilson dated November 10, 1614. Tracing the activities of the *Liefde*'s other survivors is not easy. There are references in Dutch accounts, and their names appear occasionally in the letters of Cocks and his men.

The description of Nagasaki is drawn, in part, from Japanese *byobu*, or picture screens. The tale of the *Nossa Senhora de Graça* (also known as the *Madre de Deus*) is covered in great detail by C. R. Boxer in his "The Affair of the Madre de Deus," in *Transactions and Proceedings of the Japan Society*, 26, 1929. There is a good description of the sea battle in Leon Pages's *Histoire de la Religion Chrétienne au Japon, 1598–1651*, published by Charles Douniol in Paris, 1867–70. For more information about the arrival of Jacques Specx and company, see W. Z. Mulder's *Hollanders in Hirado*, published by Fibula van Dishoeck in 1985; Derek Massarella's *A World Elsewhere*; and Anthony Farrington's *The English Factory in Japan*. See also C. R. Boxer's *Jan Compagnie in Japan*, published by Martinus Nijhoff, The Hague, 1936.

The account of Specx at the shogun's court is contained in Volume 7 of the ten-volume 1725 edition of Constantine de Renneville's *Recueil des Voyages*. The mission of Sebastian Vizciano is published in Michael Cooper's *They Came to Japan*. Vizciano was preceded by the Spanish governor of the Philippines, Rodrigo de Velasco y Vivero, whose account is published in the same volume. See also E. M. Satow's "The Origin of Spanish and Portuguese Rivalry in Japan," in *Transactions of the Asiatic Society of Japan*, 18, Tokyo, 1890.

Chapter 6, pages 132–154

The best general history of the East India Company is John Keay's excellent *The Honourable Company*, HarperCollins, 1991. Other good (although somewhat dated) histories include *The East India Company* by Marguerite Wilbur, Stanford University Press, 1945, and *Ledger and Sword*, by Beckles Willson (two volumes), Longmans, 1903.

My account of Bantam is drawn largely from the journal of Edmund Scott, which is published in *The Voyage of Sir Henry Middleton to the Moluccas, 1604–1606*, Hakluyt Society, 1943, as well as from the ships' logs of other Jacobean captains, all of whom complained about "this stinking stew."

The journal of the *Globe*'s voyage can be found in *Peter Floris: His Voyage in the Globe*, published by the Hakluyt Society, 1934. For more information about the English factory in Siam, see John Anderson's *English Intercourse with Siam in the 17th Century*, Kegan Paul, 1890. An excellent sixteenth-century account of the East Indies and Indo-China can be found in John Huyghen van Lindschoten's *Voyage to the East Indies*, Hakluyt Society, 1885. The letters of Antheunis and his men are published in *Letters Received by the East India Company*, various editors (six volumes), 1896–1902.

For a more detailed account of King James I's correspondence with the shogun, see Derek Massarella's "James I and Japan," *Monumenta Nipponica*, 38, Tokyo, 1983.

The journal of Captain Saris's voyage to Japan, *Voyage to Japan, 1613*, was published in 1900 by the Hakluyt Society. The appendices include letters as well as Saris's report on Eastern trade goods. This edition covers only the voyage from Bantam to Hirado and Saris's months in Japan. For the earlier stages, see Takanobu Otusuka's *The First Voyage of the English to Japan by John Saris* (two volumes), Tokyo, 1941. See also *Letters Received* for details of onboard wrangling.

Chapter 7, pages 155–182

The chief sources for the *Clove*'s arrival in Japan are John Saris's *Voyage to Japan* and Richard Cocks's diary (see notes to Chapter 8).

There are numerous European accounts that testify to the casual violence of the Japanese. Padre João Rodrigues's observations, published in translation in Michael Cooper's *They Came to Japan*, were originally in his *Historia da Igreja do Japão*.

Li Tan is mentioned frequently in the English letters. The most informative analysis of his business activities is "Li Tan, Chief of the Chinese Residents at Hirado," by Seiichi Iwao, published in *Tokyo Bunko Memoirs*, 17, Tokyo, 1958.

Hirado is today a modern, if provincial, backwater; there is no trace of the ten-year English presence. There are plans afoot to build several mock-Jacobean houses in the town center.

Chapter 8, pages 183–207

Captain Saris's "remembrance" is published in Anthony Farrington's *The English Factory in Japan*. Cocks has been the subject of several articles in recent years. The best of these are Derek Massarella, "The Early Career of Richard Cocks," in *Transactions of the Asiatic Society of Japan*, 3rd series, 20, Tokyo, 1985; and Michael Cooper's "The Second Englishman in Japan," in *Transactions of the Asiatic Society of*

Japan, 3rd series, 17, Tokyo, 1982. See also Anthony Farrington's "Some Other Englishmen in Japan," in *Transactions of the Asiatic Society of Japan*, 3rd series, 19, Tokyo, 1984.

For many years, the only readily available edition of Cocks's diary was the Hakluyt Society's two-volume edition published in 1883. This omits many interesting observations and is now supplanted by the excellent Shiryo Hensan-jo, *Diary kept by the head of the English factory in Japan—Diary of Richard Cocks, 1615–1622* (three volumes), Historiographical Institute, Tokyo, 1978–81. Unfortunately, very few copies were printed.

Cocks's erratic accounts are published in Anthony Farrington's *The English Factory in Japan*, but see also Peter Pratt's *History of Japan Compiled from the Records of the English East India Company*. This was edited by M. Paske-Smith and published in two volumes by J. L. Thompson in Kobe in 1931. A good, if brief, account of the English factory can be found in L. Riess's "History of the English Factory at Hirado, 1613–22," in *Transactions of the Asiatic Society of Japan*, 26, Tokyo, 1898. See also M. Paske-Smith's *A Glympse of the English House and English Life at Hirado, 1613–1623*, Kobe, 1927. There have been several recent articles in the *Study of Hirado City History*, published by the Hirado Historiography Committee. The third issue (November 1997) includes a ground plan of the English factory. The most detailed account of the factory's establishment is in Derek Massarella's *A World Elsewhere*.

Francesco Carletti's account of Nagasaki's prostitution is included in Michael Cooper's *They Came to Japan*. Other fascinating details about Japanese cleanliness, cooking, architecture, and art can be found in Padre João Rodrigues's *This Island of Japon*. Rodrigues includes a lengthy account of the tea ceremony.

The description of acupuncture was written by Padre Lourenço Mexia and is published in Michael Cooper's *They Came to Japan*. See also the third volume of Engelbert Kaempfer's *History of Japan* (p. 263 ff.), republished in Glasgow in 1906.

Chapter 9, pages 208–236

The description of Saris's return to England is drawn from the introduction to his *Voyage to Japan, 1613*, and from various notices in the *Calendar of State Papers*, Colonial Series, Volumes 2–4, 1862–78.

There are two printed editions of Adams's voyage to Ryukyu: "The Log Book of William Adams, 1614–19," in *Transactions and Proceedings of the Japan Society*, 13, Part 2, 1915; and Anthony Farrington's *The English Factory in Japan*. The original manuscript is held in the Bodleian Library.

The account of the Jesuit mission and of Ieyasu's 1614 edict against Christianity is drawn primarily from C. R. Boxer's *Christian Century in Japan*. See also Michael Cooper's *Southern Barbarians* and L. Sadler's *The Life of Tokugawa Ieyasu*. The siege of Osaka is covered in detail in James Murdoch and Isoh Yamagata's *History of Japan*. A more lively and graphic account, drawn from original letters, can be found in Pierre François Xavier de Charlevoix's *Histoire et description générale du Japon* (two volumes), Paris, 1736.

Rowland Thomas's journal of the *Hosiander*'s voyage can be found in Anthony Farrington's *The English Factory in Japan*, Volume 2, pp. 1030–44.

Chapter 10, pages 237–264

News took many years to reach London from the East. The most comprehensive collection of documents can be found in *Letters Received*, as well as in the *Calendar of State Papers*. Very little correspondence was catalogued at the time; an account from 1682 describes the various letters and diaries as being "in a confused manner, laid up in the garret of the [East India] house."

The journal of William Keeling's 1607 expedition was published in Samuel Purchas's *Purchas His Pilgrims*, Volume 2. Keeling's 1615 journal was published and annotated by Michael Strachan and Boies Penrose in their *The East India Company Journals of Captain William Keeling and Master Thomas Bonner, 1615–1617*, University of Minnesota Press, Minneapolis, 1971. John Jourdain's diary of his time in the East is published in *The Journal of John Jourdain, 1608–1617*, Hakluyt Society, 1905.

François Caron's description of ritual suicide is to be found in Michael Cooper's *They Came to Japan*.

For more information on Christianity in Japan, see Pages's *Histoire de la Religion Chrétienne au Japon*. The growing hostility to Christianity has been studied in detail by George Elison in *Deus Destroyed: The Image of Christianity in Early Modern Japan*, Harvard University Press, 1973. This includes lengthy quotations from original sources.

Chapter 11, pages 265–280

This chapter is drawn almost entirely from Richard Cocks's *Diary* and Anthony Farrington's *The English Factory in Japan*. An inventory of Richard Wickham's possessions is given in *The English Factory in Japan*, Volume 1, pp. 729–36.

The account of Adams's voyage to Ayutthaya is also contained in *The English Factory in Japan*, as is his voyage to Cochinchina in the *Gift of God*. This latter voyage was also documented by Edmund Sayers in *The English Factory in Japan*, Volume 2, pp. 1128–40.

Chapter 12, pages 281–301

A portion of Richard Cocks's diary—from January 1619 to December 1620—has been lost. Information from those years has been gleaned from letters written by him and his men. Cocks's finest letters are those that he wrote to his old friend Sir Thomas Wilson.

The story of the battles for the Spice Islands—and in particular the Banda archipelago—is told in my *Nathaniel's Nutmeg: or, The True and Incredible Adventures of the Spice Trader Who Changed the Course of History*, Farrar, Straus and Giroux, 1999. This book also contains an account of an attack by Japanese pirates in 1605 on the Jacobean adventurer Sir Edward Michelbourne.

There is a lengthy discussion of Sir Thomas Dale's disastrous mission, and Jourdain's assassination, in George Masselman's *The Cradle of Colonialism*. For more on Dale's time in Virginia, see my *Big Chief Elizabeth: The Adventures and Fate of the First English Colonists in America*, Farrar, Straus and Giroux, 2000.

Chapter 13, pages 302–324

The decline of the Jesuits is dealt with in considerable detail by C. R. Boxer, *Christian Century in Japan*. Individual persecutions are covered by Masakaru Anesaki in his detailed *A Concordance to the History of Kirishitan Missions* (supplement to Volume 6), 1930. Among the more interesting accounts are those published by Jesuits at the time. See Pedro Morejon's *A Briefe Relation of the Persecution Lately Made Against the Catholike Christians in the Kingdome of Japonia*, translated by William Wright and published at St. Omer in 1619; *Exhortation to Martyrdom* (extracts printed in C. R. Boxer, *Christian Century in Japan*); and *The Palme of Christian Fortitude*, translated by Edmund Sale and published in St. Omer in 1630. Other, grisly descriptions of torture are contained in François Caron's *A True Description of the Mighty Kingdoms of Japan and Siam*, written in 1636 but not published in English until 1663. C. R. Boxer's edition, published in 1935 by the Argonaut Press, also contains Reyer Gysbertsz's horrific account of public burnings, first printed in 1637.

Adams's will has been published several times; the most accurate version is in Anthony Farrington's *The English Factory in Japan*. For more on the Fleet of Defense, see Derek Massarella's *A World Elsewhere*. This is one of the few books to consider in detail the fleet's failure to deliver.

William Eaton—the sole factory member to return to England—must have had an iron constitution; he was still alive in the late 1660s. At that time, the East India Company was pondering a return to Japan and made contact with him at his home in Highgate. Eaton refused to cooperate, and the company plans came to nothing.

There have been numerous attempts to trace descendants of Adams, but with no success. During the long period of *sakoku* (the closed country), anyone with foreign blood was expelled from Japan on pain of death. If Joseph Adams had children or grandchildren, he would have kept secret their English ancestry.

Acknowledgments

The story of *Samurai William* has been drawn from Jacobean letters and journals. I am extremely grateful to the scholars who have collected and published these colorful records. The relevant sources are cited in the Notes and Sources, but one work must be singled out for special mention. Anthony Farrington's magnificent *The English Factory in Japan*, a monumental collection of original material, has proved invaluable in compiling a portrait of the English in Japan.

I have received much help from researchers and translators. A thank you to Laura Inoue in Tokyo for her advice, hard work, and hot plum brandy. My thanks, as well, to the staff of the Japan Foundation Library in Tokyo. I am also most grateful to Takako Suga, my guide/translator in Hirado.

Thank you to Marjolein van der Valk for translating scores of pages of *De Ries van Mahu en de Cordes*. And special thanks to Peter ten Arve in Rotterdam for locating and translating original Dutch manuscripts.

In London, my thanks to Maggie Noach and Jill Hughes; to Roland Philipps, Lizzie Dipple, and Celia Levett. Thank you also to George Tiffin, for photographing many of the illustrations; to Frank Barrett and Wendy Driver; and to the ever-helpful staff (and friends) at the London Library, where much of this book was written.

I am particularly grateful to Paul Whyles for reading and rereading the manuscript at short notice and suggesting much-needed changes.

Lastly, I wish to say a huge thank you to Alexandra for her encouragement, support, and friendly advice; and to Madeleine and Héloïse for their banter and jokes.

Index

Figures in *italics* indicate captions; those in **bold** type indicate maps.

Illustration Sources

Pages 6, 57, 61, 65, 70, 72, 77: from *De Ries van Mahu en de Cordes*, Lindschoten Society, 1923. Pages 11, 86: details from early-seventeenth-century *Namban byobu* by Kano Nizen, Kobe. Pages 24, 27, 37, 40, 96, 112, 121, 160, 169, 170, 175, 176, 189, 191, 202, 219, 228, 232, 239, 277, 286, 295, 309: Arnoldus Montanus's *Atlas Japannensis*, 1670. Pages 47, 97, 199: with kind permission from Okura Shukokan Museum, Tokyo. Pages 93, 256: from C. R. Boxer, *A True Description of the Mighty Kingdoms of Japan and Siam*, 1953. Page 106: from the *Zohyo monogatari*. Page 118: detail from *Tawara-kasane kosaku emaki*, Tokyo. Page 136: from Willem Lodewyckszoon's *Premier livre de l'histoire de la navigation aux Indes orientales*, 1609. Page 143: from Johann Theodor de Bry and Johann Israel de Bry's *Indias orientales*, 1607. Page 151: from *Miyako meisho zu byobu*, Tokyo. Pages 260, 310: from Nicolas Tigault's *De christianis apud Iaponicos triumphis*, 1623.

FOR THE BEST IN PAPERBACKS, LOOK FOR THE

In every corner of the world, on every subject under the sun, Penguin represents quality and variety—the very best in publishing today.

For complete information about books available from Penguin—including Penguin Classics, Penguin Compass, and Puffins—and how to order them, write to us at the appropriate address below. Please note that for copyright reasons the selection of books varies from country to country.

In the United States: Please write to *Penguin Group (USA), P.O. Box 12289 Dept. B, Newark, New Jersey 07101-5289* or call 1-800-788-6262.

In the United Kingdom: Please write to *Dept. EP, Penguin Books Ltd, Bath Road, Harmondsworth, West Drayton, Middlesex UB7 0DA.*

In Canada: Please write to *Penguin Books Canada Ltd, 10 Alcorn Avenue, Suite 300, Toronto, Ontario M4V 3B2.*

In Australia: Please write to *Penguin Books Australia Ltd, P.O. Box 257, Ringwood, Victoria 3134.*

In New Zealand: Please write to *Penguin Books (NZ) Ltd, Private Bag 102902, North Shore Mail Centre, Auckland 10.*

In India: Please write to *Penguin Books India Pvt Ltd, 11 Panchsheel Shopping Centre, Panchsheel Park, New Delhi 110 017.*

In the Netherlands: Please write to *Penguin Books Netherlands bv, Postbus 3507, NL-1001 AH Amsterdam.*

In Germany: Please write to *Penguin Books Deutschland GmbH, Metzlerstrasse 26, 60594 Frankfurt am Main.*

In Spain: Please write to *Penguin Books S. A., Bravo Murillo 19, 1° B, 28015 Madrid.*

In Italy: Please write to *Penguin Italia s.r.l., Via Benedetto Croce 2, 20094 Corsico, Milano.*

In France: Please write to *Penguin France, Le Carré Wilson, 62 rue Benjamin Baillaud, 31500 Toulouse.*

In Japan: Please write to *Penguin Books Japan Ltd, Kaneko Building, 2-3-25 Koraku, Bunkyo-Ku, Tokyo 112.*

In South Africa: Please write to *Penguin Books South Africa (Pty) Ltd, Private Bag X14, Parkview, 2122 Johannesburg.*